Adolescent Lives in Transition

Adolescent Lives in Transition

How Social Class
Influences the Adjustment
to Middle School

Donna Marie San Antonio

State University of New York Press

Published by
State University of New York Press, Albany

© 2004 State University of New York

Printed in the United States of America

For information, address State University of New York Press,
90 State Street, Suite 700, Albany, N.Y., 12207

Production by Diane Ganeles
Marketing by Susan Petrie

Library of Congress Cataloging-in-Publication Data

San Antonio, Donna Marie, 1951–
    Adolescent lives in transition: how social class influences the adjustment
to middle school / Donna Marie San Antonio.
        p. cm.
    Includes bibliographical references and index.
    ISBN 0-7914-6035-5 (alk. paper) — ISBN 0-7914-6036-3 (pbk. : alk. paper)
        1. Middle schools—United States—Sociological aspects—Case studies.
    2. Middle school students—United States—Social conditions—21st century—
Case studies I. Title.

LB1623.5.S26   2004
373.236'0973—dc21

                                                                  2003050532

10 9 8 7 6 5 4 3 2 1

For my father, Ugo,
who encouraged a passionate response to life and
awareness of injustice.
And for my mother, Caterina,
who taught me to live with imagination and
persistent optimism.
Your love and example have helped guide the way through
life's extraordinary transitions.

Contents

Illustrations

Figures

Maps

Tables

Acknowledgments

When I began this inquiry I knew immediately that the thirty re-search participants whose wisdom fills these pages would be amazing teachers, but I did not know that they would continue to bless my life in wonderful ways. Their generosity, compassion, and insight carried me through this process with a sense of wonder and joy. To each and every one of you: thank you for your inspiration, for your enthusiastic commitment to this project, and for helping me tell an important story that others will find useful. Thank you to all the parents who coordinated busy schedules, provided transportation to research sessions, responded to my questions and requests with unfailing consistency, and allowed me into the private realm of home life. This is a precious trust that I shall appreciate forever.

To the principals, teachers, guidance counselors, and secretaries of all three schools: thank you for opening the school doors to me and for responding to my questions and interpretations with thoughtfulness and patience. I am deeply grateful to the sixth grade teachers for the hours they spent helping with the selection process, and to the seventh grade middle school teachers who allowed me into their classrooms. It was a privilege for me to watch you work and to benefit from your openhandedness when I questioned teaching practices and classroom policies.

The twelve members of the community advisory groups provided valuable and diverse perspectives on the transition process and helped to make this work relevant, useful, and real. I frequently relied on the generosity of community agencies and local churches to provide space for meetings, copy machines, and telephones; thank you for opening your doors. I also relied on local readers for editing and fact-checking assistance. Thanks expecially to Ernie Bainton and to the parents, teachers, advisory group members, and friends who read drafts of chapters to check for accuracy, to provide technical advice, and to offer suggestions, criticism, and encouragement.

This work was especially influenced by professors, students, and staff members at Harvard's Graduate School of Education, who read and commented on the manuscript and whose work and inspiration gave this book meaning and substance. First and foremost, thank you Charles Willie; without you, this book would not have happened. You have walked with me each step of the way, knowing when to push hard, to encourage, to direct, and to let it be. As my advisor, mentor, and teacher, you took many hours from your own scholarship to provide me with your legendary wisdom, kindness, generosity, and guidance; you continue to be a steady beacon in my life.

To my closest colleague and good friend, Mike Nakkula, you will always be a guide whose counsel and confidence I seek, and whose integrity, perspective, intellect, and advising skill I admire. It alarms me to think of what my life would be like if you had not introduced me to hermeneutics.

Eileen de los Reyes, you demonstrated to me how democratic and empowering research relationships can be formed and sustained. Thank you for making sure that I kept my own high standards in interpreting my research findings with political and social awareness.

The social development work of Robert Selman gave my years of practice with adolescents new meaning and provided a valuable theoretical foundation on which to build my questions and interpretations. At a time when the world is looking for ways to create compassionate understanding across borders of identity, your work has profoundly changed the way we think about adolescent development, social and moral education, and how to create working multi-cultural classrooms.

No one was more a source of inspiration in terms of style, method, sociological imagination, and cross-disciplinary interpretation than Sara Lawrence-Lightfoot. Every page of this book carries the result of Lawrence-Lightfoot's work imprinted on my soul. When searching for role models in research, in teaching, and in living generously and passionately, I look to you more consistently than anyone else.

I am deeply grateful to eminent statistician, John Willett, for taking the time to read my work and for suggesting ways to convey the numerical self-esteem data so that it would be consistent with the narrative style of the book. Thank you Dean Whitla for believing in me from the start and for your good-natured supervision and encouragement in matters of mind, spirit, and body.

Jim Garbarino, as someone who writes with clarity, purpose, and visionary insight, you have helped us to think about the multiple influences on adolescent development and the democratic values we must preserve in our communities and schools. Your endorsement of this book means a lot to me.

Meg Turner's steady, skilled practice and essential intellectual work have been vital forces behind this project, and to me personally. As I authored this book, you helped me with a parallel process of authoring my life in a new way; as I became familiar with that new-old story, each page of this book became stronger.

Diamond Cephus, I cherish our friendship, the important influence you have been in my life, and the way you have set an example for getting through this process without compromising integrity, intelligence, compassion, and sensible priorities. Weekends in NH, Monday nights at Charlie's, and countless conversations about our work, our families, and our lives: these have been essential in my life over the last few years. Jane Lohmann and Lamont Gordon, extraordinary teaching fellows, practitioners, and intellects: you bring such integrity to your work with adolescents that those around you do better work because of it. The students in H381 were the first real audience for this work. It meant a lot to me—more than you can imagine—to have you read this work and find it provocative and useful.

I particularly relied on four good friends for technical assistance: Kathy George, an amazing transcriber whose comments on the interviews pushed my understanding and helped me to consider other interpretations; Lisa Soricone, who patiently and adeptly took the numerical information and turned it into beautiful graphs; Christina Nikitopolous, for the hours of work (and fun) entering data and writing the statistical programs; and Sang Curtis, who made the wonderful maps that appear in the first part of the book and whose generous spirit has benefitted me in many ways. I am deeply grateful to you all. My day-to-day life and work at Harvard is made immensely more reasonable by Matt Slayton. Your competence, thoroughness, good nature, and focused insight help me in numerous ways and were particular assets in the proofreading of this book—thank you for your valuable suggestions and for all you do.

This work benefitted a great deal from Craig Howley of Ohio University and his important research in rural education. Thank you for twice reading the manuscript, for your enthusiastic and encouraging review, and for moving me more into the realm of rural education and sociology. Your research challenges us to realize that if this large middle school works well, it is an anomoly to be celebrated rather than an example of what is common.

To all the people at State University of New York Press, especially marketing manager, Susan Petrie, senior production editor, Diane Ganeles, and SUNY Press director, Priscilla Ross: thank you for treating this work with exceptional skill and care. Priscilla, you played an essential role in bringing this work to publication and putting the idea forward that research on education can be both rigorous and useful to teachers, parents, and school administrators.

My sister Nadine and nephew Christopher were a constant source of affirmation. Our discussions about adolescence and watching Christopher competently negotiate his teen years while I was engaged in this process were tremendously helpful. Dan Kusch, Jeff Martel, and Cindy Weisbart, gifted practitioners and good friends, I have learned so much from listening to you talk about your work and I have benefitted from your patience when this book took up precious time and space at the office. Steve Blum's encouragement, words of wisdom, and sense of humor helped me keep a reasonable perspective throughout this project. Thanks for letting me turn your study into a safe haven all these years, Janet Singer; this generous gesture and your interest in my work make my time in Cambridge comfortable and productive.

Finally, no one has lived with this project day-in and day-out more than Holly Manoogian. I am deeply grateful to you for reading endless drafts, for your technical assistance, for the many hours of conversation when your insight and wisdom helped me understand what I was seeing, for your unrestrained and honest critique, for your support and encouragement and for your patience when this project took up too much space, time, focus, and thought.

I am profoundly thankful to all of you, and to others not mentioned here, for the distinct contributions each of you individually made to me and to this work.

List of People

Students

Hillside-Two Rivers	Lakeview
Alexeia	Artie
Allen	Becka
Amber	BJ
Analysa	Bob
Arianna	Christine
Britney	Daria
Chris	Dez
Ethan	Isabelle
Frank	Jeff
Fred	Maia
Jake	Micky
Jaz	Olivia
Matt	Simon
Oceana	Trent
	Will
	Zoe

Teachers

Striders Team:	Mr. Jordan	Ms. Lyons	Mr. Walden
Horizon Team:	Ms. Streeter		

Guidance Counselor:	Ms. Young
Music:	Ms. Jackson
Physical Education:	Ms. Olivier
Spanish:	Ms. James

Social Class and Adjustment to School in Rural Places

Christine,[1] a perky seventh grader and research participant, is a perceptive and articulate observer of seventh grade life. In the eighteen months since we began meeting, Christine left her beloved elementary school teachers and transitioned to her new school, a regional middle school for grades seven and eight. She approached the transition like many of her peers—with combined emotions of sadness, apprehension, enthusiasm, and hope. We met in May 2000, at the end of her seventh grade year, for our third and last interview. She is taller, no longer wearing pigtails; she is a bit disappointed in her grades, and her manner of speech is more modulated and deliberate. However, it is immediately clear to me that her openness, self-understanding, and desire to help others have remained intact. As I set up the tape recorder, she begins to demolish the plate of cookies I have ready for her. Throughout the interview she is constantly in motion, using her hands for emphasis, plucking at her black tights to pull them up, and yanking at her too-short skirt to pull it down over her knees.

When we talk about her future plans which include acting, music, and working with disadvantaged children, her enthusiasm is unrestrained and contagious. Christine's sharp insight, her frank critique of life at the middle school, and her altruism are cultivated out of extreme early-life hardship. She is a resilient thirteen-year-old who knows that the conditions for success are not something to take for granted. "I work my butt off to be kind to classmates who are struggling," she says; "I know what it's like."

In our last interview, I asked Christine what you have to do to be a successful seventh grader:

> You have to be yourself. You've got to be organized and keep focused, not just on school, but keep focused on . . . what you want, for the present and future. And you have to feel good

1

about yourself. If you don't feel good about yourself, you're not going to make it.

But, I wanted to know, why do some students feel good about themselves and others do not? How can all students be motivated to keep focused and set goals?

You provide somebody with a better support system. If their family is not supportive . . . they have to get themselves a good support system through friends or teachers.

In an interview with Trent at the end of seventh grade, I asked if there was a connection between social class and middle school success:

Yeah, there's a connection with everything . . . If their family's doing bad, they will concern themselves with their family and not with their academics. If they do bad in school, then they'll get more pressure from their family. More pressure can sometimes lead to behavior problems; behavior problems can go to lower social problems . . . behavior problems can lead to lower grades. It starts with the economics.

This research project explores the experiences of thirty students from economically diverse backgrounds over an eighteen-month period as the students transitioned from elementary schools in their own towns, to a large six-town regional middle school in a rural, northeastern school district. I was educated by my twelve- and thirteen-year-old informants about the social and emotional implications of this transition and the conditions that lead to success or struggle in academic achievement, self-esteem, and connecting with peers. Through observations, interviews, and questionnaires, I learned how community culture, peer relationships, family values, teacher practices, and school policies influence the adjustment to middle school and I learned the meaning of Trent's wise observation, "There's a connection with everything."

On a regular basis, I was brought up short by the students' subtle, discerning insights and I was saddened that their vast knowledge, analytic abilities, and altruism were not cultivated and tapped more regularly in school and community settings. I learned things I could not have known, even though I had spent many years of my life working in middle schools.

By listening to students, I found myself at the end of this two-year study in a place that was far from my initial orientation to these issues. I expected to hear that students from the economically struggling communities of Hillside and Two Rivers faced barriers to success when they arrived at the middle school—barriers that were a result of social class stereotypes and experiences of exclusion. And I expected to hear the reverse story: that students from the affluent community of Lakeview enjoyed a system of advantages derived from their economic security and a ready validation of their values, interests, goals, and manners of interacting. However, while some of my original presuppositions were confirmed, many were called to question.

Stories of Struggle and Stories of Strength

Prior to this study, my understanding of social class influences on schooling was informed by twenty-five years of work with children and families in small, rural communities. Over the years, I have encountered examples of injustice resulting from social class prejudice and discrimination. Not too long ago, for example, I accompanied a mother and her fourteen-year-old daughter to the high school to register the student for ninth grade. They were homeless after leaving an unsafe domestic situation. In a painful, public encounter in the high school guidance office they were told that the student could not be enrolled without proof of a permanent residence. We were eventually able to register the student but not without a visit to the superintendent's office and a lot of frustration, humiliation, and hurt feelings.

Another student reflected on her transition to middle school and said, "They tell kids [in the sixth grade] that when they go to the middle school they can have a new beginning, but they get labeled [Hillside] as soon as they walk in the door." Her grades and her self-concept plummeted in seventh grade and in the eleventh grade she withdrew from school to be home-schooled, a choice more and more disenfranchised parents and students are making in this region. A girl from Hillside demonstrated the devastating effects of internalized class stereotypes when she announced in a group of her peers that the people in her town are all "in-bred, not very smart, and always in trouble." A boy who eventually dropped out of school told me, "Teachers don't have time for students like me." A student who graduated from high school said that when she ran for class president, classmates ripped down and wrote on her campaign posters. She got the message loud and clear: "Students from Hillside do not become class officers." On a regular basis, I hear references to rural working-class people as hicks, bubbas, and greasers and I witness the pervasive and detrimental effects of social class stereotypes.

These stories indicate that social class inequality persists through a variety of means: inequitable and insensitive school policies; labeling by peers; internalized class stereotypes; uneven distribution of teacher time and attention; imbalance of power and influence among students; and the devastating effects of labeling that one student referred to as the "name tags" everyone is given in school.

Sacrifice and betrayal, the fight for dignity, lost dreams, and the experience of no "reciprocal respect across class boundaries" (p. 47) are themes in Sennett and Cobb's (1972) account of working-class life in *The Hidden Injuries of Class.* Countless examples of no respect led me to wonder how we can help students from working-class and poor families maintain a sense of hope, pride, and connection to school during the critical adjustment to middle school.

While I *did* indeed find examples of inequality and disrespect, I also discovered conditions that broadened my understanding of the influence of social class on school experience. First, adjusting to their new school was a challenge for students of *all* social class backgrounds, not just for students from low-income families. For some students from wealthy families, the tacit expectations of high social class turned out to be an impediment of a different sort to healthy development. Second, students and their families demonstrated a variety of creative, adaptive strategies that pushed against the barriers they faced. And third, I found that students had a flexible and adaptive way of understanding social class. When research participants were asked to define their own social status in the seventh grade, many less-affluent children ranked themselves high relative to their peers and seldom attributed their experiences to be the result of social class biases alone.

Alongside the stories of struggle I expected to hear from Hillside-Two Rivers students, I heard stories of extraordinary strength and resilience, and alongside the stories of success I expected to hear from Lakeview students, I heard stories of vulnerability and loss. Yes, social class makes a difference, but the conditions that led to student success or failure turned out to be far more complex and far less universal than I originally thought. I failed to find easy adaptation to the middle school for Lakeview children and difficult transition for Hillside children. I found instead a complicated combination of factors linking community culture and values, social class, gender, divorce experience, access to information and resources, and prior school experience. *All* students made the transition to grade seven with both vulnerabilities and assets.

Children, parents, and teachers influenced their environments and used strategies that enabled adaptation in even very difficult situations.

For example, I found that in the absence of abundant material resources, children from financially struggling families were adept at constructing interpretations of their experiences that were self-preserving and hopeful. Most of the students in this study cared a lot about their teachers and their school, and their parents intentionally nurtured these positive feelings. Importantly, I also found a well-functioning middle school with diverse and effective teaching styles that gave students a full range of learning possibilities.

However, I discovered many potential threats to successful middle school adjustment as well. First, I found policies and practices that inadvertently divided students by town and social class background, such as ability grouping and a selective sports program. Second, the school district lacked coherent and articulated principles concerning diversity and there was some hesitance around probing social class and equity issues. Third, I observed countless ways that sociocultural phenomena play a heavy hand in shaping early adolescent consciousness. The commercial exploitation of children as consumers threatens to replace school, family, and community-oriented values with a material-driven value system. The "neurotic desire to have everything" (Horney, 1950) is very much a part of life for too many people in the U.S. today. Finally, I noticed an alarming increase in aggressive and anxious behavior in middle- and upper-class students that is inadequately addressed.

Held in the balance of these discrepant conditions that can facilitate or threaten success at school, are twelve- and thirteen-year-old children who must make the difficult journey from home to school. I have written about this journey as it takes place in a large, rural school district—a place that is often described as idyllic and serene and seemingly unencumbered by the challenges facing inner-city schools and communities.

Mountainview Regional School District

In the seventh grade, students transition from the elementary schools in their own communities to Mountainview Middle School (MMS), centrally located in the relatively affluent community of Lakeview. The summer-resort veneer of Lakeview disguises the reality that nearly one-third of the children in this school district live in families with limited financial resources. Hillside and Two Rivers have the highest rate of poverty in the school district; between 35% and 55% of the students from these towns received free or reduced lunch in the years between 1997 and 2000.[2] Appendix 1 provides a comparative chart of educational and economic indicators for Lakeview, Hillside, and Two Rivers.

Mountainview Regional School District (MRSD) was formed in 1964 and today serves six rural towns in northern New England. The kindergarten through twelfth grade population of 2,763 includes only thirty-two students who identify themselves as students of color: thirteen Asian, twelve African American, four Latino, and three Native American.[3] Sixty-five miles from one end to the other, Mountainview Regional School District is, in population and square miles, one of the largest in the region. Lakes, mountains, deep pine forests, small farms, and dirt roads characterize the geography in this non-industrial area. Tourism replaced agriculture many years ago and it plays an important role in the economic life of these communities. Demographically, economically, and geographically, Mountainview Regional School District is typical of hundreds of northern, rural, school districts in the United States.

Rural Education and Cultural Survival

More than 28% of the public schools in the United States are located in rural places. These schools educate 6.9 million students—16.7% of the nation's total number of students (Stern, 1994: p. 14). Nearly all rural districts have enrollments of less than 2,500, making Mountainview Regional School one of the largest in student population—only 3% of the rural districts in the country are larger (ibid., p. 17). Rural education has typically relied on property taxes for its income, a setup that has been litigated in about half the states because of the unfair burden and the inequitable education it imposes on property poor communities. When all costs are considered, people in rural areas pay more for public schooling than people in urban and suburban areas, yet teachers are paid less well and fewer rural children go to college (ibid.).

Rural education researchers have focused on concerns that are both unique and universal: the role of rural schools in community development (Miller, 1995); the aspirations of rural adolescents vs. actual vocational opportunities (Hektner, 1995); the social costs of school busing (Howley, 2000); school size and student participation, achievement, and self-esteem (Coladarci and Cobb, 1996); and the economics of school and school district consolidation (Killeen and Sipple, 2000).

School consolidation has been the consistent policy when rural schools look for ways to improve educational options and decrease cost; however, increased transportation costs eliminate the hope of an economic solution, and enhanced education has been found to be dubious as well. Perhaps no other rural education issue is written about with more urgency than the academic, social, and cultural implications of school consolidation and the resulting increase in school size. In a recent study, Johnson, Howley, and Howley (2002) added to an already impressive body of research demonstrating that large school size has a negative impact on student achievement. These authors demonstrated that the negative effect on educational achievement is stronger in schools that have a large population of low-income students and they argue that small schools can help to moderate the negative impact of poverty by facilitating better student achievement.

However, research in school consolidation and school size has brought to light something less tangible than student achievement and school financing. Small local schools are social and cultural centers in rural communities. They have active and involved parents and students, low student: teacher ratios, and a sense of community that is both nurtured by, and nurturing to, the total community culture (DeYoung, 1995, Hinsdale, Lewis, and Waller, 1995). But rural communities and lifestyles—especially poor ones—are expendable in an era when material consumption is the benchmark for the value of life. In his sensitively written narrative about the demise of one school in West Virginia, DeYoung (1995) mourned the displacement of rural communitarian values: "Rural school consolidation symbolizes the economic transformation of this country from an agricultural one to an urban and suburban one," he said. "Local community identification [is] no longer required in a society based upon urbanization, industrialization, consumerism, and moral universalism" (pp. 297–298).

Educational and Vocational Underachievement

In this rural region, the majority of towns are in the lowest of five economic categories based on average per capita income. The percentage of children living in poverty increased 25% between 1980 and 1990, while nationwide, overall poverty among children decreased by 5%.[4] The 2000 census data show that in the 1990s poverty remained at the same high level.[5] As the economy grew stronger and unemployment declined in some areas across the nation, many small rural towns did not benefit from the prosperity.

Poverty has multiple social, health, and education-related implications. Births to single mothers are higher in poor communities; inadequate nutrition and the lack of accessible prenatal and neonatal care result in lower birth weights and higher rates of early-life illnesses. Children who are born into families deprived of adequate income, health, and education are more likely to arrive at school with cognitive and neurological needs that require special attention (Garbarino and Abramowitz, 1992; Garbarino and Benn, 1992). Before a child ever steps foot in a classroom, these conditions impact early learning and development.

Successful transition from one environment to another is threatened when a student does not have a secure base as their point of departure. These factors may be additionally reinforced by social stereotypes and practical constraints. As a result, some students arrive at middle school psychologically, physically, emotionally, and academically unready and the implications are long-range. Researchers have found that low socioeconomic status may be the most pervasive characteristic associated with dropping out of school exceeding the effects of race (Rumberger, 1987; Wehlage and Rutter, 1986). Nationally, less than half of the students whose family incomes are in the bottom 20% enroll in college right after high school, while more than three-quarters of the students in the top 20% income bracket enroll in college right out of high school. Of those students who enroll in college, students from low-income families are less likely to graduate.[7] In this state, dropout rates are twice as high in economically distressed towns than in affluent towns.[6]

Stories of courage, survival, and resilience (Corwin, 2001; Suskind, 1998) remind us, however, that many students manage to beat the odds. When an individual's hope and determination are met by opportunity, caring, and thoughtful guidance, students from even the most underprivileged backgrounds can go on to accomplish extraordinary things. This research supports the reality of such potential while also documenting how fragile this possibility may be.

The Myth of Sameness and Security in the Rural North

Everywhere I looked in the school and community settings I explored, I saw the dormant possibility of acknowledging and utilizing the diversity in these communities. Regions that are populated by mostly white residents are often not accustomed to thinking about diversity; however, I found social class, lifestyle, cultural, and political diversity to be vibrant in these communities.

Community history and culture and the interdependent nature of our personal lives can be a source of strength. Willie (1985) used the term "complementarity" to describe the ways people can "recognize mutuality" and "complement and complete each other through cooperation" (p. 270). But competition, misunderstanding, and suspicion create environments that disable values of compassion and cooperation, and prevent healthy reciprocity between diverse people. Embedded throughout this work are illustrations of how diversity in these communities can be a tremendous resource for improving options for *all* children.

At the same time, I have become aware of the tragic outcomes when misunderstandings result in conflict rather than complementarity. During this study, I was motivated by national news and local observations of the connections among intolerance, youth depression, poor social adjustment, and violence. Youth homicides went up 168% between 1985 and 1995, giving the U.S. the highest youth homicide rate among industrialized nations (Garbarino, 1999: p. 7). And rural areas are not exempt; Garbarino reported that,

> . . . while the overall youth homicide rate dropped in 1997, the rate among small town and rural youth increased by 38 percent. And that last statistic highlights my conviction that no longer can any of us believe that we and our children are immune to lethal youth violence, because today almost every teenager in America goes to school with a kid who is troubled enough to be the next killer—and chances are that kid has access to the weapons necessary to do so (p. 8).

For some youth, life becomes unbearable due to a pervasive sense of disconnection from significant others such as peers, teachers, and parents. School failure, peer rejection, hopeless home and community environments, and excessive media violence provide an unprecedented and volatile combination of factors. In rural areas, youth may experience troubled emotions in isolation and without access to mental health services. Still, many of us who work with youth feel a great deal of hope in the presence of the creative commitment of citizens, collaborative efforts among youth workers, and the talent, insight, and energy of youth. This work, I hope, points the way toward measures that would recognize the benficial aspects of diversity and enable successful school experiences for more children.

Democratic Ideals, Social Class Realities

In his groundbreaking sociological study on social class status and stratification in a midwestern high school with a primarily white student population, Hollingshead (1949) described conscious and pervasive social grouping and disproportionate participation in leadership roles, extracurricular activities, decision-making, and school completion. In Hollingshead's study, grubbies, elites, and scum were the labels students used for different groups. Different terms but essentially the same designations existed in Mountainview Middle School. Social hierarchies in schools mirror broader social stratification in a country with deep inconsistencies between an espoused set of ideals based on justice and equality and the actual conditions of inequality in education, housing, healthcare, opportunity, litigation, and income.

Public schools, or "common schools," as they were called in the nineteenth century, represent the noblest aspirations of a just and democratic society and, perhaps, its greatest ongoing challenge. In the first half of the nineteenth century, a movement gained momentum calling for a common school system for all free children paid for by taxation. Advocates ". . . aimed at more schooling for each child, more state involvement, more uniformity and a more pervasive public purpose for schooling" (Kaestle, 1983: p. 105). But no sooner had this new public school initiative been implemented, that efforts to keep certain children out became common. The *History of the New York African Free School* (1830) cited by Kaestle (1983), makes this point very clear: "[Some of the children] are too dirty, too ragged, and carry too much vermin about them, to be admitted to the public school" (ibid., p. 107). Later, the same attitudes served to exclude the children of immigrant families.

Despite two centuries of discourse about equal opportunity, communities across the United States have remained ambivalent about how to educate *all* children. The vision of public education heralded by Horace Mann as the "great equalizer" of humanity becomes mired in local conflicts about how to pay for education and how to educate children with diverse needs.

Inequitable and ineffective policies and practices are fueled by theories that poverty is the result of a self-perpetuating subculture in which people have low educational motivation, lack ambition, are nonconforming to middle-class ideals, and make self-defeating choices based on immediate gratification rather than long-term planning (Leacock, 1971). This interpretation of poverty ignores economic injustice and seriously distorts family and community life, omitting examples of health, generosity, and creativity, such as the networks of interdependence and the abundant resources and strengths that exist in many economically struggling communities. Children are capable of interpreting and acting on their own experiences, often with amazing insight and flexibility. Stereotypes of poverty render children as helpless victims and disregard their role as vital and active contributors in their communities.

Some researchers have documented ways that cultural stereotypes affect teacher expectations, recognition and utilization of student resources, student assertiveness, modes of interacting, and the distribution of school resources, like books and teacher time. Becker (1952), Rosenthal and Jacobson (1968), Rist (1970), and Oakes (1985) all found evidence of widely disparate teacher-pupil interactions that were influenced by race and social class biases. They each documented instructional and relational differences that hampered educational aspiration, performance, and motivation in children from low social class backgrounds.

Others have asserted that communities, schools, and classrooms have concentrated their attention, reciprocity, and resources on those who fit the norm. There's a "hidden curriculum," some authors theorize, institutionalizing middle-class values and ways of thinking and learning; school structures and patterns of communication encourage and reproduce certain lifestyles and world views, while simultaneously discouraging and constraining others (Bourdieu and Passeron, 1977; Bowles and Gintis, 1976; Freire, 1970; Giroux, 1983).

These viewpoints echo those expressed earlier by Warner, Havighurst and Loeb (1994) in their classic study, *Who Shall Be Educated?* These authors argued that the tacit curriculum of schooling teaches some children to "keep their place" and not strive too high, while encouraging others to be ambitious, noticeable, and interactive (p. 13). Educational institutions are biased toward middle-class values of occupational mobility, material gain, and social status, they said, and ignore the values and lifestyles of working-class, immigrant, and black families. These authors further stressed that the drive toward greater material gain was a value supported by schools that would threaten democratic ideals. "Unless the middle class values change in America," they said, "we must expect the influence of the schools to favor the values of material success, individual striving . . . and social mobility" (p. 172). They worried about the devastating effects of ignoring spiritual and humanistic values in school like "friendliness, cooperativeness, tolerance, and love of beauty" (ibid.). In my research, I found that parents from both communities shared these concerns.

In a diverse country like the U.S., real democracy relies on self-determination, a fair and truthful representation of people's lives, understanding, acceptance, and the power to be heard. Distortions persist where there is a lack of accurate information about families and communities, and research participants were acutely aware of the ways others (mis)perceived their communities. Take, for example, this exchange between students in a focus-group session at the end of seventh grade, recorded in my field notes, April 5, 2000:

> "When we were in sixth grade, we thought Hillsiders would be like the scum of seventh grade (Zoe)." Oceana visibly winced at the word scum. Later, I asked if Hillside and Two Rivers students had preconceptions about Lakeview students. Oceana replied, "We always thought, all those Lakeview preppies." BJ was offended and quipped, "Preppy is better than greasy." A few minutes later, BJ asked, "Isn't Hillside and Two Rivers the same thing?" Oceana, amazed by the ongoing ignorance of some of her classmates so late in the school year, responded with an emphatic "NO"

One teacher who taught in both Lakeview and Hillside used the language of race diversity to explain, "The difference is like night and day . . . People from Lakeview do not have a clue what it is really like [Hillside], just like white people do not have a clue what it is like to be black."

The Ecological Landscape of Adolescent Development

In the following chapters, the transition from elementary to middle school is explored in multiple domains of student interaction: peer, home, school, and community. Bronfenbrenner's (1979) theory of ecological environments was a useful conceptual framework for this study and enabled me to resist unilateral explanations. I found that adjustment to middle school was not a function of any single factor: it was not just individual temperament and ability, nor was it school policy and teacher quality, nor family functioning, nor peer acceptance, nor the economic and social supports a child had in place, but rather a combination of these things. Likewise, I found that students were not simply passive victims of injustice or beneficiaries of privilege, but they were active participants in shaping their environments, determining their interactions, and interpreting their day-to-day experiences.

Using the multilevel framework proposed by Bronfenbrenner, I explored how social adjustment is influenced at the micro, meso, and macro levels of interaction. Sociopolitical, historical, cultural, and economic structures are macrolevel influences that permeate interactions in all environments. Mesolevel interactions exist in the milieu of school environments and are studied in this work by looking at patterns of participation, leadership, and academic grouping. At the microlevel are the exchanges between individual students and their peers, families, and teachers at home and in the classroom, lunchroom, and school bus. Moving from macro to micro, as I have done in the chapters that follow, I will briefly describe the theoretical lens through which I interpreted each level of influence.

The Cultural Contexts of Children's Lives

There is a sense of incongruence for some early adolescents who face the task of negotiating the sometimes enormous gap between home and school, making the transition to middle school an anxiety-filled time. People want and need a sense of consistency and "desire wholeness of identity across domains" (Noam et al., 1990: 89). Some students may experience coherence from one setting to another when they transition to a new school environment, but imagine how strenuously some children have to work to accomplish a coherent sense of identity across domains when they find little resemblance of the skills, values, and ways of interacting they bring with them from home in their new school setting. For many of the students in this study, working to reconcile vastly different home and school environments was strengthening; for a few it was defeating.

Part I of this book, chapters 2 and 3, are ethnographic accounts of Hillside and Lakeview, which uncover the often unseen aspects of life in these communities and how they are influenced by broader economic and social policies and priorities. The ethnographic exploration of these two communities illustrates the ways history and economic development have linked these communities—and pulled them apart. In writing these chapters, I hoped to provide a framework for understanding the resources, values, and worldviews children from both communities bring with them to the school and to demonstrate how community culture facilitates or impedes adjustment to school. These chapters present the contextual background for answering the questions that are asked in subsequent chapters: What personal, familial, peer, school, and community resources do students engage to help them during the transition to middle school? Does social class background influence the extent to which students can successfully integrate their familial and community assets and knowledge within the school setting?

The Fit Between Students' Needs and the School Environment

Eccles and her colleagues (1993a) have suggested that the fit between students and schools is especially problematic during school transitions in early adolescence. They suggest that "behavior, motivation, and mental health are influenced by the fit between the characteristics individuals bring to their social environments, and the characteristics of these social environments" (p. 91); and they have found a "mismatch" between adolescents' needs and the opportunities available to them in their new schools (p. 90). The introduction to Part II reviews the middle school transition literature and begins to provide answers to questions about the patterns of interaction and participation that emerge over the transition from grade six to grade seven.

Chapter 4 takes us from the towns of Hillside and Lakeview to Mountainview Middle School to get a sense of the physical space, tone, pace, and feel of the school. This chapter provides a context for understanding how disparate community values and students' needs and resources are understood and integrated, or *not* understood and *not* integrated, in school policies, structures, and symbols.

Chapter 5 presents what students said about their hopes and worries as they thought about the transition while they were sixth graders and it reports what they discovered about the seventh grade by the end of the first quarter. The structure of the transition and the efforts school staff members take to ease the transition are outlined in chapter 6.

Chapter 7 portrays teaching styles and interactions within classrooms where the power of the teacher to shape the environment, and the limitations of that power, becomes clear. In this chapter, we begin to appreciate that *classroom interactions are negotiated*, not only between teachers and their students, but also *between teachers and the economic, political, and social realities outside of school*. A question that becomes important in this section is, "Which economic, political, and social realities are brought to the table in this negotiated process, and which ones are left outside the school doors?"

Chapter 8 describes how students shape their environment during unstructured times of the day. The material for this chapter came from observations of students at the beginning of the third quarter when they were well into the seventh grade year. By spending time in less-regulated settings—the school bus, lunchroom, and corridors—I witnessed the anticipated and surprising ways students interacted by their own rules, and I pondered whose rules had more sway in these peer interactions.

School Adjustment: A Central Task of Childhood at the Microlevel

The transition to a diverse, supportive, and challenging middle school environment may provide expanded opportunities and more flexible ways of viewing oneself and others but in environments that do not acknowledge diversity, fail to afford adequate support, or fall short in providing academic rigor, this transition may pave the way for misunderstanding, anxiety, and underachievement (Carnegie Council on Early Adolescent Development, 1989). Part III probes the multifaceted world of adolescent self-esteem, sense of belonging, social development, and academic status.

Peer acceptance cannot be overstated for its universal, vital importance to students and its impact on overall well-being. Research participants spoke frequently about the significance of friendship and being accepted by their peers. I learned from them that peer relationships in middle school are filled with potential, passion, danger, and distress. One research participant described her friends as a "sanctuary," another named her friends as her main source of support, and another found her classmates to be mean and harassing. One boy said that if you are not accepted at the middle school, life is a "living hell." The interpersonal lives of middle-school students have deep implications. How children get along in school influences academic achievement, self-concept, and personal and school safety for all students. School and community violence, dropout rates, and adolescent anxiety and depression make this point eminently clear.

Adaptation to school is considered a central task of childhood development, demanding increasingly more complex social and cognitive skills (Lynch and Cicchetti, 1997; Rutter, 1985). For the students of Mountainview Regional School District, and many other students nationwide, the transition to middle school marks the students' first immersion in a more diverse environment, at a time when the need for peer approval is intensified.

Healthy adolescent development and positive self-esteem are associated with successful peer, home, school, and community interactions marked by a sense of acceptance and competence; feelings of mutual affection and connection with peers and adult mentors; and opportunities to make meaningful contributions to the community (Bandura, 1977; Coopersmith, 1967; Erikson, 1950, 1968). When these criteria for healthy development are not met, adolescence may be a difficult time marked by loneliness and poor academic performance.

In Part III, I explore how self-esteem (chapter 9), extracurricular participation (chapter 10), and academic performance (chapter 11) influenced microlevel interactions between the students and their immediate relationships with peers, teachers, and families. How do students succeed at the task of "feeling good about themselves," to echo Christine's words, and why do some students struggle with self-concept? The central unifying theme in these chapters is the way students construct a sense of themselves as friends, athletes, and scholars as part of their peer, family, and school communities. Part III examines how students' needs for acceptance, sense of competence, and belonging are met or not met by middle-school policies and practices.

Recognizing and Documenting Success

This research explores the complex interactive forces of youth development, school and community structures, and broader sociocultural economic conditions, as they influence students of different social class backgrounds. I found examples of struggle and many reasons to re-evaluate how diverse students in rural areas are integrated in the seventh grade. But I also found in these thirty students what Willie (1973) referred to as "quiet courage." Though he was writing about black and white children in newly integrated schools, his observations hold many truths for this study on social class integration. "The difficulties and disorders have been recorded and preserved as public information. But the quiet courage of these students has been ignored . . ." (p. 2).

This is a story about *successful* adjustment of students and a *successful* middle school. When we do not stop to take our successes seriously, we place the actions that lead to success at risk of being ignored, taken for granted, or thrown out. This is also a story of struggle. Lakeview children, in the symbolic language of dress and behavior, are telling us something about loss and vulnerability that must not be ignored. Hillside and Two Rivers children are still left behind, as graduation rates, test scores, and post secondary education statistics aptly demonstrate, despite the efforts of parents who encourage and plan for their children's education, despite the students' courageous and creative efforts to do well in the regional middle school, and despite the school's balanced curriculum and teaching styles.

This is the story of an economically hard-hit town and a tourist haven, side by side, and the children from these communities who go to school together for six years. It is the story of a well-resourced school with experienced teachers, involved parents, and a generally supportive community. And it is a story of thirty extraordinary children who generously allowed me into their lives.

CHAPTER 1

A Methodology for Research
with Young Students

Interpreting Webs of Significance

It quickly became clear to me that if I wanted to compare experiences of social adjustment to middle school, I needed to understand the cultural contexts in which this adjustment was taking place. Clifford Geertz (1973) describes culture and the study of culture in this way: ". . . man is an animal suspended in webs of significance he himself has spun, I take culture to be those webs, and the analysis of it to be therefore not an experimental science in search of law but an interpretive one in search of meaning" (p. 5). Searching for meaning is a fundamentally relational endeavor.

The story that emerged over the two years of data collection is one that is perhaps best described as a web or tapestry: multiple strands, woven together, in varying colors and textures. In order to understand the transition to seventh grade from the perspective of the thirty students in this research project, I needed to listen to many stories, simultaneously told, in a variety of languages. This was not easy to do, first, because I was nearly forty years away from the experience I was trying to understand, and second, because we often tune our ears to the loudest, or most urgent, or most familiar voices. We seldom expect children to be the *primary* experts in conveying important knowledge, and without caution, preconceptions based on past experience can limit what we hear to what we *expect* to hear.

These concerns were made clear to me when I realized that I had to hear the same thing several times from several sources before I *really* heard it. Once I realized this, I tried to listen differently. I took several actions, explained in this chapter, to help in the ongoing process of genuine listening, challenging assumptions, and noticing discrepancies in the data.

The students in this study were members of diverse groups and operated in a number of environments. Every day students navigated, at the very least, the contrasting environments of home, bus stop, school bus, a variety of classrooms, school corridors, lunch room, and after-school activities, each with their own set of rules and distinct pace, tone, purpose, and people. Students were members of many groups, such as family and friendship networks, summer camp, church and civic organizations, and community recreation programs. Some students whose parents were divorced had two homes—one with their mother and the other with their father.

Rather than a pursuit of the one or two most influential factors leading to successful or difficult adjustment to grade seven, this study was a search for deepening complexity; it was, in every possible way, an interpretive analysis in search of individual and collective meaning. Contrary to the fears of some empirical social scientists, interpretation need not be a subjective analysis, laden with bias, and driven by ideological standpoints. The challenge of interpretive work is to operate from beginning to end in the presence of alternative points of view, skeptical guides, clear questions, and a sense of direction articulated and used. Interpretive work is consciously flexible and relational. This study had these components in the form of a local community advisory group, critical readers, and a conceptual framework that I invoked continuously.

In order to document complexity and development within a variety of contexts, there were multiple data collection points over an eighteen-month period and multiple methods: group and individual interviews, school and community observations, questionnaires, and an assessment of student grades, attendance, and test results.

While I agree with the viewpoint that qualitative research needs to be flexible, creative, and open to modification (Marshall and Rossman, 1995), I could not venture into the lives of thirty young students and their families without clear ethical and methodological guidelines, expectations, and questions. The following sections give readers a sense of the many factors that influenced how information was given and interpreted, and the special circumstances that require thought when children are research participants.

Underlying Assumptions and Guiding Questions

Elias et al. (1992) studied academic and interpersonal adaptation to middle school and advised researchers to consider these points: first, they said, the child's appraisal of adaptation difficulties is phenomenological; second, the experiences of children often go unnoticed by adults in the environment; third, adjustment is linked to the context of the environment, as well as to individual child factors; and finally, sources of information about the child's behavior outside of school should be obtained.

Despite this counsel, I found in a review of the literature on middle-school transition and adjustment that researchers have not examined middle-school experience from the students' perspective, nor have they considered school and community contexts. Little research has been conducted in rural areas, how students understand and experience social class diversity has not been explored, and inquiries that uncover the profound interpersonal lives of middle school students are few and far between. This research project responds to these gaps in the research literature.

Addison (1989: pp. 41–42) described interpretive research as a "co-constitutive" and "dialogical" process in which the researcher's prior experience leads her to enter the field with certain expectations that are tested through interactions with research participants. My research questions were informed by twenty-five years of practice with adolescents in rural areas. What social-emotional issues would students from different social class backgrounds face when they transitioned from the elementary schools in their own communities to a six-town regional middle school? What personal, familial, peer, school, and community resources would students engage to help them during the transition year? Does social class background influence the extent to which students successfully integrate their familial and community "funds of knowledge" (Moll et al., 1992) within the school setting? What patterns of interaction and participation would emerge over the transition from grade six to grade seven? Is there evidence in these patterns that the school environment provides a better fit for some than for others?

A number of assumptions are embedded in these questions and in the methods I used. First, I believed that students would be reliable and valuable sources of information; I believed, in fact, that they would be the *best* sources to answer these questions. Second, I assumed that social class would play an important and visible role in student adjustment to middle school, and I believed that socioeconomic and town diversity would be salient factors for students when they transitioned to their new school. Third, I believed that students would arrive at the middle school with a variety of skills, styles, and resources derived from their unique temperaments, home and community cultures, and past experiences. Students would be met by a school environment that is a composite of many factors: teacher personalities and styles; school policies, rules, and norms; classroom resources, such as books and computers; subject matter and curriculum; and student evaluation processes. Finally, I began this project with the hypothesis that the middle school environment would provide a better fit for some than for others and that students from lower social class backgrounds would not easily be able to integrate their familial and community knowledge and resources into the middle school setting, which I assumed to be an environment influenced more powerfully by middle-class values and norms. I searched for data that might contradict these assumptions, and indeed, these preconceptions were challenged over and over again by the research participants.

Human lives are lived much more idiosyncratically than sociology would have us believe and are much more normative than psychology would have us believe. I needed a methodological and theoretical foundation that would capture that reality. The theoretical frameworks for this study are interdisciplinary, drawing from sociology, history, and developmental psychology; the conceptual framework takes its shape from the work of social psychologist, Urie Bronfenbrenner.

Bronfenbrenner (1979) depicted human development as the "progressive, mutual accommodation, between an active, growing human being and the changing properties of the immediate settings in which the developing person lives" (p. 21). So the relevant question here is not only how do students adjust to their new environment, but also how does their new environment shift and change over time to adjust to them? How do teachers, parents, mentors and the broader culture mediate this experience?

Research Design Overview

In this research project I worked to understand how and why students from different social class backgrounds and communities interact with each other, participate in extracurricular activities, hold leadership positions, access resources such as teacher attention, provide assistance to their families, and make friends across social class and town-of-residence lines.

After students were selected using a criterion-based random selection procedure, I began the project by visiting each family in their home between January and March 1999. Data were collected from students in three waves: spring of 1999 when the students were sixth graders, fall of 1999, when the students were new to the middle school, and spring of 2000, when the students were experienced seventh graders. I wanted to grasp the sixth graders' expectations and hopes as they approached seventh grade, the new seventh graders' initial experiences and reactions to the middle school, and the experienced seventh graders' interpretations and adjustment strategies.

The matched group of students from two elementary schools represented an economically diverse group of students who had, so far, been academically and socially successful. The study group had sixteen students from Lakeview (eight boys and eight girls) and fourteen students from Hillside-Two Rivers (seven boys and seven girls). These thirty students were 18% of the total student population in the same grade from these towns. All thirty students attended every data collection session, so I had the unusual advantage of having complete questionnaires and interviews from all research participants at all data collections points.

Each data collection point included individual in-depth interviews and student focus-group sessions, during which students also completed questionnaires. I consulted town history books, historical societies, local newspapers, and school documents, such as newsletters, the middle school handbook, and correspondence sent from the middle school to the families of incoming seventh graders. At the end of the sixth and seventh grades, I collected grade reports and standardized test scores for all students. Interviews with elementary and middle school staff and conversations with parents provided important contextual information.

Since I had lived in the school district for nearly eighteen years, it could be argued that I had been collecting data for a long time and that I was always collecting data. The long history of interactions with students, teachers, and parents of this school district formed what Heidegger (1962) referred to as a "forestructure of understanding"—an interpretation that precedes formal data collection and analysis. I learned to use this forestructure as background context and as a hypothetical stand—a possible explanation to be *disproven* rather than proven. In the end, some of my early assumptions were strengthened, but many were found to be inaccurate or incomplete.

More than fifty hours of community observations were conducted at local coffee shops, on the street, and at public events like community suppers, holiday fairs, and the Fourth of July parade. Casual conversations about the towns and schools had an entirely different meaning to me (and still do) because of this project. I also attended school and community meetings, sixth grade promotion nights, a middle-school information night for parents, and school district meetings. During the observation, or immediately after, I took notes and recorded them in the computer as soon as possible.

School observations were conducted over six days and more than fifty hours, during the winter of 2000. I got on the school bus before

6:00 a.m., attended all classes with a group of students, ate lunch in the cafeteria, stayed after school, and took the bus back to my car at the end of the day. I tried to spend some time in classes with all the students in the study group. The purpose of these observations was to get a feel for the middle school environment—the sounds, smells, sights, challenges, and emotions that students faced every day. I did not intend to observe individual students during this time but I could not help but notice how the research participants interacted in the classroom setting. However, I maintained our confidentiality agreement during this time and did not single out or pay special attention to student research participants, unless they made it clear to me that they wanted my attention. Students liked the covert connection we shared; we acknowledged each other in subtle ways.

Another component of the research design was the use of community advisory groups in each town. I convened these groups to provide resource and factual information and to be skeptical advisors throughout the project. Each group met four times over a two-year period, with consistent attendance from ten people. Getting this project off the ground required a rigorous negotiation process with the school district. It took a full year to negotiate entry with the school district. Politics, community relations, and methodological concerns were central to this process. Having a group of interested, informed, community members helped tremendously.

Selecting Matched Groups from Two Communities

As soon as I got the go ahead from the district office in early December 1998, I contacted the principals of both elementary schools and arranged to begin the selection process, with the help of sixth grade teachers. A criterion-based random sample selection protocol was established with clearly defined procedures. I supplied teachers with sheets of paper for selected, alternative, and not selected students, a basket, and numbered chips. As teachers drew numbers and looked to the class list for the student that number represented, they needed to be able to answer yes to all these questions before placing the name of the student on the selected list:

Has the student lived in the school district for two years or more?

As far as you know, is the student reasonably likely to remain in the district and make the transition to middle school?

Does the student have three or less discipline referrals so far this year?

Does the student have at least a C– average so far this year?

Is the student without a significant physical, emotional, cognitive, developmental, or learning disability?

In order to clarify "significant" and to help teachers decide whether or not a student fit the above criteria, I gave these instructions: "If you answered 'no' to any of the questions, you will have to make a judgment about whether or not you feel this 'negative' factor is likely to be a risk to that student as he or she makes the social adjustment to middle school" (Selection memo, December 7, 1998). Also, I asked teachers to keep a record of the reasons why they decided that a student did not fit the criteria. The process proceeded in this way until the selected and alternate lists were filled, or until all the chips were drawn.

Finally, I asked teachers to look at the list of students carefully to make another judgment: "As far as you know, does this group of students accurately and proportionately represent the social class and lifestyle demographics of your community? If the group is unbalanced in a way that you think might cause distorted results, please draw another name" (ibid.). Again, teachers were asked to document how and why they made the decisions they made along the way.

To protect student privacy, I did not see the names of students on these lists. A letter to parents explaining the project and requesting their child's participation was in a stamped envelope ready to be addressed and mailed by school staff. The mailing included a stamped, addressed, return envelope and reply form that requested parents to check either "Yes, I am interested in hearing more about this study. Please contact me." or "No. Please do not contact me." Forms were returned to the school and I received only the yes responses. By requesting an active response, the process fully met the concerns of the school district regarding family privacy.

Hillside Elementary School has students from Hillside and from the small neighboring town of Two Rivers; Lakeview Elementary School has a few students from the neighboring town of Meadow. After consulting with teachers, we decided to include students from Two Rivers and Meadow. One Hillside teacher said, "Two Rivers students come to Hillside elementary in the fourth grade, when they go to the middle school, they are thought of as Hillside kids." Once data collection started, I heard this from students as well. In the final study group, there were seven students from Hillside, seven from Two Rivers, fifteen from Lakeview, and one from

Meadow. These groups were diverse economically, but well matched in terms of grades, school attendance, participation, and social development.

Teachers from Lakeview and Hillside reported striking differences in the way they experienced the selection process. Lakeview teachers said it was quick and easy, and they filled both the selected and alternative lists with names to spare. In Hillside, however, they found that they had to draw every name to fill both lists because so many of their students did not meet the criteria. Hillside teachers said they found the experience validating. As they thought about each student and evaluated whether or not he or she met the selection criteria, they recognized the enormous challenges they faced. "No wonder we're so tired," one of them said.

In Hillside, seventy-six names were drawn. Forty-one students (54%) were excluded because they did not meet the criteria. Seventeen students (22%) did not meet the residence longevity criterion for selection; twelve students had a significant learning disability (14.3%); eight students had average grades lower than C– (10.4%); and four had too many discipline referrals (5.2%).

Lakeview teachers drew only fifty-six names out of ninety and filled the selected and alternative lists with thirty-eight names altogether. They had to exclude eighteen students (32.1%) because they did not meet the criteria. They gave the following reasons for excluding students from the potential sample: eight moved to town less than two years ago or were planning to move away before grade seven (14.3%), four had more than three discipline referrals (7.1%), four had a significant learning disability. By contrast, only two students had low grades.

As a teacher, I knew the sad experience of coming to school one morning to find one of my students gone—suddenly withdrawn from school. In low-income communities this happens often, sometimes without warning, and frequently under highly stressful circumstances, causing a disruption in classroom life. In Lakeview, teachers reported that children were less likely to move in or out during the school year, less likely to move because of stressful circumstances, and less likely to move suddenly. These differences in student population and the fact that fewer Hillside students met the selection criteria is an indication that the Lakeview students selected for the study may have been more representative of their classmates than the Hillside students.

Building Rapport by Visiting Homes

Information packets, including a letter of introduction and a summary of the research project, went out to sixty parents. In all, twenty-six families—fifteen from Lakeview and eleven from Hillside—responded to the mailing. Five other families became involved through word of mouth.

Right after the holidays I began what was one of the many enjoyable and memorable parts of this project: visiting each family at home. In all, I went to thirty-one student homes in the winter of 1999 (two families had two sixth graders each). All but one family decided to participate in the study and another family moved out of the school district before the children went to middle school.

There are a few things I would change if I were going to do this research project all over again; one of them is that I would not design the project in a way that would require thirty-one home visits in the middle of a northeastern winter! What I recall most vividly about these visits, aside from the blinding snowstorms and ankle deep mud, are the warm conversations, often over tea and cookies at the kitchen table, with enthusiastic parents and their children. From January through March I drove all over this rural, hilly, school district, enjoyed the hospitality of wonderfully generous people, and began to feel comfortable in my researcher role.

At each visit I met with the sixth grader and at least one parent; sometimes, curious siblings or friends joined us. Usually mothers met with me but in Lakeview, two fathers were actively involved in the meeting, and in Hillside, *six* fathers were actively involved and stayed involved throughout the project. The home visit folder that I left with each family included a three-page overview of the project, a time line with interview and questionnaire schedules, a draft of the questionnaire and interview questions, ethical guidelines concerning informed consent and confidentiality, and a permission form. Parents and students were encouraged to take their time thinking about whether or not they could make a commitment to this project, but almost all parents and students signed on to the project during the home visit.

The home visits gave me the important opportunity to establish a connection with parents and students in their own territory. I believed that the success of the project—the retention of students and the quality of the information they would give me—would be positively influenced by this initial visit and the trust and openness that it encouraged. The conversations we had during these home visits gave me a chance to take in parental concerns about the transition to middle school and attitudes toward education. These visits gave me a glimpse of family life and the physical surroundings that were home to each of the students—the tone, pace, and sensations of their lives. Images from these encounters remain clear: the goat that bounded over to meet me in the yard, the fifteen disassembled motor vehicles scattered here and there around the house and surrounding woods, the mother who showed me an oily hand when I offered a handshake and said, "Sorry, but I just changed the oil in the car," the artifacts from international travel, the happy dog present in each and every household, the family photos on the walls, refrigerator reminders to organize intensely busy lives, the interruptions of visiting neighborhood children and curious siblings, the television or CB radio going as we talked, the special treats picked up just for my visit, the smell of wood stove burning, the question asked by one mother, "Do you have biases about this?" All these and countless many other experiences gave me an essential (and, of course, incomplete) contextual understanding of the lives of the children in this study.

Meeting with families in their homes, making my intentions, biases and research goals known, and asking for their trust and commitment made me feel vulnerable and this vulnerability helped me grasp what I was asking these children to do. The home visits were my first negotiation at defining the boundaries of our relationship. I had signed permission forms from everyone from the start, but requesting parental permission, explaining informed consent and confidentiality, and providing information were a part of every interaction for the duration of the study. Throughout the project and beyond, I stayed in touch with research participants and their families through letters, cards, phone calls, and visits.

Characteristics of the Research Group

The fifteen boys and fifteen girls who were research participants in this study were reliable and earnest sources of information about the transition from grade six to grade seven and about life in the middle school. In the spring of sixth grade, the students ranged in age from eleven to thirteen years old. There were eight girls and eight boys from Lakeview, seven girls and seven boys from Hillside-Two Rivers. They were all shapes and sizes, dressed in a variety of ways, and had very different communication styles. They impressed me over and over again with their observations, insights, and self-understanding.

In the process of exploring issues together, we developed a common language for understanding their transition to middle school. The students not only generously shared their experiences of being seventh graders, but they were actively involved in the process, regularly making suggestions about research procedures. One day a girl from Two Rivers told me I needed to see a certain part of her town if I wanted to grasp some of the issues townspeople face, and so she took me there. They often offered recommendations for how the transition to middle school or the middle school itself could be improved.

These young research participants, on the cusp of their teen years, lived complex and full lives. They were serious players of lacrosse, ice hockey, baseball, field hockey, track, soccer, and basketball. They played paintball, rode their four-wheelers, and took their horses out for long walks. In a beautiful, quiet gesture of caring, one Hillside participant had her gorgeous, waist-length auburn hair cut short to give to a cancer patient. Another student lovingly cared for his three younger siblings most days after school because his mom, a single parent, was either at her waitressing job or at school, working hard on her baccalaureate degree. By grade six, one of the girls had published two of her poems, and another wrote a regular column for the local conservation newsletter. One boy frequently joined his father doing electrical work to raise money to go on a People-to-People trip to Europe.

They had dreams of playing in the NFL, becoming a lawyer, teaching kindergarten, writing books and comic strips, having careers as vets and in acting, and being the first in their family to go to college. They listened to Korn, Garth Brooks, Slipknot, P.O.D., Tupac, and Metallica. Some got up in the morning when it was barely light to bring in firewood and to feed chickens and rabbits and goats. Some had family members who were ill and some had lost grandparents and beloved pets. In the fall of seventh grade, one student was seriously injured while she rode her four-wheeler alone on steep, rocky terrain. They were amazingly different, yet they shared a lot in common and treated each other with respect.

Research participants were from rural northeastern communities with a year-round population of less than 5,000 people. They were of white, mixed European heritage. Half of the thirty research participants had experienced their parent's divorce at some point in their lives. Seven of them lived with a stepparent and eight lived with single mothers. Their relationships with non-custodial biological parents ranged from nonexistent to consistent, full, and supportive.

Ascribing Socioeconomic Status

Since I wanted to know how social class influenced social adjustment to middle school, I needed to find a way to determine socioeconomic status. Drawing from the work of Entwisle and Astone (1994), four factors were considered: property value, the number of parents in the household, the occupation of the adult with the higher status job, and the level of education of the adult with the most advanced certificate or diploma.

This information was gathered through telephone conversations with parents and public property tax records.

Values from 1 through 5 were assigned to each education, occupation, and property value category, and the added value of 1 was assigned to a household with two adults as care takers. These values were added together to obtain total scores and then divided into categories to define high, middle, and low social status. Scores of 5 through 7 were considered low; 8 through 11, middle; and 12 through 15, high. Appendix 2 provides a more detailed summary of the categories and values used.

A few students lived in homes that were rented; others lived in properties that ranged in assessed value from less than $25,000 to nearly $500,000. Some of their parents had graduate degrees and some went to work before finishing high school. Occupations spanned a similarly diverse spectrum, from owners of international corporations to carpenters, electricians, teachers, and waitresses. A few parents were disabled or unemployed.

My own background shared some similarities and some differences with the students in the study. In many ways, the culture of Hillside reminded me of the working class, Italian-American neighborhood of my childhood located in an urban mill town of a neighboring state.

The Gap Between Observed and Perceived Affluence

Using level of education, occupation, property value, and number of caretakers in the household to assess social class status, more than half of the Lakeview children and *none* of the Hillside-Two Rivers children were in the highest social class group. Hillside-Two Rivers children were split between the lowest social class group where there were six (out of 14) and the middle group where there were eight. Talking with people from these communities, I often heard the misperception that everyone in Lakeview is middle or upper class, but in this study group, two of the Lakeview children were in the lowest social class category. Some of the children in the research group lived with a considerable amount of economic stress in their lives.

Figure 1.1 shows the number of students from Lakeview and Hillside in each of three social status categories. However, social status is much more than economic indicators and is, therefore, hard to assess. For example, families with a high level of involvement in their communities may benefit from "social capital" (Putnam, 1993) that contributes to overall social status and levels the playing field for some lower income

Figure1.1. Number of Lakeview and Hillside Students in Low, Middle, and High Social Class Categories

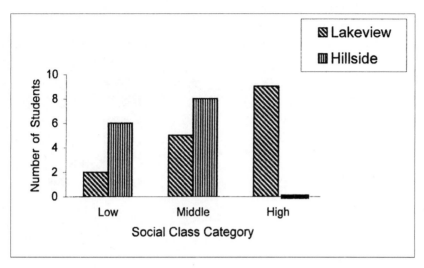

families (Duncan, 1999). Researchers had previously found what I found, that students of this age tended to report, "We are all the same," when answering comparative questions about social class (e.g., Rosenberg and Pearlin, 1978).

The subjective complexity of social class status is clear in how the students in my study responded to the question, "On a scale of 1 to 10, where would you place your family in terms of affluence, compared to the other students in your school." I asked this question of all students at the beginning and at the end of seventh grade, and categorized their answers into low, middle, and high scores of perceived social status. In general, their responses remained stable over time, indicating that perceptions of social class status were not influenced to a large degree by exposure to greater economic diversity. These responses do suggest, however, that students made within-town comparisons that influenced how well off they perceived themselves to be. Figure 1.2 combines perceived social status by town, at the end of grade seven, with the calculated indicators of social status reported above.

In general, Hillside-Two Rivers students perceived themselves to be better off and Lakeview students perceived themselves to be worse off than the objective signs indicated. Two Hillside-Two Rivers children placed themselves in the highest social class group; four Lakeview children and

Figure 1.2. Calculated and Perceived Social Class by Town

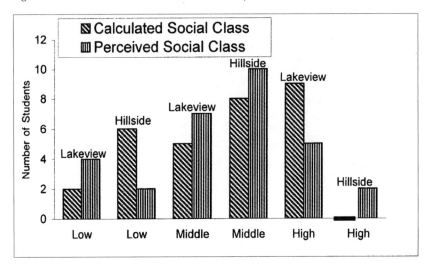

only two Hillside-Two Rivers children placed themselves in the lowest group. Most students placed themselves in the middle.

The Flexible Role of the Researcher

Some ethnographic researchers have studied middle schools using a participant-observer approach (e.g., Wells, 1996). I chose not to use this approach because, being considerably older than twelve, I was skeptical of the idea that I would blend in with the research participants. It was immediately clear that I needed to have personal clarity regarding my research role, and I needed to make my role and purpose explicit to research participants, their parents, and school staff. However, as I interacted with students and their families, I found that the way I defined this role was a negotiated process, requiring constant reflection and modification.

For almost two years, I never left my house without a research notebook and often a tape recorder. My residence and work in the same area gave me many opportunities for informative casual observations and conversations. As the director of a youth service organization, I also had access to educational and counseling services and information. Occasionally, parents sought information from me that was connected to my youth development work. I saw this as a part of my commitment to families and students, a very small exchange for the enormous generosity they showed me. When necessary, I referred parents to other youth counselors and resources, so that my role with students remained as a researcher throughout the research period, albeit a researcher who was mindful of, and open to, the mentoring potential in adult-child relationships.

Rapport was established more easily with students because we had something else in common: a love for our dogs. Hollingshead (1949) brought his dachshund with him on research visits with students to "break the ice," and I often had my Siberian husky along for that same purpose. Each time I reconnected with students to set up the next round of interviews, I paid close attention to any signs of emerging reluctance on their part but research participants remained eager and accessible informants. They seemed to appreciate my interest in them and they reciprocated by treating my requests with kindness and generosity.

The way research relationships require flexibility in role definition is evident in this end-of-interview exchange that took place between Arianna, a Two Rivers student, and me when she was in the sixth grade:

> Donna: Is there anything else you'd like to tell me, anything more about yourself or things I didn't ask that I should have asked?
>
> Arianna: No, I think you asked me real good.
>
> Donna: Yeah, we covered a lot of ground. Is there anything you want to ask me?
>
> Arianna: Did you go to college?
>
> [I explain to her in some detail that I went to college after high school and later went to graduate school, and still later, went back to school for more graduate work.]
>
> Donna: For someone who was very nervous in school, like you, I sure spent a lot of time in school. I think half of my life I've been in school.
>
> Arianna: Has this been a goal for you?

I was so touched by this question from Arianna on our first encounter and after I answered how this was indeed a goal for me, we talked for a while about her own goals. In this moment I was extremely aware of my mentoring role.

Sara Lawrence-Lightfoot (1997) wrote that much of social science seeks to uncover failure and pathology, and this tendency overlooks health and resilience, "magnifies what is wrong and neglects evidence of promise and potential" (p. 9). She continued, "Portraiture resists this tradition-laden effort to document failure. It is an intentionally generous, and eclectic process that begins by searching for what is good and healthy and assumes that the expression of goodness will always be laced with imperfections" (ibid.). I did not begin this study looking for goodness but I indeed found "goodness laced with imperfections." I couldn't help it. Through my relationships with research participants, I came to understand the complexity of their lives. The more complex my understanding became the more goodness and health I saw.

Student Focus Groups

Small group sessions gave students an opportunity to share their impressions, opinions, and feelings with their peers. Students became important sources of information to one another. Not only did they come to anticipate hard questions about their beliefs, values, and experiences, they also looked forward to the special time with their peers. The focus-group sessions were held after school or on Saturday mornings, for between ninety minutes and two hours, with usually four to six students at a time. We used space in local churches and agencies. I had the time of my life doing these sessions and the students enjoyed themselves too; none of them missed a single meeting. We met in March and April 1999, when students were sixth graders, October and November 1999 and March and April 2000, when students were seventh graders.

These field notes, written in March 1999 just after our first session together, reveal the enthusiasm, energy, diligence, and humor I experienced throughout the project:

> I picked up the boys [all from Lakeview] right after school at 3:30. They were all anticipating our time together and they were very excited. They continued to be excited when they saw the pizza in the car: "Wow, we are getting a lot for doing this: pizza, a ride home . . ." They thanked me over and over again. At first they played with the church-school toys, and then they easily settled in, eating, drinking root beer, and talking nicely to each other and me. After we finished [the questionnaires], I taped

their discussion, which they were so excited about they wanted to listen to it in the car as I was driving each of them home. They took the tape recording very seriously, speaking clearly and moving closer to the tape recorder in order to be sure to be heard. They had heard about seventh grade organizational planners and talking right into the tape recorder they protested, "No planners! Do you hear me? No planners!" When we listened to the tape again in the car as I was dropping them off at home we laughed a lot when we came to this part.

Every session followed basically the same format. A letter home announced the meeting times and locations and a phone call arranged the specific day each student would attend the group session. I always made a reminder call a day or two in advance. Students were picked up at school or they were dropped off at the meeting place by a parent. We always had food and talked informally at the beginning, then they completed questionnaires for about fifty minutes while I wrote notes on their interactions, what they were wearing, and so on. Finally, we had a discussion that I sometimes taped.

Many purposes were filled by this research component. Most obviously, I was able to get all the questionnaires filled out, and while students were still there, I checked them quickly to be sure they were complete and legible. While they filled out questionnaires, they sat separately and worked quietly. Their automatic demeanor was to act like they were taking a test, and for these academically successful students, test-taking was mostly a positive experience.

During the discussion time, I let students lead the way with whatever issues they wanted to discuss. On two occasions, seventh grade girls talked about sexual harassment, both surprising and, I think, embarrassing the boys with their bold honesty. These sessions also gave me an opportunity to watch students interact with their peers in single-gender and mixed-gender groups, and in single-town and mixed-town groups. I noticed, for example, that Lakeview children seemed more sure of themselves:

> There is a sense from most of the Lakeview kids that they feel sure of themselves, aware of their own voice, confident and self-possessed with their peers and with adults, and sure that what they have to say is worth listening to. At no time did I have the impression that Lakeview students were at all surprised that I would value what they have to say—they expected my attentiveness. (Field notes, April 1999)

I did feel, however, that some Hillside children were less sure that what they had to say was valuable. It was not until after they filled out one of the questionnaires that the Hillside students took snacks on our first day together. Did they now feel they were more deserving of the reward? I found that most Hillside children did not take my attention or this experience for granted. If I was not careful, Lakeview children could have easily dominated these sessions, risking the loss of insights the Hillside students had to offer. The initial reticence on the part of Hillside students may sadly be misinterpreted by some as resistance, distrust, dullness, disinterest, or even defiance, to the great detriment of these students *and* their Lakeview classmates who have much to learn from them.

The gender differences were also evident during these sessions: single-gender groups seemed far more relaxed and covered a much wider range of topics than coed groups in both sixth and seventh grades. The girls often wanted to meet in coed groups, while the boys said they did not mind either way, but boys in mixed groups were more quiet and, perhaps, self-conscious. Single-gender sessions just happened by chance depending on who was able to make it on that day and were an opportunity for important and rare social interactions and exchanges of information. My field notes from April 2000 documented a memorable interaction between the boys about getting a girlfriend— something that had become very important, frustrating, and confusing to some of them by the end of seventh grade:

> These 12–13 year old boys from both towns go from cutting-edge insights about interpersonal and group relations at the middle school to expressing their young and innocent desire for romance and connection.
>
> [One boy] was especially exasperated by the situation at the middle school—the girls seem to go for the boys who get into trouble, not for the respectful boys.
>
> [Another boy] "Yeah, like that saying, 'Nice guys finish last.'"
>
> "I don't get it," said the first boy. "When I was in the second grade *all* the girls had a crush on me."
>
> His classmate, another boy who said very little the whole meeting, quipped, "When we were in the second grade, even *I* had a crush on you!"

They were totally unselfconscious as they shared these intimate longings with each other—this exchange between early adolescent boys could not have happened in a coed group and, I fear, will not happen as they get older.

In another instance, students talked about their parents' divorce and shared hope and comfort with their friends also dealing with parental discord and separation. Research participants also learned new things about themselves during these sessions. One student handed me her completed self-esteem questionnaire and said, "I guess my self-esteem is lower at home than at school." Another student said he was beginning to see himself "through the eyes of other kids." It is easy to see how children can be harmed in research relationships if there is not careful attention to understanding our role as researchers and the impact of research participation in the lives of children. It is essential to establish norms of interaction that are appropriately responsive.

Emerging social class-consciousness was also evident during these sessions. In fact, meeting in this way *encouraged* students to think about social class differently than they might have. On one occasion, two students from Lakeview traveled with me to Hillside for a meeting. My notes from that day demonstrate how increased social class awareness may have resulted from participation in this project:

> As we drove into Hillside Center, I wondered what the two Lakeview students riding in the back of the van were seeing and taking in. We pulled up in front of Hillside Crossing, the location of several social service programs, where our meeting would be. The Two Rivers girls climbed out of a faded, red Pinto whose approximate age could be guessed by the generous amount of rust along the doorframes. They seemed happy to be there and ready to go. I remembered the large sports utility vehicles that dropped off the two Lakeview girls riding with me and I wondered what they were thinking. For an uncomfortable moment, they remained seated in the van. Did they feel out of place? Once we got going they were friendly to each other. One Lakeview girl asked a girl from Two Rivers, "Are you like middle class?" (Field notes, October 1999)

These girls were working out a definition of class right in front of my eyes. The conversation that pursued was an amazing comparing of notes about where they buy their clothes, why some students are called "snobs," and misunderstandings about Hillside and Lakeview. The Lakeview students had never been to Center Hillside before—a fact that Hillside and Two Rivers students found incredible. At the end of this session, the Lakeview students rode with me as I dropped off Hillside-Two Rivers students at home. This session helped to reduce the mystery and stereotypes that prevail in the minds of children who had never been to Hillside but had "heard things." Over and over again I noticed how exposure to each other enhanced student's self-understanding and awareness of others.

However, on another occasion I picked up silent cues from a Hillside student that he would have been uncomfortable with Lakeview students seeing where he lived, so I arranged the transportation to drop off Lakeview students first. These are the important subtle kinds of things researchers who work with children are responsible to figure out. These children signed up to be research participants, not to have their lives insensitively exposed. We can do harm if we are not astute to the sometimes fragile nature of early adolescent self-esteem and peer acceptance.

These brief snap shots of the focus-group sessions portray how the sessions were used to gather information, but they also reveal something equally important in research work with children: the research experience was a powerful and meaningful intervention in the lives of the children involved in it. I have no doubt that it changed the way they thought about and experienced the transition to grade seven. My unambivalent position throughout the project was to acknowledge that out of their relationships with me and each other would come new insights and new ideas about school, social class, gender, future plans, and so on. While I used a great deal of caution to facilitate interactions rather than dominate them, and while I was careful to explore *their* opinions and feelings rather than disclose my own, I was also committed to allowing them to enlist me as an adult mentor and guide. Discussions about provocative issues such as divorce, sexual harassment, and social class stereotypes required very careful facilitation. In addition, I encouraged and sometimes even advised students around educational issues when I worried that students lacked the requisite information to make important decisions or envision future plans. When I occasionally worried that a student might be in danger of emotional harm, I spoke with the student and his or her parents.

From the start, the students in this project were fully and actively engaged. I referred to students as "research participants" throughout the project to reflect this active and influential role, and I have chosen to maintain this active phrase in my writing rather than the more passive, "research sample." Throughout this book when I refer to "research participants," I mean the thirty students selected for the project.

In-Depth Individual Interviews

As soon as focus-group sessions and questionnaires were complete at each data collection point, I began to meet individually with eight of the thirty students for a one- to two-hour interview. The four Lakeview and four Hillside-Two Rivers students were selected for in-depth interviews because they were interested and able to talk freely with a microphone present. In these individual sessions I explored beliefs, values, and attitudes concerning popularity, school achievement, peer relationships, and the future; and I tried to gain a deeper understanding of the meaning of social class and the transition to middle school in their lives. The interviews were all recorded and transcribed.

As I grew to know students better and better, I was often deeply moved by our interactions. It was during these sessions that students revealed their deepest feelings and fears, and explored with me, bravely and honestly, the treacherous emotional territory of peer group acceptance. Occasionally, I glimpsed the early childhood tragedies several students had experienced and how these circumstances transformed the way they interacted with others and interpreted the world.

I pushed students hard during these sessions: I asked difficult questions, listened carefully, and looked for deep and thorough answers. Neither students nor I settled on facile definitions or responses. By our third session together, the connection between us seemed so filled with mutual respect and trust that I sensed some sadness when our individual time together was about to end.

The Power of Community Advisory Groups

In order to end up with a story that was credible, applicable, trustworthy, and recognizable to the community, I convened advisory groups, one in Lakeview and one in Hillside-Two Rivers with twenty members, ten of whom attended meetings regularly. These groups provided feedback and gave direction at all points of the study. They discussed the meaning and implications of my findings; they provided resource information and made suggestions; and they were a political presence ready to generate community dialogue and identify practical applications for the results. They represented, in function, purpose, and character, the unique cultural context in which they operated.

Meetings were in the fall of 1998, before the project actually began, the spring and fall of 1999, and the spring of 2000, as I wrapped up data collection. In the first Lakeview meeting, seven people arrived right on time and turned their attention immediately to the agenda and handouts that included a brief summary of the project. Right away, my reasons for convening this group were confirmed: a middle school teacher remarked, "You want to look at 'school environment?' Which environment is that? There are multiple environments. Every classroom is a different

environment." There was also an important discussion about the connections between academic and social adjustment. The Lakeview meetings followed an agenda and relied on my facilitation. We started and
ended on time and focused on technical and methodological issues.

A week later, most of the nine people attending the meeting at
Hillside Crossing came before the starting time of 3:30 and they stayed
late. As soon as they all crowded around the oval table, they started the
meeting without me while I was in the kitchen making tea. At this and
all other Hillside meetings, the discussion was an associative one focused on substantive issues, rather than a sequential one focused on
technical issues. My notes from November 22, 1998 describe the power,
purpose, *peril*, and potential of these advisory meetings. These notes,
recorded after the first Hillside meeting, draw a sharp contrast to the
Lakeview meeting:

> I never even had a chance to provide an overview of the meet-
> ing. They knew what they were there for and they weren't wait-
> ing for me to get to it. Immediately, they launched into a
> discussion about class issues in the school district. For the next
> two hours I heard one example after another of exactly the con-
> ditions that have spurred me on to do this study. The tone was
> fast-paced, energetic, hard to get a word in, lots of laughter, and
> perspectives that were told from a position of certainty. No
> apologies, no questions, mostly bold, clear statements about
> how things "are" in the school district they all know so well. This
> meeting was in substance, volume, energy, and style remarkably
> different than the November 4 meeting, which focused more
> on the technical aspects of the study and stuck to the agenda.
> The idea of having this group ensure my accountability to the
> community is a sure thing. One mother wanted to know if I
> would be making recommendations at the end of this study.
> This is an activist group looking for change. At 5:00 I pulled out
> the agenda and tried to get people to take a look at it. "An
> agenda?" someone said. "You've got delusions of grandeur!"
> Everyone laughed.

These advisory groups played an important, even contentious,
role throughout the research project. My fear that the advisors might
ask for more ownership than I was willing to give never materialized
into an actual threat, but I learned through this process to consider
many alternative possibilities and interpretations. The divergent styles
and perspectives provided another opportunity to observe town dif-

ferences and a mechanism for keeping my work grounded, purposeful, trustworthy, and credible.

Limits of Generalizability

Maxwell (1996) makes a distinction between external and internal generalizability (p. 97). This work can make no claims of external generalizability when geography, community culture, racial background, and economic conditions differ. In fact, it only has internal generalizability to students who would meet the same selection criteria. However, when I present these findings publicly, teachers, administrators, and parents in other rural, regional school districts frequently say they recognize these issues in their own communities. To some extent, generalizability lies in the reader's ability to locate themselves and their own realities in the detailed descriptions of towns, classrooms, and students. Therefore, I believe this study has relevance, if not generalizability, to other demographically and economically similar school districts.

Students in this study were selected with specific criteria and, therefore, their transition experiences are representative of the experiences of other students who meet the same criteria. My research group represents a low-risk group of students who had, so far, been academically and socially successful. I am certain that many of the findings reported here would look very different in a group of students who were at higher risk for difficult adjustment. Still, the issues that are raised in this study, and the students and situations described, will be familiar to many people who work with early adolescents.

Validity and Reliability

Twenty-five years of prior work with early adolescents and familiarity with the school district posed both an asset and a threat to the validity of this project. In order to ensure valid and reliable results, I used these strategies: a well-planned research design that I followed or modified with purpose (Maxwell, 1996); dialogical and reflective methods for examining biases (Patton, 1990); careful and consistent documentation (Nakkula and Ravitch, 1998); and a mechanism for uncovering discrepant data and alternative interpretations (Giroux, 1988). These procedures supported what Lincoln and Guba (1985) referred to as "truth value" in qualitative research. These authors proposed that to have truth value, findings must be credible, transferable, dependable,

and confirmable. Miles and Huberman (1994) provided these questions as a guideline for truth value: "Do the findings of the study make
sense? Are they credible to the people we study? Do we have an authentic portrait of what we are looking at?" (p. 278). To authenticate
my findings, I incorporated the following strategies.

First, when I heard or saw something unexpected, I asked other students and adults *not* connected to the study about it. For example, when
I observed the surprising difference between Lakeview and Hillside-Two
Rivers buses described in chapter 8, I checked my observation with other
students from both communities. This was an important strategy because
the research participants were very much aware that I was writing about
what they told me and, as often happens with research participants, they
became more thoughtful and reticent about those things that had particular power and meaning, such as the patterns of social grouping
among their peers. Students not in the study were noticeably less cir-
cumspect about their answers than the research participants, who became increasingly concerned about giving me a fair, balanced and,
perhaps, self-protective, point of view.

Second, I searched for corroborating evidence in multiple methods.
For example, when students told me in individual interviews about a
popularity hierarchy in the middle school, I searched for confirming and
disconfirming evidence in lunchroom and classroom observations, student focus-group sessions, and questionnaires.

Third, local knowledge was regularly consulted to answer all sorts of
questions: How much does a dressed deer weigh? How much time does
it take to cut a cord of wood? What are the wages at local department
stores and grocery chains? When I wanted answers to these kinds of questions, I asked around.

The research advisory group previously discussed served as an
"outside audit" (Lincoln and Guba, 1985) to ensure the inclusion of
multiple and alternative interpretations. Finally, when I had a draft
ready in early March 2001, I sent letters to research participants and
their families, sixth and seventh grade teachers, and members of the
community advisory group notifying them that copies were available
through the school and town libraries for them to review and give
feedback. It was especially important to me that research participants
would have a chance to read the story they helped me construct. I nat-
urally hoped for positive responses but I also braced myself for responses of disappointment, surprise, maybe even hurt or anger, as can
sometimes be the case when research participants find their stories in
print. When a retired teacher and member of the research advisory

group read the draft, he wrote, "Needless to say, knowing the communities as I do, I found your observations fascinating and completely valid" (Personal correspondence, March 25, 2001). One mother, a parent of a research participant, called to say that as she read about her community and the schools she attended, she felt a lot of emotion—it resounded with her own knowledge and experience. She and three other parents got together one evening for dinner and read excerpts from the manuscript to discuss them. I had not dared to expect something as wonderful as this parent-initiated discussion and I was deeply moved by its occurrence.

Of all the checks and balances I placed along the way to ensure valid and reliable results, it was my relationships with the thirty students in this study that provided the most compelling assurance of validity. I found that the more I felt the privilege and responsibility of their trust, and the more I realized they believed in me to tell their story honestly, the more determined I became to tell an authentic story, one that research participants could recognize and verify. It was our relationship more than the rules of validity that inspired a deep commitment to understand and convey, as clearly and carefully as possible, what these students shared with me. This became my most important and challenging standard.

A political view of validity, described by Gitlin and Russell (1994), calls for a "mutual process" of knowledge production fully involving research participants, leading toward practical change in schools and communities:

> The validity or "truthfulness," of the data can no longer be understood as something extracted by an individual armed with a set of research procedures, but rather as a mutual process, pursued by researcher and those studied, that recognizes the value of practical knowledge, theoretical inquiry, and systematic examinations. The influence of the research process on who produces knowledge, who is seen as expert, and the resulting changes at the level of school practice are also part of an expanded and political view of validity (p. 187).

Alongside my commitment to engage the expert knowledge of research participants, understand their meaning, and report it as best as I could, was a commitment to engage *my* knowledge and experience in the service of a mutual process that would lead to a positive application of the research findings.

Researching a Changing Reality

One research challenge was the elusive nature of adolescent feelings, beliefs, and values at a time in life marked by rapid growth and development and heightened social and physical awareness. Peer group acceptance is paramount and self-identity is crafted and re-crafted in continuous transactions with others in and out of one's social group. Although I found student understanding of themselves and others to be fairly stable and consistent across time, I also noticed remarkable changes in the depth of their understanding, their ability to find personal meaning in their experiences, and in their psychological complexity. As the study progressed, students sometimes surprised me by saying things that sounded less aware of social class issues rather than more aware. Was their analysis becoming more simplistic? Were students "forgetting" important social knowledge because it was too painful or because they discovered that it was not okay to say some things? Were they learning to be more protective of their peer group and cautious about sharing their knowledge? Or had students developed a more complex repertoire of responses, drawing from a wider range of information and experience? It was important for me to fathom these developmental issues at every step of the way and consider the effects of development on the information I collected.

Writing It Up

During the data-collection period of the research project and beyond, I wrote notes almost every day resulting in literally hundreds of pages of descriptive notes on a variety of topics in different folders. There was so much to notice, I began to record all sorts of things, relevant and irrelevant. For example, I began to record when students forgot about meetings and realized that Lakeview students forgot more often than Hillside-Two Rivers students, and I later found that this seemed to fit an overall pattern in Lakeview of feeling overwhelmed with too many things to do.

Besides voluminous field notes I occasionally wrote memos. Nakkula and Ravitch (1998) addressed the usefulness of memoing to encourage researchers to reflect on assumptions, to tie research findings to theories, and to trail emergent questions, analyses, and interpretations.

One of the most challenging ethical considerations I faced was what to include and what to omit in the telling of this story and how to tell it. With children twelve and thirteen years old, this concern is especially salient. Their development during these years was so dramatic and so quick it had my head spinning and I knew that some ideas and perceptions would have changed substantially by the time I finished writing. Furthermore, although I had permission to write about what I heard and saw at the outset of the project, it was impossible for any of us to really understand the shape, tone, direction, and meaning the writing would eventually take.

During our sessions I always encouraged students to shut off the tape recorder if they wanted to say something off the record, and I often clarified my interpretations with them to be sure I was getting it right. However, the tape recorder was never off, and the information that added to my understanding was collected from more sources and in more ways than I could have ever guessed. I made some judgments in writing to respect students and protect them from potential harm. For example, I sometimes identify the student speaking (by pseudonym) and sometimes I don't, depending on the topic. Even though everyone chose an alias for himself or herself, I knew they and their families would be recognizable to each other. Therefore, some stories and interpretations are left unsaid, exercising my own judgment about where to draw the line to protect student and family privacy. I have tried not to identify individual students with particular social class indicators like the value of their home. Still, there is risk of offense, not only by what is said, but also by what is left unsaid.

In addition to these cautions, I also corrected spelling and punctuation when I used information from questionnaires. I did this for two reasons: first, my students were absolutely credible informants and I did not want to risk the reader's skepticism based on poor spelling. Second, their spelling and punctuation skills changed so much over the course of the study that it seemed unfair to use a way of writing they had outgrown by the time the study was completed. However, I never changed their grammar or the particular way they said something.

Another consideration was the writing style to use in reporting findings. For me, the research process was an aesthetic, creative, and relational process. I needed a way of conveying what I learned that upheld these elements; I needed a style of writing, therefore, that was not sterile, linear, and void of subjective reality. When she discusses research and writing, Lawrence-Lightfoot (1997) recalls Dewey: "If we want education to be artful—beautiful, not merely pretty, creative, not merely competent, discovery, not merely mimicry—then, suggested Dewey, we would have to find ways of envisioning and recording the experience that would not distort its texture and richness. This would require joining aesthetic and empirical approaches, merging rigor and improvisation, and appreciating both the details and the gestalt" (p. 6). It is this counsel I relied on throughout this writing process.

In the end, I know I have authored an incomplete and imperfect story, clouded and illuminated by my own experiences and interpretations. Countless precious moments and insights have gone untold, reminding me of one research participant's comment, "I could write a whole book just on *my* experiences in seventh grade. How will you ever write about thirty of us in one book?"

Authentic Relationships—the Heart of Qualitative Research

When children are research participants, confidentiality, boundaries, honesty, and interpretive integrity are ethical and methodological issues that are all the more urgent. Among these many issues, one seems to emerge more frequently for me: the reality that qualitative research is fundamentally a relational process and, therefore, a powerful intervention; a transformative experience for research participants, researchers, and the communities in which they work. It is not only how we collect data, and what we write, but also how we engage in research relationships from the start that matters. Like all relationships, the development and maintenance of these precious personal connections require special consideration.

At the core of this work are the contrasting evolving stories, told by the students themselves, of their emerging sense of belonging and alienation, competence and under-achievement, emotional well-being and struggle, empathy toward other students and harsh judgment, self-confidence and painful self-consciousness. The decision to write about these issues from the perspective of children is a methodological choice based on my belief that children possess important experiential knowledge, "legitimate knowledge," as Gitlin and Russell (1994) would say, based on their day-to-day experiences in school. This source of knowledge is unfortunately rarely consulted in curriculum development, scheduling, planning, educational reform strategies, and policy-making.

Also central to this work are the parallel stories, theirs and mine, of the development of thirty unique and temperamental relationships. Day-by-day, and sometimes minute-by-minute, I made choices about how to develop and maintain a research relationship with my young informants that was genuine and responsive. The ongoing negotiation of this relationship fundamentally influenced what I heard, recorded, interpreted and wrote. In *The Art and Science of Portraiture*, Lawrence-Lightfoot and

Davis (op. cit.) asserted that, "relationships are more than vehicles for data gathering, more than points of access . . . [they are] central to the empirical, ethical, and humanistic dimensions of research design, as evolving and changing processes of human encounter" (p. 138). These relationships govern the interchange and determine the quality of data we get. They are, as Ricoeur (1979) suggested, the "extra text" that must also be explored and deconstructed.

One Saturday morning, I sat around a sunny table with a group of seventh graders, listening to their sharp and detailed descriptions of life in their new school. I realized that this was a rare, perhaps unprecedented experience for them. To be able to have a critical discussion in which *they* are the experts on school experience, and an adult is the learner, changes the way we both think about that experience.

I assume these conversations have shaped the students' interpretations of their experiences in the middle school. I also assume that in our conversations, the students carefully sought to accommodate what they perceived my viewpoints and interests to be. This is something I have come to understand as a wonderful and necessary part of relationship building. They knew my purpose, they were invested enough to imagine what they thought I might want to hear, and they were altruistic in their desire to share what they were experiencing to make things better for other students. With this in mind, my first job was to be a *believing* listener; my second job was to be a *critical* listener. While I listened with openness, I needed to remain conscious of the extra text of our relationship, their development and mine, and the contexts of home, school, community, and culture.

At the end of seventh grade, I wanted to say thank you to the research participants and acknowledge them for the enormous contribution they made to educational research. So we marked the end of the project with a trip to Harvard's Graduate School of Education where students addressed a small audience in a large lecture hall about "successful transition to middle school." The morning of the trip I arrived at the middle school before 7:30 and was moved beyond words to find all thirty students, excited and ready to go, along with fifteen of their parents and several siblings.

We can easily underestimate how important we become in the lives of research participants. The researcher-in-relationship seems to me to be an evolving character, balancing the roles of academic, friend, mentor, counselor, teacher, and ordinary community member. Like any relationship, it is a risk. Some, like Judith Stacey (1991), wonder "whether the appearance of greater respect for, and equality with research subjects in the ethnographic approach, masks a deeper, more dangerous form of exploitation" (p. 113). I believe that betrayal, disillusionment, and exploitation are all dangers, but not necessary outcomes of this relationship, and I have faith in the possibility of respectful, mutually transforming research relationships. Together, I hope, my research participants and I will do a lot of good with the information we co-constructed on these pages.

PART I

—————

The Towns

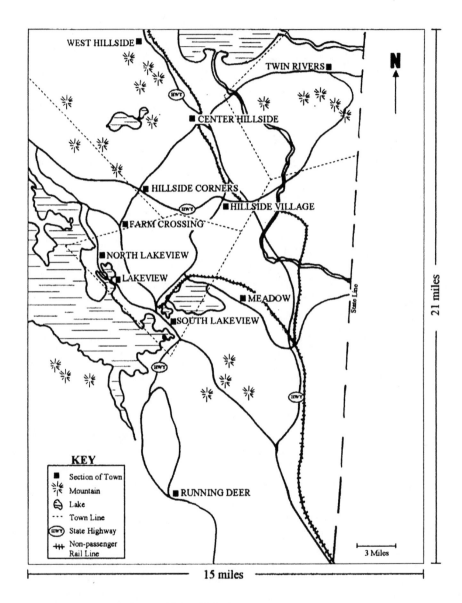

Map 1. Mountainview Regional School District

Introduction

Lakeview and Hillside[1] are geographically beautiful small towns located in the northeast, surrounded by lakes and rolling hills. In the eighteenth and nineteenth centuries, they shared a similar social and economic development history. First farming and then manufacturing helped these communities to flourish. However, in the last hundred years, tourism brought a different economic base to Lakeview, and with it, different opportunities, lifestyles, aspirations, and values. Hillside lost its manufacturing economy to southern towns where laborers were paid less; the shoe, textile, and tanning factories have not been replaced by tourism or other industries. The economic disparities between these communities are reflected in the overall town per capita incomes, land values, occupations, and educational attainment. However, both communities thrive with active social networks and an involved and industrious populace.

The 2000 census reports Lakeview's population to be 6,083—a 26.54% increase since 1990, when the population was 4,807. The combined population of Hillside and Two Rivers was 5,484 at the 2000 census, a 29.04% increase from the 1990 population of 4,250.[2] The populations of Lakeview and Hillside, and therefore of its schools, are almost exclusively white. In the 2000 census, Lakeview's population included ten Black, twenty-two Asian, fourteen Hispanic, and four Native American residents; in Hillside and Two Rivers there were eleven Black, twelve Asian, fifty-two Hispanic, and twenty Native American residents.

Although there is little (but growing) racial diversity in this region, socioeconomic diversity is significant. Students from Lakeview, Hillside, Two Rivers, and three other towns come together for the first time in the seventh grade, and this transition to middle school marks the students' first immersion into a more economically diverse environment. When schools work well with diverse populations, students benefit emotionally and developmentally from what Willie (1985) referred to as "complementarity." Interactions across lines of difference not only improve understanding, but also improve opportunities for all students, argued

Willie. His research shows that integrated schools enable students to learn from each other what they may not learn from their own cultural backgrounds, expanding possibilities and enhancing development and adjustment. As the following two chapters illustrate, there are many opportunities for complementarity between these two communities; each community has much to gain from its neighbor and each community has much to offer. Students often demonstrated a drive toward mutual sharing but, in some cases, the struggle to establish reciprocity between the student's background and the school environment ended in frustration.

Town and school cultures reflect each other in meaningful ways that are sometimes hard to discern. Sociologists, anthropologists, and historians interested in schooling have illustrated how communities influence schools. For example, Metz (1978) compared authority, discipline, and teaching patterns in two recently desegregated high schools in a midwestern city. Heath (1983) lived for ten years in the rural Piedmont Carolinas and described the different ways white children and black children from two distinct community cultures learned to use language. Politics, history, race, immigration, and community activism were examined by Ravitch (1974) who chronicled community power and educational decisions in New York City over a 165-year period. More recently, Wells (1996) studied how students' literacy skills were affected when they transitioned from a progressive middle school to a traditional high school. Common to each of these works is the concept that the structure of schools and pedagogical decisions are influenced by local history and by the economic, social, and political conditions of the community. Community culture shapes attitudes toward education and schooling; schooling, in turn, shapes the economic, social, and political structures of the community.

Curriculum decisions, discipline, teacher-student interaction patterns, scheduling, instructional methods, and enrichment activities are all decided within the context of local aspirations, lifestyles, economic conditions, and values. In this regional school district, as in many others across the country, these decisions must balance the sometimes conflicting messages from widely disparate community cultures.

In the often contentious process of educational decision-making, it is essential to remember that it is the *student* who takes the ". . . precarious journey from home to school, experiences the contradictions . . . and must incorporate the myriad and often dissonant norms and expectations" (Lawrence-Lightfoot, 1978: p. 21). Children are the ones most directly influenced by these tensions as control of schooling is played out with diverse and sometimes competing interests. But children are not just subject to their environments, they also shape them; they are agents of change in their classrooms and they use endlessly creative strategies to adapt to and change their surroundings. Children bring to school interests, social interaction styles, values, skills, and desires shaped by their families and communities. Schools receive and integrate, or ignore and perhaps even reject, what children bring with them. The way children participate in class, behave, and develop relationships are affected by what they bring and how they are received.

Students adjust to school more easily when their schools consciously receive and integrate the assets students bring that are cultivated within the network of family and community relationships and environments (Moll et al., 1992). The roles children can hope to assume as they grow older; the ways children and the adults around them contribute to their families and communities; family structure, communication patterns, and gender expectations are all influential in shaping how early adolescents move toward the middle school. For the students of Hillside and Lakeview, these "funds of knowledge" are developed in communities with considerably different social and economic conditions.

The concept that schools are the "repository for communal values" and the expectation that schools will transmit those values to its students has implicit public approval (Seeley, Sim, and Loosley, 1956: p. 262). But there is little consensus on *which* community norms should become the standard, and *whose* values should inform curriculum decisions and teaching styles, as home-schooling families, fundamentalist Christian schools, alienated students, and irate parents aptly demonstrate.

When I went to Hillside and Lakeview as an ethnographer, I was seeking to understand the community contexts that prepare children from very different social class backgrounds for the transition to middle school. These chapters provide a context for interpreting how students adapted to their new environment, their ways of interacting and perceiving the world, and their interests, values, and expectations.

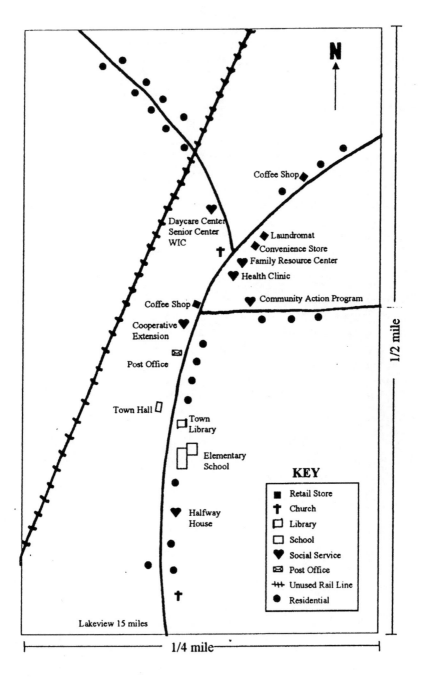

Map 2. Center Hillside

CHAPTER 2

Hillside—On the Way to Somewhere Else

Thou art the fairest spot on Earth
  Hillside, my Hillside!
Oh, mountain home that gave me birth
  Hillside, my Hillside!
No hills in all the world so blue,
No hearts in all the world so true,
    I'll love and guard and work for thee
    Hillside, my Hillside!
Thy Sons are brave, thy Daughters fair,
  Hillside, dear Hillside!
Thy highest good shall be their care
  Hillside, dear Hillside!

Though far from thee their feet may roam
They'll ne'er forget their mountain home
    But love and guard and work for thee
    Hillside, dear Hillside!
Thy fields are broad, they forests green
  Hillside, fair Hillside!
Thy lakes are bright with silv'ry sheen
  Hillside, fair Hillside!
Long as thy hills around thee stand
In beauty decked by God's own hand
    We'll love and guard and work for thee
    Hillside, dear Hillside![1]

A Place of Contrasting Beauty

Hillside is a northern New England community of subtle beauty and ecological diversity. It encompasses an abundance of geographic gems—the gentle Hillside Mountains, deep pine forests, and dozens of ponds, lakes, bogs, and marshlands. Three rivers run through it, as well as three state highways. It is a large area with more than 44,000 sparsely settled acres sprawling 20 miles north to south and 15 miles east to west.

In the fall, the foliage on trees along serene country roads is bright with color: the lemon yellow poplars, bright red and orange sugar maples, and rich amber oak, intermingle with evergreens. It is at this time of year that the high mountains 40 miles to the north get their first snow; icy white peaks rising beyond the warm colors of Hillside's foothills create a striking image. The brisk, fresh air and the peace that arrives once the summer people leave enliven and renew the souls of people weary from a summer of too much traffic and low-paying service work in the tourist industry of neighboring communities.

Winters can be harsh, but many residents welcome the solitude that comes with deep snow and freezing temperatures. As a year-round resident in a community adjacent to Hillside, I can attest to the feeling of satisfaction that comes with knowing how to live, and live comfortably, even appreciatively, in such a demanding environment. Many homes are heated with wood stoves and few Hillside children are free from the year-round chores of splitting and stacking cordwood and replenishing the firebox all winter long. When I taught seventh grade in the regional middle school that Hillside children attend, one of my students, a thirteen-year-old boy, lost two fingers in a wood-splitter. There are often similar and other less-gruesome injuries to children caused by a momentary gap of awareness while "doing wood."

People joke that the seasons are really summer, fall, winter, and mud season. With occasional snow flurries in May, and ski areas to the north open through mid-April, spring seems nonexistent. Driving can be treacherous six months out of the year and many residents travel in 4-wheel drive vehicles. Very occasionally, school buses cannot make their complete hour-long circuits, giving children who live in remote areas an unexpected day off and, perhaps, increasing their feelings of isolation in their realization that school can go on without them.

Summer, when it comes, brings lush vegetation, humidity, and spectacular evening lightning storms that bear down through the valleys with gusty wind and pelting rain. During July and August, the heat and the population soar. There are more than 8,000 seasonal residents, adding to Hillside and Twin River's year-round population of nearly 5,500.[2]

From the fire tower atop the 2,000-foot high Pine Mountain, the area below looks like a desolate wilderness of woods and wetlands. In the center of this vast area is a large lake, and on its shores are the homes of hundreds of summer residents and several residential summer camps. Smaller ponds and lakes glisten amidst deep green woodlands. There are two state forests and several conservation areas in Hillside that are protected from logging, but the scars of clear-cutting operations interrupt the dense cover here and there.

A state highway bisects Hillside and serves as the thoroughfare for leaf peepers, skiers, and hikers heading north. Loggers with loaded trucks speed their way toward the paper company nearby. In this region, where many long-time residents are property rich and income poor, some people lease their land to logging companies and turn their property into short-term profit. The Hillside library has a table set up in the children's section with stacks of coloring and game books printed by the paper company and given away free. The books tell the story of logging and how it safely and economically brings paper and other necessities to the public. However, clear-cutting angers a small but growing group of local environmentalists who mourn the diminishing wood and wetlands that are habitats for diverse animal and plant life.

Hillside's forests are a treasured resource for their economic value in lumber and fuel, and for their recreational and sport value to hunters and snowmobilers. Cutting and selling cordwood ($100–$125 per 4' x 4' x 8' stack) provides a partial income for many Hillside families. During the summer and fall, an active snowmobile association of adults and youth work to maintain the maze of trails that wind scenically all the way to Canada. On winter weekends, cross-country skiers and snowmobilers use these trails to enjoy the out-of-doors in their own very different way. Many Hillside families, including the children, have snow machines and all-terrain-vehicles (ATVs) and talk about them knowingly, in the way some Lakeview boys talk about fancy sports cars.

By the second day of hunting season in mid-November there is already a dusting of snow on the ground and Hillside is busy with pick-up truck traffic. Before the morning light, hunting groups in camouflage and bright orange jackets will have quietly consumed a hearty breakfast with several cups of coffee and scattered off to Hillside's expansive forests hoping to take down a deer by mid-morning. Weeks before the official opening of deer hunting season, rifles are mounted in the rear windows of 4-wheel drive trucks and hunters take time to scout their favorite areas for evidence of deer activity. By the age of thirteen, many boys and a few girls have taken hunter education and gun safety courses and hunt with older family members. A state fish and game officer told me that while men are hunting less, women are hunting more and now represent about 7% of the total, keeping the number of hunters in the state at about 10% of the eligible population.

Many people regard private property and gun ownership as inalienable rights. There are few zoning ordinances to interfere with the desires of landowners, and the one-acre minimum requirement for new homes makes Hillside a more affordable option than neighboring towns where the minimum is two to five acres. But despite safely guarded private property rights, very few acres are posted with no hunting signs and hunters roam free without regard for boundaries. Restricted areas are regarded as inhospitable and evidence of Hillside's changing population. During the one-month deer-hunting season, even dogs sport orange jackets and most people do not venture out in their own yards without wearing precautionary bright colors. In the dooryards of some neighborhoods, a gutted deer hangs by its hind legs within a week after hunting season starts.

Most of the kill is more than trophy; it is going on the dinner tables of people who are grateful to have it and who may not be able to afford store prices for 100 pounds of red meat.

Hillside is full of these sorts of complexities. Long-time residents cherish the geographic beauty of this area, and also defend and encourage logging operations and the influx of franchises like Rite Aid, McDonald's, and Dunkin' Donuts. Hillside's rich local history and everyday neighborliness are in sharp contrast to outsider perceptions of Hillside as a place that has little to attract visitors. I have come to know Hillside as a once-thriving community, now struggling due to over-exploited natural resources and the arbitrariness of development. It is a place where many experience a daily effort to make ends meet and where many hands are available when tragedy falls on any of its families. But the comments I hear in surrounding communities foster cruel stereotypes of Hillside as a place that is rampant with small-mindedness, in-breeding, illiteracy, primitively rough women, and children with special needs.

From this home environment and these outsider-created myths, Hillside children go to the six-town regional middle school. Because of the distance they must travel, most Hillside students get up by 5:00 to get the bus between 6:00 and 6:30 to begin school at 7:25. But the *real* distance between home and school is represented in ways more subtle than miles. This chapter portrays a town, and the values, experiences, and legacies the children from this town are likely to bring with them to school that are unknown to most nonresidents.

The District System and the Hierarchy of Place in Hillside

From the fire tower on Pine Mountain, it is possible to discern the state highways and natural boundaries that roughly section Hillside into its smaller, but historically significant, districts. Occasionally a cluster of white houses and a church steeple, the quintessential architecture of northern New England, interrupts the dense forest. Hillside Corners, West Hillside, and Center Hillside each have their own volunteer fire department, post office, zip code, and Grange Hall, and different social and economic histories. Hillside Village is a fourth area close enough to Hillside Corners to share its services. Along with these more formally designated areas, there are other districts that in years past made up the population base for one-room schoolhouses. These districts, like ethnic urban neighborhoods, gave residents a sense of identity, as well as the economic and social support needed to survive life on the northern frontier.[3]

The town of Hillside was incorporated in 1785, with fewer than 300 residents. Abenaki, Wabenaki, Mic-Mac, and Pemigewasset: these indigenous names for rivers, lakes, and streets are ironic reminders of a displaced lifestyle and culture. By 1831 there were nearly 2,000 people living in twenty districts, each named after the most prominent family in the area, and each with its own schoolhouse. The current population of 5,484 (4,211 in Hillside and 1,273 in Twin Rivers) is mostly concentrated in Center Hillside.

In 1886 the district schools were consolidated into nine rural elementary schools and this system slowly dwindled until World War II when schools were unified in one location. Hillside residents voted to open a two-year high school at the 1924 annual school meeting. People of Hillside had historically regarded education as primarily a means toward employment; they were becoming increasingly aware of the need for education beyond elementary school to keep pace with the changing economy and job market. In 1949 the decision was made to close the high school and send students to neighboring communities with four-year high schools. The regional school district was established in 1964 and since then Hillside students have gone to the neighboring town of Lakeview for middle school and high school.

Though the tiny district schools are of days gone by, a contemporary reincarnation of them exists in the increasingly popular decision to home-school children—often a cooperative venture among several neighboring families. This choice thrives in areas where there is dissatisfaction with public education and conservative religious and political viewpoints. According to home-schooling parents, this school district has the highest rate of home-schooled children in the state. Ninety-one students received their education at home in the 1999–2000 school year—an impressive number considering the time and energy commitment that is required of parents who choose this option.

Contemporary native residents are careful to say which part of Hillside they are from because of historically based social status and political differences, which persist today. Even now, when people from Hillside are asked where they live, the response is often the name of the district rather than the name of the town. Outsiders do not make these critical distinctions, however. They imagine Hillside to mean *Center* Hillside, and this is a generalization many Hillside residents living outside of the impoverished Center are eager to correct.

The southernmost section of Hillside, and the closest to Lakeview, is Hillside Corners, a tiny settlement tucked a quarter mile off the state highway. It is the location of a magnificent, brick, Greek revival Superior Court House, constructed in 1920 to replace the original court building that met its demise in a fire, like so many other nineteenth century buildings made of wood. Nearby are also several lawyers' offices in stately old homes, a post office, fire department, and playing fields. Across the state highway and up the road a little are other county buildings, including the nursing home, county jail, probate court, registry, and administrative offices. A few miles beyond the county complex is Hillside Village. Both these districts are characterized by rolling fields, colonial and Victorian-style residences, austere Protestant churches, and neat little family cemeteries marked out with stone walls.

While the Corners and the Village are more pastoral locations, West Hillside, the farthest district to the north, is centered on the crossroads of two state highways and was once the site of a tourist tramway and small ski area, now overgrown and abandoned. In recent years, as the mountain areas to the north overflow with summer and winter visitors, there has been a slow renewal of tourism in West Hillside. Small shops and businesses have sprung up along the highway, sometimes making a brief stand and disappearing the next season. Dunkin' Donuts, McDonald's, a barbeque chicken-and-ribs restaurant, a gas station-convenience store, and a sub shop are accommodations to tourism but also satisfy the local need for jobs and evolving taste for convenience stores and fast food. These businesses also tell of Hillside's struggle for sustained economic development. In a service-based economy, jobs are plentiful enough for half the year but are low-paying and do not provide benefits, security, or opportunities for advancement.

Center Hillside is the main part of town, a mile from the highway and halfway between Hillside Corners to the south and West Hillside to the north. The tired, defunct railroad station, the paint-worn Purina grain tower, the abandoned storefronts, the row of run down tenements, and several elegant, Civil War-era Main Street homes are evidence of the once thriving commercial center of years gone-by. After the 1940s, Center Hillside lost much of its industry—furniture, shoe, and textile manufacturing—to southern and international locations, and the economy never recovered.

Differences in economic and social status among Hillside's districts persist today. During one meeting I attended in Center Hillside, a comment was made that the people of Hillside Village do not consider themselves to be part of Hillside. The feelings of some people in Center Hillside are that people in other parts of town "think they are too good for us." These distinctions continue to be salient for the younger generation. Students in my research groups were asked to write whatever came to mind on encountering the word Hillside on a questionnaire. One seventh-grade resident of West Hillside wrote, "A town next to mine that I had to go to school for a couple years, it is a town that I don't like."

What Through-Travelers Miss

Traveling north on the highway, the entrance to Hillside is marked by a big yellow sign that warns, "Moose Crossing Next 6 miles." Along this stretch of road are several antiques dealers, the grain store for garden and farm animal supplies, a large furniture store, a John Deere tractor business, a tire dealer, discount and second-hand stores, a welding shop, a low-income housing apartment building, and two campgrounds where several dozen families live in small camper vehicles all year long. A couple of restaurant businesses are closed up and for sale. At the intersection of two state highways is Hannaford's grocery, Rite Aid, Dunkin' Donuts, a gas station, an empty department store that closed down in 2002, and two real estate offices where I have never, ever seen a soul. For many out-of-towners heading toward other destinations, this business area, and its duplicate ten miles farther north in West Hillside, are the only places in Hillside where they might stop and get out of the car. Unknown to most through-travelers are Hillside's wealth of natural areas and historic treasures, like the nearly 220-year-old water-powered mill and the narrow 1870 covered bridge.

The two-lane highway that runs down the center of Hillside has a steady stream of cars three seasons out of the year—summer, winter, and autumn—and town residents have learned to make the most of this by-passing traffic. There are several makeshift stands along the highway where you can buy fresh corn, plants, lawn ornaments, and those mysteriously popular two-year-old-sized cloth dolls made to look like they are crying in the corner, known as "time-out kids." No where do I see signs of the more savvy, contemporary tourist industry that exists in neighboring towns, where windows are packed with expensive L. L. Bean-style clothing and coffee sells for $1.50 a cup. Hillside's wares are more modest and lack the commercial stylishness of typical tourist areas.

Taking the turn off the highway toward Center Hillside, it is suddenly peaceful. In less than a mile, there is another turn but the faded road sign pointing the way to Center Hillside can hardly be read. Hillside Central School, public buildings, social services, the post office, town library, and tenement buildings dominate the busy heart of Center Hillside. All of this is contained in an area about the size of a football field. The K–6 elementary school was enlarged and renovated in 1993 and across the street the town hall underwent substantial improvements in 1995. Residents are proud of these public buildings where they feel welcome and known. Whenever I visit the elementary school office I am struck by its open warm atmosphere and the common presence of parent volunteers, usually mothers of students, who help out in a variety of ways.

Although I worry that I may be naively nostalgic for the character and lifestyle that Hillside's agricultural past suggests, when I visit Hillside and talk with children and adults there, I am always impressed by the friendly easiness of the conversation, the welcoming wave from people as they pass me in their cars, and the generous and accommodating ways of people in the town hall, the library, the school, and the local coffee shop. On questionnaires, students from Hillside described their town as "safe," "trusting," and "boring," but when I asked seventh graders from the neighboring community of Lakeview about Hillside, they often replied that they had never been there. Their answers reflected common stereotypes focusing on Hillside as a "poor town" where "people are different." The few who had been to Hillside said they were passing through, "on their way to somewhere else."

Before the state highway was built in the 1930s, the road north brought travelers right into the center of town where there were hotels, restaurants, and entertainment. Now, people say, the only tourists in Center Hillside are lost and looking for their way back to the main road.

The primarily white population native to this area has a distinct linguistic style, which is often imitated by outsiders for a laugh. This indigenous Yankee dialect has become an unfortunate cliché to some, but for the students and their parents who speak it, this way of talking marks a tacit cultural and social status difference. These differences perhaps become more clear to students when they leave their Hillside sixth grade to go to the regional middle school located in the more affluent community of Lakeview.

The elder generation of this community remembers well when life was slower and more gritty. They remember when the road by their house was finally paved, when the state highway came through, when the schools were the one-room kind, when the snow was packed down by horses pulling a gigantic wooden roller, and when many residents did not have access to the rest of the world all winter long. Many people in Hillside still live quite a lot like people did a century or two ago, but now with the welcome assistance of tractors and electricity. They plant big gardens, put away food in the fall, heat with wood, raise chickens, goats, and cows, and stick close to home, busy with chores and visits with friends.

There are sayings from the older generation that suggest the reality that good luck is temporary, and hard luck is expected. Two of these sayings I call "Inezisms," after a 90-year-old neighbor whose family was one of the first to settle in this region: "I'd rather see the devil than a robin in March" and "So far the sun shines in, so far the snow blows in." Luck and weather are discussed with respect, and many people keep emergency supplies on hand for the half dozen or so times a year the electricity goes out. "I hear we're goin' to get some weather," is the warning, stated non-chalantly, that soon all hell is going to break loose in the form of pelting rain, snow, cold, or wind.

The population has historically been of northern European ancestry. Names like Smith, Merrow, Eldridge, Moulton, and Tibbetts are plentiful in the tax records and can be traced back many generations. An increasing number of Native American people are claiming their ancestral past and there is a well-attended powwow that is part of Old Home Week, an annual celebration of Hillside community and culture. This two-week summer event blends old and new—fiddling, demonstrations of the volunteer fire department, a fishing derby, a 1960s street dance, car races, a casino night, and an Italian supper. Although ethnic names from southern Europe are still rare in Hillside, their increasing presence indicates that a fair number of people are relocating here from the urban areas of neighboring states. These are the people to whom residents sometimes refer when they speak of the problems brought into town by an influx of newcomers with city-ways.

This town is also home to a growing number of alternative lifestyles people. The old folkways, such as fiddle-making, organic gardening, canning, and woodworking, attract a new generation of residents who sometimes move into the area because the town lends itself well to this more self-sufficient lifestyle.

It is not uncommon for children to refer to friends and neighbors as cousins, aunts, and uncles. This feeling of extended family not only suggests a sense of community, but may also indicate that, for some, life is so stressful and demanding, it needs to be shared. Historically, the town paid a small sum to families for boarding children, women, and disabled men who were unable to live on their own. There is an indication that this kind of arrangement perseveres today without the aid of local or state government. During home visits, I heard and witnessed over and over that this is a town where people are graciously willing to set another place at the table, where there is an ethic of both respect for privacy and a communal pitching-in-together, where children with working parents can go to a neighbor's house after school, and teens not getting along at home can live at a friend's house until things settle down a little.

There is a weekly free community dinner at one of the churches, popular bean suppers all summer long, and one of the most active volunteer fire and rescue departments in the state. The volunteer crews include local teens that meet weekly, attend trainings, and support firefighters and rescue workers during emergencies. In the summer, the town recreation program involves about one hundred children, ages six through twelve, five full days a week for eight weeks. This is double the number of children involved in the larger community of Lakeview, where the recreation program has twice the budget. One Hillside seventh grader explains this sense of community to me: "In Hillside people really care about each other. Like when that woman who used to clean the laundromat died when she was having a baby—*everyone* came together to help that family." At a time when people nationwide are looking for answers to how they can reconstruct a sense of community in their towns, Hillside lives its traditions of caring for one another with unpretentious simplicity, not seeming to grasp its unique strength.

Entangled Influences of Education, Geography, and Development

In the center of town there is a cluster of worn-out storefronts with upstairs apartments, an Evangelical church, and many social and public services that have been enlarged and renovated over the last ten years. As private businesses have struggled to survive in this town, public services have simultaneously grown, with the help of federal and state block grants. Statistics show Hillside to be one of the most impoverished areas in the state. The 1990 census showed that 31.7% of the people in Hillside did not have a high school diploma, compared to 18% statewide.[4] The median family income at the 2000 census (recorded in 1999) was $34,709 in Hillside and $36,000 in Two Rivers compared to the state median family income of $49,467.[5] In 1999, 10% of the people in Hillside and 15.30% of the people in Two Rivers were living in poverty, compared to 6.5% statewide. Only three towns in the state have poverty rates higher than Two Rivers. In the 1998–1999 school year, 53.7% of Hillside's elementary school children were eligible for free and reduced hot lunch.[6]

On one corner, Hillside Crossing houses Hillside Concerned Citizens, the senior center, a daycare center, and the WIC Program (a preventive nutritional program for women, infants, and children). Next door is the County Cooperative Extension Service that offers community education on a variety of topics, including child development, nutrition, and gardening. Across the street are a family medical clinic and a small store with limited supplies. All these programs operate within a stone's throw of one another, usually cooperating handily, but occasionally competing over funding, recognition, and scarce resources. There are two laundromats in this section of town, perhaps an indication of how few people have their own washer-dryer.

In the nineteenth century, Hillside was an agricultural community that survived through a system of resource interdependence—farm animals and tools were collectively owned and families grew different crops to share. After a forty-year period (1820–1860) of agricultural prosperity, the call of townsmen to the Civil War and a desire to make an easier living initiated a steady decline in agriculture. The population of Hillside was about 2,000 at the beginning of the Civil War, but was not that high again until 1980. Tourism is not as vital a part of the economy as in neighboring towns, fated by the fact that the railroad brought city people to areas with bigger lakes and mountains. To Hillside, the railroad brought industry rather than tourists. As farming became less viable, it was replaced by manufacturing. From 1870 until the 1940s, Center Hillside had several thriving textile and lumber mills and a tannery. Center Hillside in its manufacturing heyday had a large hotel, taverns, and several successful dry goods stores. Hillside entered the 21st century with neither industry nor tourism, and little promise of strong economic development in the near future.

Today, Hillside has 70% of neighboring Lakeview's population but only 20% of Lakeview's town budget.[7] Hillside does not have the infrastructure to support tourism. Without business and valuable property to tax, Hillside residents have a higher tax rate than other towns in the region—an average of $22.36 per $1,000 compared to $15.72 per $1,000 in Lakeview. The unreasonably high tax burden on residents of economically stressed towns, used primarily to fund education, was the basis for a successful 1998 class action suit in which the state supreme court mandated that legislators come up with a plan to fund education equitably. Five years later, a funding plan is still not in place and the controversy is more heated than ever.

Retail trade, health services, such as the nursing home and rehabilitation center, and schools are the three largest employer categories. More than 20% of those employed commute to out-of-county jobs. The unemployment rate of 15% in 1990 has improved to just over 5%, but is still higher than most towns in the state.

Right in the center of town, across from the abandoned Purina grain tower with its faded checkerboard design, the old, unkempt railroad station now serves as Center Hillside's only coffee shop. The entrance looks more like the doorway to an abandoned warehouse than the entrance to a restaurant. The McCain for President bumper sticker in the doorway symbolizes this town's independent and Republican voting habits. One September morning I stopped by for coffee. Four people sat smoking and talking around one of five tables. I immediately felt self-conscious, as though I had just walked into a stranger's kitchen. This is not a place where new customers are likely to come, but a middle-age woman who helps out the owner quickly and cheerfully gave me a menu. The atmosphere and the prices are from days past: a two egg special with toast and coffee for $1.49, $1.99 with home fries, omelets for $2.25, and hamburgers for $1.60. I expressed my astonishment at the prices and the owner, who told me that her friends come in all day long from before 6:00 a.m. until after 7:00 p.m. replied, "I have to keep the prices down, my customers can't afford more . . . My prices haven't changed in 15 years but I don't know how much longer I can do it."

An artificial Christmas tree, decorated and lit, stands in one corner. On the walls are an announcement for the food pantry, an award from the Hillside Old Home Week committee, and shelves with games and kids' toys. In the midst of this homey disarray is a poster of a smiling Hitler, his arm raised in the Nazi salute and the disturbing words, "All in favor of gun control, raise your hand." When my breakfast was delivered I asked the meaning of the poster and was told that it means, "If you want gun control then you want a dictatorship."

I lingered, trying to sort out the possible civic and social roles this place plays in the community, and the politics that drive the conversation. Everyone who came in knew each other and sat at the same table. It is, I imagine, a place where opinions and biases are formed and affirmed, complaints are aired, reputations are made and broken, social issues are reiterated as worse and more horrible and hopeless than ever, and plans for action are made. At different times of the year, town and school politics are hotly debated topics. On the morning of my visit, the talk was about children and grandchildren, a recent divorce in town, and whether or not the predicted hurricane would amount to much.

This unpretentious gathering place was a key organizing site for the taxpayers association during the two years I served on the teacher's negotiating team in the early 1980s. The teachers association fought for improved teacher salaries; they were among the lowest in the state at that time. The taxpayers association appealed to people struggling to stay above water when inflation and taxes were high and local wages were low. It was a bitter struggle pitting teachers and the school district's poor families against each other. In the end, after months of careful organizing and community outreach on both sides, the teacher's negotiated contract was defeated at an historic volatile meeting of 1,400 people. The Hillside community spoke in one voice against the negotiated pay raises. As a member of the teacher's negotiating team, I was stunned by this decisive defeat, and at the same time, I was made acutely aware of the economic realities facing Hillside residents who pay unfairly high tax rates to support education.

The tensions between school staff and local families have a long history. Hillside families have historically supported education that enabled citizens to properly exercise their civic responsibilities and that gave their children employable skills. Edward Cook's 1989 history of Hillside suggested that during the agricultural era, the attitude toward school was that it needed to be practical: "Higher education, and higher knowledge were a fine thing—for city folks. Ordinary country people had no time to learn such things, and little money to pay for them. Once a country boy or girl knew the basics, it was time for them to leave school and get on with the hard work that went into making a living" (1989: p. 214). The 1855 school report, cited by Cook, explains that some people "thought that there was a danger of children knowing more than their parents" (p. 222). Schooling was interrupted whenever more important home responsibilities needed attention.

Teachers' salaries remained low in this school district until recently. In 1920, despite standardized test scores higher than the national average, the superintendent observed that Hillside teachers could not possibly make as much as a factory worker, but "at least they should receive as much as the average domestic servant" (ibid., p. 236). Today, teachers' salaries are at about the state average but test scores in Hillside are among the lowest in the state. As educational achievement, employment standards, economic development, and technology advanced through the twentieth century, it appears that the gap between affluent and poor communities grew wider.

At Home

In this rural town there are no sidewalks. Heading out from the center of town are two narrow country roads that wind their way up to the surrounding hills to the sites of some of the oldest settlements. Newly painted ranches and capes, with landscaped yards, flowers, and cut lawns, sit alongside homes that can use some repairs, a new roof, or replacements for broken windowpanes. One of these houses is so badly in need of paint that I cannot tell what color it might have been at one time. Some of these single-family homes are rentals belonging to people who have moved out of town. Several houses are for sale and, in this part of town, real estate is hard to sell and sells low, even if the house is in good condition.

In my new role as researcher, I find myself resisting the task of observing and logging into my memory the sights, smells, and sounds of this somewhat impoverished neighborhood. This is a neighborhood I have visited before in my role as counselor-advocate for children and families. These are homes I have been in, families I might know. In this neighborhood, where poverty and stereotypes disenfranchise adults and children alike, I have been welcomed by families who see me as a respectful ally. I know I can and must maintain this respectful alliance with people as I write about their community and their children, but at this moment I feel humbled by the challenge. No matter how respectfully I look and listen and write, I know that many people are quick to couple poverty with carelessness, lack of ambition, overly rigid discipline or permissiveness with their children, less intelligence, and lack of concern about education. I have heard too many demeaning Hillside jokes over the years and have known too many Hillside children who quit school, exhausted by the sheer effort it takes to navigate the disparate environments of school and home. I have felt the sting of knowing that I too am an outsider here despite my involvement. But I also realize that my commitment to this community would be hollow without my willingness to look and listen and, finally, to tell a story that needs to be told, from the perspective of people who live here.

So, I sit for a moment and take it in: the blue tarp duct-taped to the roof to cover places where the weather comes in, the smell of rotting wood, the broken windows covered with cardboard, the damaged window shutters, the missing floorboards and railings on the porch, the old cars in the driveway used to replace parts in the newer old car. I try to imagine and feel what it is like to grow up in this neighborhood: the noisy mealtimes, kids from all over the neighborhood coming and going, slamming the screen door all summer long, the squabbles that spill into the street as children arrive home from school with different agendas, a television going in the background, the smell of cigarette smoke, the cold and the snow that blows in through the cracks in the windows during the winter, the aroma of dinner cooking, the dust and mud that makes its way into the house from the yards where children, animals, and cars have worn the grassy covering down to bare dirt.

One chilly school-day afternoon in spring, I am in the center of town as kids in grades one through six leave school. The cars being driven through town come in all shapes and sizes but are decidedly U.S. made. "Walkers," kids who live within a mile of the school, head home, many of them are wearing book bags that look too heavy for such small children. Boys are almost all dressed in T-shirts, sneakers, and cords or jeans. Shorts are not as popular here as they are in the middle school where even in the winter a handful of students come to school dressed in them. Some girls are dressed as the boys, but many of them are wearing ankle-length dresses and skirts. A small group of friends or siblings walk hurriedly in one direction and then back again. An older girl, perhaps the older nine or ten-year-old sister of a smaller boy, walks with urgency in her step and her thin arms swinging. She continually shifts her small frame to keep her over-stuffed book bag from sliding off her back. She is wearing a lime green jumper that goes down to her heels, and white high-heeled sandals. Despite their hurried pace, it seems they are not going anywhere. I wonder how many children get themselves home at the end of the school day, and perhaps start homework or chores while they wait for working parents.

One redheaded boy has a checkerboard design in his crew cut, but all the other students I observe have more simple, homemade hairstyles. A number of boys zip down the center of the street on skateboards and free-style bicycles, testing new "extreme sport" moves, and defying what little traffic there is. There is a lot of energy or apathy, but nothing approaching rough or rude behavior. These are children who seem to have the rules of public decorum deeply imprinted on their beings. By comparison, when I think of children leaving school in Lakeview, these Hillside children seem smaller and younger, less worldly, and more self-conscious of a public eye. In a town like Hillside, where everyone knows everyone else, stories of bad behavior can make it home to the ears of older siblings or parents before the child arrives.

Sixth Grade Promotion Night

In mid-June, I attended Hillside School's sixth grade promotion celebration. At 5:30, the sun is still high, the air is warm, and parents coming from work rush to get to the packed gym before the program starts. It is nice to see so many familiar and friendly faces. Whole families sit in rows of folding chairs facing the sixth graders who are arranged in V-shape in the front, diagonally facing the audience and each other. On the stage are the three sixth grade teachers and the principal, looking a bit awkward amidst the happy commotion as parents locate their children in the mass of seventy-five sixth graders, friends loudly greet each other, and younger siblings join the ruckus, determined not to be sidelined.

It is after 5:30 but we are all waiting for a student who was left home by her parents, each one coming from work thinking the other would pick her up. Another ten minutes go by. Everyone is seated; they chat and wait patiently for the forgotten student to arrive. Finally, the event begins. It is quick and unceremonious. There is a very brief greeting from the principal who does not appear to enjoy public speaking. Citizenship, fitness, academic, and most-improved student awards are given to individual students who are called up to the stage. Then homeroom teachers read each student's name and all seventy-five students come up on stage and quickly collect a certificate and T-shirt from their teachers.

There are varying degrees of enthusiasm as each name is called but every student receives applause. The clapping and cheering becomes rowdier as the forty-five minute program continues. No one tries to tone down the noise, which is coming from both the students and the audience. "These are signs of things to come," I think to myself. Later, someone observes that "the students are acting like seventh graders."

Most parents and children are informally dressed—baseball caps, jeans, shorts, and T-shirts. But a few girls wear elegant long dresses and beautifully done hair. After the program, there are cookies and punch served by the two school counselors and assistant principal. The students seem self-conscious in their special position as the focus of attention, but they are all friendly and polite when I speak to them and to their parents. Over and over again, students, parents, and teachers thank me for coming. Some students are anxious to be with their friends; others hang very near their families with no sign of wanting to stray.

Here, the students represent what is most touching to me as they move from their community elementary school to the regional middle school. The image of students with friends and families represent the very crux of this transition: the increasing importance of social connections, emerging interests away from home, and the longing to stay close to their families, all at the same time. Their new school, like most middle schools, will place a very high premium on developing autonomy, individual accomplishment, and personal responsibility. I hear concerns expressed by middle school teachers that over-protective parents might interfere with the child's need for independence. Hillside's complex history, geography, social, and economic conditions are not well known outside of this town. Hillside parents harbor concerns that their child may not be treated fairly at their new school. The sixth graders are cautiously enthusiastic as they approach their new school, yet, at this moment, their last night at Hillside Central School, they seem awkward and unsure. How will the middle school meet them and what will these students, coming from this abundantly rich and complex town culture, be encouraged to bring with them from this environment to their new school?

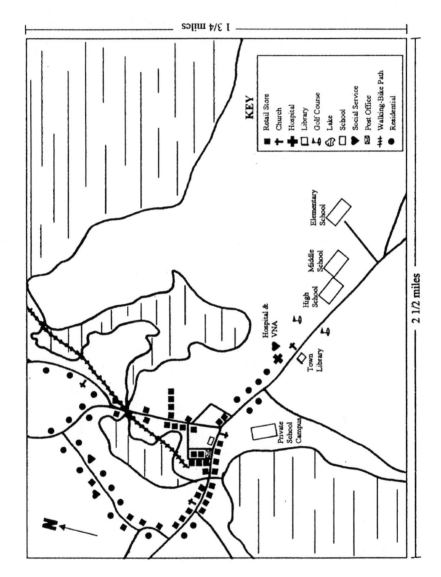

KEY

■ Retail Store
✝ Church
✚ Hospital
▢ Library
⌐ Golf Course
🜋 Lake
□ School
▶ Social Service
⊠ Post Office
✛✛✛ Walking-Bike Path
● Residential

Elementary
School

Middle
School

High
School

Hospital &
VNA

Town
Library

Private
School
Campus

N

2 1/2 miles

Map 3. Downtown Lakeview

CHAPTER 3

Lakeview—Journey's End

The night after Hillside's sixth grade promotion, I went to promotion night at Lakeview Elementary School. The difference is so remarkable, it is hard to imagine that the students are the same age and attending schools only twenty miles apart. I hurry toward the entrance with small groups of parents and students and I am immediately aware that the dress seems more formal. Once in the auditorium, a look around confirms this observation; jeans, caps, and T-shirts are nowhere in sight. A few men and women are dressed in suits, perhaps having stopped here directly from work.

This is only the second sixth grade group to be promoted from the two-year-old school, which houses grades four to six. Generous playing fields separate Lakeview Elementary School from the main road. Big windows look out from this handsome, redbrick one-story building to surrounding woods and fields. The school is on a campus that also includes the high school, vocational center, and the middle school, and it is a mile south of the center of town. For Lakeview Elementary School students, transition to seventh grade means going to school just a few hundred yards away from their old school.

The promotion takes place in the school's auditorium/gym, larger and better equipped than Hillside's. Just before the program begins, all ninety sixth-graders clamor up the stage tiers to their places. Clearly, *they*, and not the teachers, are the main attraction tonight. Unlike promotion night in Hillside where teachers played a prominent role, handing out T-shirts and certificates to officially pass each student on to the middle school, Lakeview's teachers are part of the audience and have no role in the program. The principal is an articulate and confident master of ceremonies from a podium on the floor in front.

The event is a finely tuned performance. Students play music, sing songs, and almost all of them give brief "I remember when . . ." snap shots in clear, sure voices. The principal delivers a short but rousing motivational speech reminding students of the importance of this educational milestone, "As you move toward the middle school, nervously and excitedly, dream it and you can do it," he encourages them. "One never fails until he or she quits."

The band director announces that the songs they are performing are at the seventh grade level of difficulty. One song has lyrics about anticipated adventures at the middle school—lockers, changing classes, new friends, and more homework—and is sung to the tune, Ob-la-di, Ob-la-da. The band and the chorus are very good and I am moved by the effort that is evident in being able to accomplish a piece of music that is slightly beyond their reach, despite an occasional off-key instrument or a complicated phrase sung by only a handful of students. As I listen, I wonder if high expectations, hard work, and determined involvement are characteristic of everyday culture in this elementary school.

Here are twelve-year-olds with an already well-developed sense of a public self. They are poised for action, aware of being watched, and seem familiar with being the focus of attention. In both promotion ceremonies, there is an atmosphere of hope, enthusiasm, promise, and possibility, but tonight I observe a confident reach toward the future—a demeanor that was not evident in Hillside.

In the last fifteen minutes of the hour-long program, there is a slide presentation of the annual end-of-the-year overnight trip to an urban area and science museum. The presentation is accompanied to music from the futuristic movie *Star Trek*. There is no such overnight field trip for Hillside students. The program in Lakeview is a brief, appreciative look back and a long, spirited look forward—ready to take on new adventures and locations. After the program, everyone is welcomed to the cafeteria for refreshments. Immediately, the students, who have maintained a reserved, good-natured stage presence for most of the program, make a noisy, hasty retreat toward the refreshments; public decorum for an adult audience quickly changes as students rush to connect with their friends. Unlike the previous evening in Hillside, most of these students make no attempt to find their parents after the program. I receive cool responses when I say hello to otherwise friendly and receptive students. "This is *our* celebration; it is not a time to chit-chat with adults," seems to be the message. Most students avoid eye contact, give me a polite, brief half-smile, and then quickly move to form a tighter, more closed circle with their peers. The cafeteria is packed with soon-to-be seventh graders generously helping themselves to refreshments, so I join the groups of parents talking to one another outside.

In these commonplace community rituals, it is possible to observe certain aspects of a community's values, hopes, and lifestyles in action. Consciously or not, school events contribute to the overall acculturation of children and are often a good indication of an unspoken but pervasive community consensus on what families value as proper training and preparation. The curriculum tonight appears to be a lesson in preparing children for public life, for performing, for being watched and judged.

As I leave the Lakeview promotion celebration, I am caught by a scene that lingers vividly in my memory and captures a stunning difference in the demeanor of students and their families from these two communities. A group of girls, several of them research participants in my study, are standing on a picnic table as a couple of parents snap pictures. They are artistically assembled: arms flung open, looking like the world is theirs as they gleefully "strut their stuff" to receptive and approving adult eyes. Almost as though they are modeling for a trendy teen fashion magazine, they arrange themselves without prompting for pictures and for the attention of their humored audience of parents. This is a far cry from the reserved, carefully arranged family pictures that were being taken after the Hillside promotion. I saw this difference in demeanor over and over again during my eighteen months of observations and interviews.

These twelve-year-old Lakeview students seem to be prepared and eager for the greater degree of independence this night represents. They seem ready and on the move, unambivalently in full stride toward their new school, confident yet, at the same time, intensely self-conscious. By comparison, the Hillside students seemed reserved and unsure, pulled by their friends yet remaining close to their families. These students were not positioned on the stage and did not speak a single public word at their promotion. They were quietly and unceremoniously passed from grade six to seven, perhaps with a degree of ambivalence shared by parents, teachers, and students alike. At the Hillside promotion event, the private and particular relationships between students and their families, and between students and their teachers, were recognized and supported. These children were expected to look toward teachers and family members for their cues. They seemed cautious about being the focus of attention, preferring to have a less public and perhaps less autonomous presence. Although some students gathered together with their peers, many others stayed near their families after the program.

There are layers of difference in these two events, in the town and school cultures that spawned them, and in the reality that students absorbed as participants of these events. What are these Lakeview sixth graders being encouraged toward and groomed for? What will it mean for Hillside students to move to the seventh grade, twenty miles away from their old school and community? What significance do these different styles and attitudes have in schooling and learning from day to day? What will Hillside students miss about the school and the community they leave behind and what might they have to give up to make it at the middle school? The journey to middle school for Hillside students requires a transition marked by distance to a new school as well as to a new community. Does the transition process offer different opportunities and prompt the development of different skills for students from Lakeview and Hillside? At a time when many sectors of U.S. society place an increasingly high value on being able to function well in multiple contexts, what might *Lakeview* students miss in their development by attending middle school in the same, familiar town? Social, economic and historic factors that have shaped these communities provide a context for understanding the answers to these questions.

A Resilient Tourism-Based Economy

Lakeview spreads out along the shore of a twenty-six-mile-long lake, surrounded by hills. A wooden sign declaring Lakeview "America's Oldest Summer Resort" has greeted thousands of visitors a year for more than a century. Lakeview has just over 6,000 year-round residents, but the population swells to more than 20,000 May through Labor Day.

Most people approach Lakeview from the south where the state highway roller-coasters its way into town for eight miles, affording spectacular views of the lake and mountains and the shorefront village of Lakeview in the distance. A sharp left turn at a dangerous intersection is the start of Main Street, two and a half miles from the center of town. On the busiest summer weekends, this is about where traffic begins to slow to a crawl all the way into town.

Retail trade employs one-third of the labor force; educational and health services are the second and third highest employers. There are several small industries also located here, manufacturing custom molding, thermal underwear, and printed plastic bags. At 2.6% unemployment, Lakeview is below the state average and half of Hillside's unemployment.[1] When the town was incorporated in 1770, fifteen years before Hillside, the economy was based primarily in farming and lumbering. These industries were then replaced by manufacturing. Textiles, furniture, saw and gristmills, and especially the production of shoes played an important role in Lakeview's economic development in the latter part of the 19th century. But for nearly a hundred years, tourism has played a much more significant role in the economy and has a dramatic influence on local values, ambitions, and tastes. More recently, retirement-based businesses have emerged including several full-service communities serving Lakeview's largest population: people over sixty-five years old.

The commercial center is along Main Street and runs parallel to the lakeshore. The expanded summer population strains town services, jams the narrow streets with cars and pedestrians, and makes a mid-day trip to the post office or grocery store a major production and a frustrating one. Seasonal employment is plentiful but the salaries of local people working in the service industry (waiting tables, housekeeping, landscaping, care-taking, etc.) hovers near minimum wage. Two bedroom year-round rentals are hard to find and run over $750 per month and people pay tourist prices for basic necessities, like gas and food. However, residents here seem mindful that tourism is their livelihood and it's what makes this rural town a bustling, thriving, active community where you can find music festivals, a talented local theater group, good places to eat, bookstores, and even a decent cup of coffee.

Several accounting offices, law firms, investment agencies, and insurance companies provide services to the Lakeview community. The medical center adjacent to the 75-bed regional hospital houses a full range of medical practices. There are several yacht clubs and marinas and a good selection of hotels, motels, and inns ranging from low to moderately high priced, most of them located on or near a lake. Construction, lumber, and nine real estate companies thrived in the 1990s with a booming building economy of mostly second homes. The locally owned community bank and two national banks have all undergone considerable expansion in the last decade. Among the many multimillionaires that have summered in this area are the founders of several major international corporations.

Six lakes are fully or partially within Lakeview's border—7,800 acres of water in a total acreage of 38,000.[2] The total assessed property value in Lakeview is $787,039,013 compared to $277,831,101 in Hillside, though Hillside is larger by more 10,000 acres.[3] The shorefront has seen heavy development in the last twenty years and lakeside building lots are few and far between. Lakefront property starts at about $350,000—cheap by city standards—and that is why so many people are still building seasonal homes here. Lakeview is only two hours from this region's largest metropolitan area. A small local airport makes it possible for people to commute to the city to work and be home at the lake by dinnertime.

Thriving tourism provides lots of incentives for young local entrepreneurs to invest in retail, restaurant, and preventive health-based businesses. Lucrative business opportunities may be part of the reason why this middle-class community sends only about half of its public high school graduates to four-year colleges.[4] Local people own and operate food, music, clothing, sports, crafts, book, and grocery stores. Local artists work in a variety of media and make and sell their wares in downtown galleries. Recently, a fitness center and dance studio joined the tennis club and gym as health-based businesses. A few family-run local companies have been stable for decades, but a national franchise drug store and donut shop moved in during the 1990s, forcing two locally owned businesses to shut their doors.

The most valuable waterfront property in town is owned by a private boarding school, whose campus of white buildings spreads generously for a quarter mile along Main Street. Craft festivals and fairs are held on the school fields almost every summer weekend and draw artists from throughout the northeast. These craft fairs are controversial; some feel they draw potential customers to town while others point out that visiting shoppers are likely to empty their pockets at the fairs before they even get to the downtown stores.

People take the yield-for-pedestrians law seriously here. Someone who makes the mistake of cutting off a cross-walker receives glares from pedestrians and motorists alike. The volume of pedestrian and motor traffic in the summer slows cars to a crawl.

Most everyone is assumed to be another tourist when visiting shops in the summer and treated with the careful courtesy meant for the economically important but less intimate relationships of our lives. Lakeview *works* at being the welcoming, quaint, small-town community tourists have come to expect. Wooden signs along Main Street point the way toward shops with names that evoke images of leisure and rustic beauty. For over one hundred years, Lakeview has been a destination for urban and suburban people seeking natural charm, relaxation, and healthy activity. Storefront windows are jammed with sports clothes and gear, kitchen paraphernalia, and gifts, looking very much like other popular tourist towns in the northeast. You can shop for New Age books, body lotions, and clothing from Asian countries and then buy a $2.50 latte and sit for long conversations at outdoor tables.

It is this downtown area that Hillside students mention when asked what they know about Lakeview. In middle school, more students are allowed to spend time in town with their friends. When asked about Lakeview, Hillside students responded that "downtown is fun to walk around with friends," "[Lakeview] is a big town with lots of stores," and "the people are not as preppy as I thought they were." Enticed by what Lakeview has to offer, some Hillside students become more disparaging of their own town.

Holidays in Lakeview are also commercial opportunities and the 2000 Fourth of July parade provides a good example. This is one of many downtown events planned by the chamber of commerce and it brings more people to downtown than any other single event. The parade is a show of local humor, history, politics, service, and commerce, with an emphasis on commerce. It kicks off another season of family vacations, one-day shopping visits, and hard work by the hundreds of local employees, many of them teenagers, who make it all happen.

Neighboring Hillside has an equally large parade but children's groups and town services make up the majority of the entrants. If these parades represent the resources that have significance in each community, in Lakeview, it is business that has prominence, while in Hillside, town and social services play a major role.

Lakeview's attractiveness to people of means makes it far less subject to economic recessions. The well-researched local history book notes that even during the depression, conditions in Lakeview were much better than in other towns in the region due to its tourism-based economy.[5] Tourism is so economically important that it is, by necessity, the town's preoccupation.

The wealthy and more cosmopolitan summer community plays a critical role in Lakeview's economic and social development and creates an illusion about life here that is not reflected in the statistics. There is a veneer of affluence in this community but year-round residents actually make less per capita than the state average. The perception that Lakeview is a rich town and Hillside is a poor town was reflected in my conversations with students and parents from both communities, some of whom said that they did not know of any poor people in Lakeview or rich people in Hillside. Lakeview is certainly economically better off than Hillside, but not as well off as one might mistake it to be. The median household income in Lakeview of $44,012 is $4,000 higher than the median household income for the county, and more than $9,000 higher than the median household income in Hillside, but it is less than the statewide median household income of $49,467.[6] In this region, people can expect to earn about 75% of what their metropolitan counterparts are earning two hours away. Here and there homes half-built and abandoned indicate dreams not realized. The inflated building industry, along with growing land costs, make new home construction a privilege of an increasingly elite group of people.

Unlike Hillside, Lakeview's various districts have little significance today. There are two post offices—one in the center of town and the other a half-mile away in Lakeview Falls. At one time, The Falls was an important manufacturing area. In the last fifteen years, the run-down

apartment buildings in this area have been renovated and a new commercial district has taken shape. Older residents remember when north,
east, and south Lakeview had social and political relevance, but today,
these designations have no bearing on daily life. The locations that have
more meaning today are the affluent residential areas defined by a section of road or point on the lake.

Four Season Charm

Summer is Lakeview's premier season. The summer people come
back and take up residence in seasonal homes, and thousands of families return for a week or two, often staying at the same lakeside cabins
each year. Swimming, boating, water-skiing, biking, walking, and jogging
are all popular activities. Lobster bakes, chicken barbeque dinners, side-
walk sales, music festivals, farmers' markets, weekly band concerts, summer theater, and sporting events keep people of all inclinations busy all
summer long.

The shorefront near Main Street has public dock space and a
restaurant serving fried clams, burgers, and ice cream. Adjacent to the
dock area is a small town park with a new gazebo where band concerts,
rallies, and weddings take place. Every year, bigger and faster sailboats
and motorboats bob up and down along the town docks all day. Dozens
of boats with names like Fat Cat, Sunshine, Shooting Star, Happy
Times, and Sweet Dreams arrive with their sunburnt cargo of people of
all ages who descend and make their slow procession up one side of
Main Street and down the other purchasing candy and gifts. It is at
these town docks that the old wharf building housed a pool hall, sa-
loon, roller-skating rink and dance hall, until it burnt down in 1899,
when the population was about half of what it is now, and visitors numbered about 10,000 a year.[7]

In the fall, busloads of foliage-viewers keep the town busy a few
more weeks. You can pick your own apples at local orchards and hike
without mosquitoes on one of the numerous trails in the area. The
maple trees along Main Street are a colorful contrast to the white colonial and Victorian homes.

In December and January white lights sparkle in house windows and
on trees in the park, small pine trees are placed in front of shops along
Main Street, and the fire department erects a three-story Christmas tree
in the center of town. Snowy days bring out dozens of amateur photog-
raphers capturing the same downtown scene people have been photo-
graphing for decades.

After the holiday season, in the coldest weeks of winter, life slows down to a still, peaceful deep-freeze. Finally, it is possible to find parking on Main Street, buy groceries without waiting in line, and drive through town without stopping for pedestrians every few yards. Year-round residents savor this time of year when Lakeview feels like a small, close-knit community, and when ordinary events, celebrations, and rituals are not intended to promote tourism but to build relationships and community spirit among local people.

In winter, on country roads just out of town, the smell of wood stoves hangs in the air and in Lakeview Bay dozens of ice-fishing bob houses spread out like an arctic shantytown. Years ago, to ward off the winter boredom and have a little fun, small replicas of town buildings were built and put out on the ice creating a mini Lakeview village. During most winters from 1888 until the 1990s, "Fisherville" had a post office, town hall, church, store, and courthouse. The events of Fisherville, including elections, town news, and court proceedings, were reported in the local weekly newspaper.

As soon as the ice begins to break up on Lakeview Bay, usually sometime in mid-April, salmon fishing marks the beginning of another tourist season. Predicting the date for ice-out is a favorite pastime. Ice-out is official when the 1,250-passenger tourist boat is able to dock at all four ports on the big lake—a reminder of the present day and historic importance of boat travel. Rail and steamship transportation benefited manufacturing in the second half of the nineteenth century and then brought tourists in droves until the car replaced public transportation as the most popular means of travel. The fact that rail service stopped miles short of Hillside's lake is a partial explanation for the very different economic fates of these two communities.

John Greenleaf Whittier wrote about Lakeview when he took a train and then a boat here in 1853 to attend an anti-slavery Free Soil Party Convention of 3,000 people.

> We have now reached the end of our land journey. Off to the right is a glorious reach of blue water. We step on board the steamer, and...look forth upon the ever varying panorama of sparkling waters, green islands, and mountains starting abruptly from the lake . . .
>
> Ten miles . . . and we enter a broad and beautiful bay, at the head of which lies the village of [Lakeview], its dwellings brilliant in white and green, scattered in their picturesque irregularity along the fertile slopes of the southward trending hills,

looking out over crystal clear waters upon long broken ranges of misty mountains on the opposite shore. Nothing finer than its site can be found . . . It has two large hotels, a flourishing academy, an orthodox and Friends meetinghouse.[8]

In this report to the *National Era,* Whittier described his journey to Lakeview in a way that captures the beauty that continues to draw thousands of famous and ordinary people to this day.

Thriving Social Capital

Lakeview is a community with a sturdy economic base, vibrant, inclusive citizen participation, and a wide range of recreational, educational, social, and artistic outlets. Foreign-made cars and utility vehicles carry all-season outdoor equipment on their roof racks—everything from kayaks and racing canoes to dog sleds and iceboats. Clubs for sailing, hiking, dancing, and ice boating have been popular for more than a century. The town is the location for several prestigious sports events that draw top-notch competitors from throughout the region: a triathlon, a bike race, a canoe race, and a relay run around the entire 65-mile circumference of the lake. These are community events drawing local athletes, spectators, and volunteers. Today, local athletes are among the country's best runners, rowers, bicyclists, cross-country skiers, and paddlers.

Volunteers provide substantial labor to local social service agencies, the hospital, and fire and rescue services. Lakeview has a community daycare center that began in 1974 and has an average year-round daily enrollment of about 115 children. In the late 1990s a teen center opened in a former church and it generates active local participation and generous contributions. Many townspeople hope the center will keep teens from "hanging out" downtown where they might bother shoppers. Other services include a community mental health clinic, a food pantry, an adventure-based youth development and counseling program for teens and families, and many services for people who are elderly or disabled, such as home health care, hospice, and meals-on-wheels. Unlike the center of Hillside where an array of social services are located within easy walking distance from low-income neighborhoods, Lakeview's downtown is a commercial district reserved for eating and shopping; social services are out of town a half-mile or more.

The Lakeview Public Library, built in 1978, is a bright airy space with big windows and comfortable chairs and study corrals. There are frequent speakers funded and sponsored by the Council for the Humanities. There is a large children's section and a weekly reading hour all year long. Local artists display their work here and the up-to-date and eclectic book selection is impressive. The bulletin board is overflowing with posters and fliers for theater and concerts and an array of services for families and individuals.

In Hillside, most residents demonstrate their altruism in personal, quiet ways, like helping out an elderly neighbor, taking in a teen who is having a hard time at home, or looking out for kids after school whose parents do not get home until later. In Lakeview, altruism is expressed in public, organized ways. Here, volunteering has social, political, and even commercial relevance. The hospital fair utilizes the assistance of hundreds of volunteers year-round and raises over $50,000 at the annual summer weekend event. In the mid-90s the local theater group raised funds to buy and refurbish an old building and turned it into a lovely town theater. The rail bed that travels through sixteen miles of woods and wetlands is a popular route for snowmobiling, biking, hiking, dogsledding, hand-railing, and cross-country skiing thanks to thousands of volunteer hours contributed by youth and adults.

When it comes to performing, everyone can have a chance at it. The theater group, chorale, and town band welcome anyone and everyone, regardless of experience or talent—a spirit of inclusivity that is rare and makes for good fun for beginners and accomplished people alike. Every summer a children's theater involves 100 or more children from the area in a production that requires active parent participation. The gazebo in the park, the restored elementary school cupola, flower beds, and the playground are other examples of accomplishments in this industrious community where people seem committed to keeping Lakeview a good place to live.

Lakeview's churches are well attended and several clergy are active in the community. A ten-minute walk down Main Street passes the Episcopal, First Congregational, Catholic, Christian Science, and Second Congregational churches. There are also Baptist and Mormon churches and several evangelical communities. Fundamentalism and liberalism coexist in this town where residents generally seem to prefer not to let religious and political differences interfere with the ease of everyday interactions.

Yet differences of opinion and lifestyle are evident from time to time and political participation is robust. Peace and social justice activists occasionally gather to hold vigils along Main Street, sometimes with dozens of people of all ages. Passersby respond with curiosity, support, and, not infrequently, hostility. In the weeks before residents vote on the town and school budgets, there are lively, contentious debates over zoning, the school budget, social service funding, and the cost of the police, fire, and emergency medical systems. In February and March, the local weekly newspaper frequently runs several pages of provocative letters to the editor. The heated exchanges are perhaps as much a welcome reprieve from winter boredom as a lesson in democracy. People are proud of the long democratic tradition this public dialogue represents. Everyone has ample opportunity to practice tolerance and patience, since opinions span a wide range of ideologies, are voiced with varying degrees of civility, and are sometimes expounded upon with righteous fervor and at great length.

Until recently, residents attended an annual town meeting in March to discuss and vote on warrant articles. But in 1996 legislation made it possible for local communities to end the town meeting tradition, and replace it with an information session (which is not well attended) and a day when polls are open to vote. Some regard this controversial new system as more fair, since many taxpayers were unable to participate in the long meetings because they were housebound or lived away part of the year. Others see the end of town meeting as the demise of an important democratic tradition where diverse opinions were aired, complaints were made, and solutions to town problems were hammered out with lively and long discussions.

In all, Lakeview has fifty clubs and organizations, eleven parks, three public beaches that welcome nonresidents, five museums, a hockey and ice-skating rink, trail systems for cross-country skiing, playing fields, two tennis clubs, and two golf clubs. All these resources are well used by year-round and seasonal residents of all ages.

Interconnected and Competing Lifestyles of Summer People, Tourists, and Townies

For many residents, the lake is a self-contained world of its own, defining social life, pace, and lifestyle. On summer weekends, motorboat traffic can make the lake feel and sound like a congested, noisy city, but fall brings the serene beauty Whittier described. There are many occupied islands and almost every foot of shoreline is privately developed with few environmental restrictions. Several residential summer camps still operate but many of them closed down, due to a decrease in camper enrollments and an increase in the value of lakefront property.

Since the 1990s the trend has been to build immense lakefront houses (my friend calls them conference centers) that are often lived in only a few weeks out of the year. The fronts of these houses face the lakeside not the roadside, drawing attention toward the leisure and action of the lake, rather than the civic responsibilities of a busy town. How and where summer people and tourists focus their attention and their considerable resources is a concern always present just below the surface in Lakeview. Summer residents provide a substantial sum of money to the tax base and tourists keep local businesses thriving, but year-round residents sometimes quietly wonder if too much consideration is given to part-time residents, while urgent local needs are not met. For example, it took years to get sidewalks in the congested South Lakeview area so that children could walk to school more safely, and the town hall, which houses the district court and all the town offices, is badly in need of expansion and repair. So far improvements to the town hall have not been supported, but roads and drainage systems in the most affluent neighborhoods seem to be consistently well maintained.

Others feel that efforts to accommodate tourists and summer residents are not sufficient enough. Many visitors note Lakeview's congested downtown area and the lack of adequate parking. There is no movie theater, high-tech services for computers and cell phones are limited, and stores and restaurants are closed by 9:00 p.m. These limitations suggest opportunities for another generation of entrepreneurs, but also tell of a community that strains, perhaps with a degree of ambivalence, to keep up with its triple identity: one as the small, aging community of 5,000 people with modest incomes and educational backgrounds, living relatively simple, working lives; another as a health and leisure-oriented tourist town, accommodating a transient population of urban and suburban visitors of all ages and means; and a third, as a summer residence to a small but influential group of people of extraordinary wealth who build elaborate homes, drive luxury cars, maintain exclusive social connections with each other, and seek a secluded respite from the public, fast-paced lives they lead away from here.

When tranquility finally comes, and the traffic moves more easily down Main Street, and parking is once again available, and shopkeepers can slow down and recognize you as someone who lives here all year, then people seem to relish the small and intimate community they share. A comment about winter weather often initiates a discussion about the thickness of the ice on the lake, when maple sugaring will begin, and how much or little snow the season has brought due to the temperamental disposition of El Niño. I no longer think of these conversations between permanent residents as trivial. They are an important way to connect with other year-round people and to talk about the things that only 12-month residents know about. Still, there is something both gratifying and enormously aggravating about the way everyone knows each

other. To avoid a brief exchange of pleasantries would go against local social conduct, although I notice that I am not the only one who tries to get
through town unnoticed on busy days.

Good emergency services and hospital facilities are priorities in
this community, but fiscally conservative taxpayers associations are especially active when there are controversial budget items. The most
contested expenditures are those proposed by the school district. More
than 60% of every tax dollar goes to fund education. Lakeview voters
have historically voted liberally on local issues but Hillside voters pay a
higher property tax rate and tend to vote more conservatively on
school and town budgets.[9]

There are a number of festivities that are local traditions for local
families. On Halloween, for example, elementary school children and
their teachers parade through town in costumes, collecting goodies from
downtown stores and entertaining parents and shopkeepers with a hilar-
ious show. But children become teenagers and this town worries about
anything that might negatively affect tourism, like "kids hanging out
downtown." Every summer, articles and letters are printed in the weekly
newspaper. Business owners complain that groups of teenagers intimi-
date shoppers, block doorways, and use offensive language. This has
prompted the town to pass an ordinance forbidding young groups from
hanging out at their favorite spots: on the small stone bridge in the center of town, and at the old railway station where tour buses drop off and
pick up their clients. It turns out that this is not at all a new issue in town.
The town history reports that "in the 1880s 'plug-uglies' who loitered on
the Main Street bridge and annoyed passersby were a problem."[10]

Across from the old railroad station, a bike and skate park was
started by a local family in the foundation of an office building that
burned down. Teens spray-painted bright, bold designs on the cement
walls that town officials soon had whitewashed back to its neutral state. Its
presence close to the center of town and across from the Chamber of
Commerce Visitor Center sparked a great deal of controversy. The issue
became a focus at a number of meetings of the board of selectman. After
a few weeks this venture was shut down, confusing and angering the adolescents who were using it. In this town where summer residents, tourists,
political conservatives, and retired persons, have sway, youth hanging out
in groups are seen as bad for business.

These three vastly different communities—tourists, permanent residents, and summer residents—are engaged in a mostly concealed competition, vying for resources, stability, cultural dominance, and political
leverage, and I suspect that it is the latter of these three communities that
provides the substance for local kids' dreams of what they want to have in

life. Perhaps the young students on promotion day demonstrated the temperament of high-status ambition as they posed for pictures with un-selfconscious flair. Perhaps the Lakeview teenagers who spend every cent of their summer job money to buy sports cars, expensive sound equipment, and clothes from Ambercrombie and Fitch, instead of saving for college have internalized the lessons of a hidden curriculum this community teaches all too well. Ambition, desire, confusion, and frustration reside together in some of Lakeview's young people trying to find their way in a town with competing lifestyles and values, as case studies in later chapters will demonstrate.

It is in the middle of this tension that children develop perceptions of the world and the life they hope to make for themselves. Decisions about educational spending, commercial development, and town policies are made in a forum of competing interests. Many clergy, parents, and youth workers are concerned that the implicit values children are learning in this context are weighted a little too far on the side of material gain.

Lakeview: Enchanted or Deceived?

A 14-foot tall papier maché Nutcracker made by high school students in the early 1970s stands outside a Main Street bookstore—an easy target for practical jokes. Every few years, the Nutcracker is damaged generating a flurry of letters to the editor and efforts to restore the landmark back to its former shape. Soon, the Nutcracker takes up its post again, looking better than ever with a new paint job and refurbished nose. This Lakeview mascot says much about a town that many people regard as enchanted. It is a town that seems, at least on the surface, relatively unfazed by national economic swings and political events. Even the tragedies of its own residents ruffle the placid image of this community only temporarily and then life, at least for most people, goes on as usual.

There are people who struggle in poverty or who live exhausting and difficult lives for other reasons. Every year, teenage lives are permanently altered or ended in car accidents. Too many local youth attempt or succeed in taking their lives. Several years ago, the town was stunned by the suicide of the postmaster, a well-known and pleasant man, who walked off his boat into the deep, icy lake one November day. Alcoholism, drug abuse, depression, domestic violence, and other problems are far more often attributed to the low income town of Hillside than they are acknowledged to be a part of the fabric of life here, frustrating the efforts of people who know these to be serious problems that impact many lives. Teachers, counselors, social workers, and parents who have lost children often speak of the veil of denial that filters the way life is portrayed here. Like the Nutcracker who stands in silent witness, what appears on the surface is not what really is. Children growing up here may internalize a distorted view of future possibilities and wealth— dreams that often cannot be realized.

On this particular fall day, as I leave the bustle of downtown to walk along residential streets, the setting sun is glistening gold on the water and fall foliage on the sugar maples is a brilliant red and orange. Many people would argue that this is one of the best places in America to raise children and make a life. Sixth graders are confident, ready for the world, eager for the opportunities the middle school will give them. Optimism, kindness, compassion, good humor, and active involvement abound in this community, expressed in countless ways.

Living in a community where tourism has primacy makes the world bigger, more interesting, and diverse, and at the same time it can make the world dangerously small, riveting attention toward material gain and status. Like the students posing on the picnic table after their promotion to seventh grade, this is a town with an alluring flair; conscious of the outside looking in and it wants to look good, even sometimes looking better than the truth.

Conclusion

These towns, one that is only known to outsiders as they are "on their way to somewhere else," and the other, a popular tourist destination, each have abundant resources, rich histories, broad social networks, and involved citizens. But there are gaps of understanding in the ways both communities are perceived. When people see poverty in Hillside and miss the cherished sense of community and the active involvement of its citizens, they miss an important part of community culture and socialization there. Likewise, when people see trendy downtown shops, fancy cars, and big houses in Lakeview, and miss the everyday struggle and frustration of many parents who know their children are exposed to material wealth that they cannot provide, they make assumptions about Lakeview that are not entirely accurate. Many Lakeview parents are concerned about the potentially harmful commercial seduction of their child's values and desires, even as they enjoy the resources their community has to offer. Many Hillside parents know that to be successful, their children will need a good education and job opportunities that may require moving away, even as they cherish the intimate connections they work to maintain.

Comparing Hillside and Lakeview, we see neighboring towns that share a strong sense of citizenship, healthy self-sufficiency, active social and political involvement, and rich natural resources. We also see two communities with contrasting lifestyles. In Hillside, life feels slower. Clothing styles are informal and practical, interactions are intimate, even homey, and extended family and neighborhood or district networks are preserved. There is an appreciation for just "being you" without pretense; social status is determined more by social and civic connections than by material wealth. Community interdependence and cooperative intimacy are highly valued, perhaps more so than individual freedom and autonomy. Teachers are thought of as authority figures rather than friends. People are connected to and aware of the past in the way they live their present lives. However, students from Hillside are quick to

87

point out that *they too* like the most popular rock groups, know how to dress, are competitive athletes, want to go to college, wish they had a skateboard park in their town, and have impressive ambitions.

In Lakeside, the pace is quicker, styles are trendier, and commercialism is savvier. Involvement in the community and social networks are carefully planned and often have commercial and political implications. Family privacy is well guarded. Social status is determined by material wealth and independence and autonomy are highly valued. Good teachers are like friends, people are future-oriented and they structure their present lives in a way that will positively impact future opportunities. Yet there are many contrary examples of these generalizations demonstrated by children and adults who have strong communal ideals, refuse to let material standards go unquestioned, and who reject status quo fashion and music trends.

Internal discord is evident in both Hillside and Lakeview. Hillside's diverse districts, each with their own social, political, and economic histories, create a hierarchy of place that is a salient symbol of internal social status tensions. In Lakeview, three distinct populations rather than locations create a subtle internal conflict. Permanent residents, tourists, and summer residents represent different social status norms and make different types of investments in the community. In later chapters, I will explore how children experience these tensions and the possibility that there may be more common ground *between* towns than *within* them.

Common ground remains hidden to most residents, however. At the end of his seventh grade year, Ethan, a Hillside student, reflected on how common interests among students from both towns are not known to one another. He thought the middle school needed to:

> . . . have some way to show kids that there are kids who are from different towns that have the same interests as them. Like a lot of kids like skateboarding; there's a lot of kids that skateboard down Main Street in Hillside, and I don't really think Lakeview kids know that. They've never been to Hillside, or if they have, they've just flown by it to go to [another town]. They think of Hillside as a little speck on the map.
>
> (Ethan, grade 7 interview, spring)

Students from Hillside know a lot about Lakeview, even before they go there to middle school. But Hillside, a mere "speck on the map" to outsiders, is not known to Lakeview students, and is therefore often defined by myth and stereotype. When I asked Ethan what he saw in Lakeview that was missing in Hillside, he said the stores and downtown area. When I asked him if he thought anything was missing in Lakeview, he said, "Lakeview is definitely missing the community thing." This "community thing" has multiple layers of meaning and significance, as following chapters will illustrate. These twelve and thirteen-year-old research participants were keen to the differences in community cultures and they were articulate about what they experienced when they were exposed to differences at the middle school.

The findings from three studies of family and community life offer a helpful framework to illuminate core community patterns and values in Lakeview and Hillside. The patterns described in these works, however over-generalized they may be, are a useful way to begin to think about the contrasting socialization experiences of children from these communities.

Crestwood Heights: A Study of the Culture of Suburban Life was written by John Seeley, R. Alexander Sim, and Elizabeth Loosely in 1956 about a small town of 4,000 in mid-west Canada. The authors describe the children growing up in primarily white-collar, professional households of Crestwood Heights as "healthy, physically well-developed, attractively dressed, poised" (p. 160). This upwardly mobile, future-oriented, middle-class town has interesting similarities to Lakeview, despite its different population, geography, history, and national location.

In *The Urban Villagers: Group and Class in the Life of Italian-Americans,* Herbert Gans (1962) wrote about a working-class, Italian-American urban community. This study by Gans, together with the 1985 work of Charles Willie, in *Black and White Families: A Study of Complementarity,* provide useful insights about lifestyles that are community and family-oriented, with a lean toward the past and an ambivalence toward an unknown future. Table 1 describes divergent, perhaps even contradictory, ways of living, working, and viewing schooling and the future from a working-class community (left column) and middle-class community (right column).

Crestwood Heights and Lakeview can be described as communities that value independence, freedom, upward mobility, future orientation, optimism, individuality, and change. There is an expectation in these communities that the schools will reflect these values and there is low tolerance for people and structures that interfere with individual career goals, personal growth, and educational attainment.

The core values of Hillside and of the families Willie and Gans described include close family and neighborhood ties, a strong sense of communal goals, an appreciation for the foundation of knowledge provided by the traditional past, and a faith in the goodness of the local community. There is concern in these communities that people in outside

Table 1. Attitudes and Values in Working Class and Affluent Families

Subject of Contrasting Attitudes	The Urban Villagers by Gans (1962) / Black and White Families by Willie (1985)	Crestwood Heights by Seeley, Sim, Loosely (1956)
Role of Families and Schools in Socialization	Cultural transmission is the primary responsibility of the family; the school is "treated with suspicion" since the culture of the school may not reflect the culture of the community (Gans, 121). Fathers share school communication responsibilities with mothers (Willie, 189).	The schools of the community exist to prepare its children, socially and vocationally, to take their places as functioning adults in this society (259). The transmission of culture is seen as the responsibility of parents (mostly of the mother) *and* the school together—active home-school alliances are forged (163).
Group Identity vs. Unique Individual Identity	Children are not expected to behave as unique individuals, they are expected to behave as part of a community. When schools expect children to behave as individuals, the response may be passivity on the part of the student (Gans, 133).	Children are encouraged to be independent; are given freedom to make choices; have a lot of range to explore and make decisions (163–164). Individual uniqueness is encouraged and supported (171). Independence, not interdependence, is characteristic of relations with others (160). A "highly individualistic culture" where family is an "aggregate of individuals" (220).
Present, Past, and Future Orientation	The future is unknown and not thought of, the focus is on the present; past tradition and culture provides an important base (Gans, 68).	Families live the present with future opportunities in mind (164). The future is thought of optimistically and the past is less important (164).
Authoritarian and Democratic Family Functioning	Authority rests with the father *or* the mother; relationships between children and parents are not equal (Willie, 266).	Form of family function is democratic (168); children are given choices, (170); it is ideal for family members to be equal (203).

Orientation to Community and Individual Goals	Children are not expected to leave their family and community for personal development and career opportunities (Gans, 245).	Children are expected to leave their families of origin and start a life of their own; "a balance must be struck between allegiance to the family of orientation and the demands of adult life" (183).
Adult Role in Child's School Life	The life of the child and the life of the adult are seen as separate, with clear distinctions. Parents see the school as their child's realm and there is little involvement in it (Gans, 57).	Children are included in adult activities and adults are involved in their child's institutions (207). The distinction between the life of the child and the life of the adult is not clear (270).
School and Community Involvement	Involvement in the school and the community may be limited due to family responsibilities and full working schedules (Willie, 191).	The community is a "highly complex, associational society" and the primary goal of joining community activities is social mobility; the secondary goal is to serve the community (211, 222).
Adaptation in Unfamiliar Environments	There is strong loyalty to culture of origin and a drive to structure new environments like home in order to behave in familiar ways (Gans, 136).	The rapid pace of change gives people a feeling of "never being completely at home;" new social behavior is always being learned (217).
Importance of Education to Achieve Social and Economic Mobility	Parents are concerned that schooling will estrange their children from them and from their community (Gans, 129). Privately, parents are ambivalent about education unless there is a link to a good job and financial security, but they speak positively to their children about school (Gans, 131). Although many parents have not gone to college, they wish this opportunity for their children (Willie, 190).	Social and economic mobility is essential (206), and education is seen as the way to achieve social and professional status.

institutions will not know enough about them to reflect the values they hold dear, and there is an accompanying wariness of outsiders looking in with judgmental eyes that lack real understanding. Lakeview residents generally like how others see their town but Hillside residents sense they are defined more by misperceptions than by real knowledge.

How, then, does the middle school, located in Lakeview, balance these disparate and competing interests? Does the school respond to the needs and incorporate the resources of both communities? Does the middle school promote equity and complementarity to allow children from both communities to integrate the knowledge and resources they bring from home? Are children encouraged to learn from each other? The next section will provide a context for answering these questions by describing the middle school, the students, and the transition process.

PART **II**

_____

The School and its Teachers and Students

Introduction

Middle grades teachers must balance the varied concerns of parents, students, and taxpayers within the context of a broader political agenda that increasingly focuses on outputs, such as test scores, rather than inputs, such as class size. Middle grades schools, at their best, encourage children to build successful bonds with adults and peers and, simultaneously, move children toward more independence and autonomy. Teachers must find ways to coordinate the curriculum to respond to the diverse values, talents, skills, and expectations their students bring with them, and they must motivate students to develop new skills and ways of viewing the world that will be useful to them in future contexts. The lead roles in this universal drama belong to twelve-year-old students who must work to establish an amicable balance between school, home, and friends. Successful middle grades schools bring this medley of objectives into sharp focus and find ways to integrate them into everyday policies and practices.

The following chapters are based on observations, student focus groups, and interviews with school staff members that took place in the winter of 2000, while my research participants were well into their seventh grade year. I took the school bus to school, attended all seventh grade classes, ate with students in the lunch room, hung out in the hallways during break, attended after school activities, and then went home on the late bus at the end of an exhausting day. During these observations, totaling more than fifty hours, I paid attention to how seventh grade students spent their school day, and the pace, tone, emotion, and physical sensations they experienced. From the chapters on town cultures, I now move to five chapters that delve into the middle school environment and the expectations, hopes, worries, and developmental needs students bring with them as they transition from grade six to grade seven. Taking cues from what I learned about Lakeview and Hillside, I went to the middle school eager to see how students from vastly different backgrounds would be received and included in their new setting.

Adaptation to school is an interplay among at least three realms: community and family cultures and educational values; the environments of sending and receiving schools; and the social, cognitive, emotional, and physical developmental needs of students (Willie, 1973). The explicit and implicit agendas of communities, families, and schools encourage and emphasize different skills and ways of interacting. During adolescence, healthy development requires opportunities to experience a balanced range of seemingly contradictory modes: competition and cooperation, autonomy and intimacy, family heritage and personal aspirations, social and cognitive development, individual growth and sense of community, ambition and concern for others (Erikson, 1968; Selman, 1980, 1990; Kohlberg, 1969). However, many educational institutions, by default, design, or inadequate resources, concentrate their efforts on one or the other, and these complementary skills often become polarized (Carnegie Council on Adolescent Development, 1989). My observations at Mountainview Middle School, my individual and group conversations with students, and the answers on student questionnaires, suggest that these skills and values are more integrated than polarized.

Middle Grades Schools: Instructional Innovation or Solution to Space Needs?

Students spend between eight and fourteen hours, five days a week, in classrooms and engaged in other school-related activities, yet few people have studied school environments as a context for understanding student experience. The research that does exist on school and classroom environments has focused attention on elementary schools (e.g., Ashton-Warner, 1963; Dennison, 1969; Jackson, 1968; Paley, 1986) and high schools (e. g., DeYoung, 1995; Grant, 1988; Lawrence-Lightfoot, 1983; Rutter et al., 1979; Sizer, 1984). But accounts of the middle grades (e.g., Goodlad, 1984; Tye, 1985) are rare, perhaps due to confusion about what exactly these schools are supposed to be doing. Should middle grades schools focus attention on moving students ahead toward high school and more rigorous subject matter? Allow students another couple of years of close academic and emotional guidance? Expose students to future career options? Concentrate on guiding positive social and moral development in children who come to them during a time of life when identity development and awareness of others are main concerns?

My conversations with teachers revealed some ambiguity regarding the primary mission of middle grades schooling. Elementary school teachers worried that their students, especially the ones who struggled in elementary grades, would not be given the care, support, and individual attention necessary to keep them on the right track at the middle school. Some high school teachers, on the other hand, claimed that the middle school provides two more years of hand-holding rather than getting on with the independent, subject-oriented schooling necessary to graduate from twelfth grade.

During my home visits, some Lakeview parents voiced concerns that the middle school would not challenge their children intellectually, while some Hillside parents wondered if the middle school would make opportunities accessible to their children so that they could feel like fully participating members of their new school. The following chapters describe Mountainview Middle School as a place where experienced teachers attempt to bridge these differences. But it is no small task to teach with clarity of purpose, support students in their social and emotional development, maintain rigorous academic standards, and respond thoughtfully to public concerns.

There is some basis in history for why people seem baffled by the mission and primary objectives of the middle grades. Tyack and Cuban (1995) traced the vision of middle grades schools to early in the twentieth century when less than 10% of the U.S. population graduated from high school. They explained, "Educational reformers—supported by social investigators, developmental psychologists, and foes of child labor—designed the junior high school as a structural and pedagogical solution to the problems of attrition" (p. 70). They went on to clarify why establishing middle grades schools appealed to many progressive educators:

> It was the hope of reformers that separating the middle grades would not only improve retention and encourage vocational exploration, but that it would also more effectively meet the special developmental needs of adolescents. Furthermore, the early advocates of junior high schools argued that these schools should be a seed ground for developing new forms of curriculum and instruction that one day may transform the entire educational system (p. 72).

But it was not until after World War II, when new schools were being built to accommodate increasing numbers of students moving into higher grades, that a majority of students in the middle grades were in separate schools (p. 71). Although the initial concept of middle grades schooling was as an educational innovation, more often than not these schools were formed as a pragmatic solution to space needs.

Despite the original progressive vision that middle grades schools would respond to the distinct needs of early adolescents, junior high schools tended to mirror high schools rather than present a model for reform. They were departmentalized and subject-oriented, teachers were inadequately trained, and tracking by ability was common (p. 72). Although junior high schools fell short of their original goals, they opened to discussion important issues surrounding how to effectively educate early adolescents.

The notion that middle-level schools are created to provide a developmentally appropriate atmosphere for early adolescents is challenged by rural education researchers, De Young, Howley, and Theobald (1995). These authors argued that middle grades schools are first and foremost a form of school consolidation rather than a pedagogical advancement and are created when K–8 schools run out of space. They questioned the concept of student-centered teaching promoted by middle schools and they challenged the argument that early adolescents need more autonomy and freedom than their elementary schools can provide. Above all, they mourned the loss of community that comes when students leave their own towns to go to school in faraway places:

> The idea of the middle school is founded on the assumption that the individual must constitute the focus of pedagogy, and that theories of personal and psychological development ought not merely to inform, but to dictate institutional practice . . . Choosing to emphasize the psychological needs of individuals implies that the needs of communities and cultures are less important (DeYoung et al., 1995: p. 32).

The unequivocal conclusion that these authors draw from their research is that, "pursuing the middle school concept in rural America is misguided and, moreover, it is harmful to small communities" (p. 33). These concerns are important ones that must be considered in the endless reorganizing of school districts in rural areas.

The Multiple Influences on Development in Context

When social psychologists, like Bronfenbrenner (1979), began to focus their attention on the role of the environment in influencing human behavior and development, some educators began to adapt their classroom environments to the social, emotional, physical, spiritual, and cognitive needs and resources of students. This theoretical framework—

one that attempts to see a complex person as an active agent in multiple contexts—is the basis for the middle schools "movement" in schools that have the resources and the means to shape their environments.

Children develop their repertoire of social behavior first within a home and family environment, and then within the increasingly more complex and diverse environments of school, church, community, and work. Children learn to read social cues and develop social perceptions from infancy (Bowlby, 1969); they arrive at school with an already well-developed framework for understanding and participating in social interactions. However, there are vast differences in what children learn from their early experiences; expectations for social interactions, relationships with authority figures, and public behavior differ, as the preceding town chapters indicate.

I learned from the students who participated in this study that personal characteristics like the color and texture of their hair, height and weight, and communication skills had relative importance subject to other interdependent factors in the student's environment. For many, individual likes and dislikes are tempered by changing peer group standards, but there are countless conditions that influence the school experience of students, many of them exerting influence in ways that are not explicit. Students described many factors when they spoke about what was most important in shaping their lives at school and at home:

- town of residence and the location of their residence within the town
- their family's longevity and history in the town
- connection to another home community where they used to live
- body size (boys worried they were too small; girls worried they were too big)
- divorce status of their parents and the timing and nature of the divorce
- relationship with their non-custodial parent
- possible presence of their parent's new partner
- change in financial status following separation or divorce
- associational and altruistic habits of parents and the social capital the family may claim from community participation

- family composition and birth order; influence of siblings

- employment of parents

- education of parents

- their ability and desire to dress fashionably

Lewin (1935, 1946), and later, Bronfenbrenner (1979), argued that human behavior is enacted within the total environmental context—a constellation of interdependent factors—the historic, economic, political, structural, symbolic, and human life space of existence. Human beings behave differently in different environments and different contexts.

Adolescence and Adaptation to a New School Environment

Early adolescents face multiple changes all at once: biological, psychological, and social. Simmons and Blyth (1987) argued that the stresses of puberty make this a particularly inopportune time to also add the demands of a major school transition. They argued that for some children in some circumstances, a transition during the middle grades results in a disruption that has a long-term negative impact. They offered as evidence convincing documentation of academic and social declines in their study samples. These authors find ample agreement in other school transition research (e.g., Blyth, Simmons, and Carlton-Ford, 1983; Eccles et al., 1993a, b; Eccles and Midgely, 1989; Simmons et al., 1979).

Grade span research in rural areas is not common, but Wihry, Colardarci, and Meadow (1992) studied eighth grade student performance on statewide achievement tests in Maine and found that, "the elementary setting (K–8, K–9, 3–8) surfaced as the most favorable location for the eighth grade" (p. 58). Junior high and middle school configurations were better for student performance on achievement tests than when eighth grades were located in senior high schools, but they did not have as good outcomes as when the eighth grade remained in an elementary school.

The notion of adolescence as a clearly defined and often problematic stage of development began with the work of Erikson (1968) who understood adolescent identity development to be particularly difficult because of the young person's heightened awareness of the contradictory nature of society's moral ideals vs. social and political realities. Erikson proposed that youth face a disconnection between themselves and a culture eager to appropriate rigid roles, work lives, lifestyles, and stereotypical ways of defining youth. For some, this disconnection erupts in crisis proportions.

Adolescence is also a time of heightened self-awareness and awareness of others. Elkind (1967) suggested that as adolescents begin to be aware of what others think of them, they become preoccupied with an imaginary audience of critical peers. Heightened social awareness and social comparisons make this a particularly volatile time for adolescent's self-perception. Their assessment of how they are doing compared to their peers can be harsh, regardless of their actual performance. Some researchers have found that for students whose families struggle economically, shifts to a higher status reference group for comparison can have deleterious effects on self-esteem (e.g., Schwarzer, Jerusalem, and Lange, 1981). Others have found only modest correlations between social class and self-esteem (e.g., Rosenburg and Pearlin, 1978).

When I began this study, I wondered how Hillside students would fare when they experienced this shift in reference group. Generally, I found Hillside students to be less concerned with social comparisons than Lakeview students who seemed oriented toward the standards of a not-so-imaginary audience of adults and peers. A few Lakeview students told me, for example, that they sometimes brought a change of clothes to school in case their first outfit received a derogatory response from their peers. Many frustrated parents of early adolescents see a lot of expensive clothing go unworn during these years.

Another common experience for the parents of early adolescents is to find that the obsession of a year ago is now disdained as an activity for "little kids" and no longer important. I was surprised to find, for example, that the boy who collected every Pokemon character card in the sixth grade, was entirely disenchanted with these little personalities by the beginning of seventh grade. At this age, activities that are more psychologically central become satisfied more quickly and soon lose their appeal (Lewin, 1946: p. 242). The fast-paced claiming and disclaiming of passions in the lives of early adolescents may be hard for adults to keep up with, but this experimental expanding of a young person's life-space is an essential part of development. Understanding this, some middle grades schools attempt to provide an array of new choices and opportunities as a chance to expand awareness of different options and provide the substance for imagination and future orientation. By midway through the eighth grade, most students are ready to move on to high school, leaving their middle school teachers with the difficult task of working with students who spend a good portion of the first year adjusting, and a good portion of the second year with their eyes on high school.

The transition to seventh grade in a regional school district marks the time when students are exposed to more diversity in their peer group and expanded opportunities and experiences. It is also a time when students must learn to operate within an increasing variety of institutions and organizations: family, school, church, teams, classrooms, cliques, clubs, etc. It comes as no surprise that the drive to fit in with one's peer group takes on extreme importance during this time of life, and the failure to fit in is cause for great concern.

Some authors have argued that some stressful experiences, like school transitions, may be functional if they lead to an improved ability to cope with future disruptive changes. Freud (1958) and Erikson (1968) viewed periods of stress as growth-producing, as long as the stress is short term and there are options for mastery in their new environment. I found, for example, that students benefited from greater diversity in their peer group—it gave them a broader range of choices and perspectives regarding things such as dress, looks, popularity, music, academic success, future goals, and material desires. Some Lakeview children were relieved to find wider variation in the dress of their middle school classmates; it took the edge off the fashion competition that dominated their sixth grade year at Lakeview Elementary School. Some Hillside students were glad to be with more classmates who wanted to get good grades and go to college.

Despite my expectation that I would find declines in self-esteem and social self-concept, particularly among Hillside-Two Rivers students, I found that most of the students in my study group continued their pattern of social and academic success at the middle school. I observed what other researchers have pointed out: early adolescence can be a period of resilience, productivity, cognitive growth, and increasing involvement at home, school, and in the community (Coleman, 1980; Rutter, 1980; and Bandura, 1972). The following three research summaries begin to explain why middle school is a period of increasing positive self-image and competence for some students, while others seem to face challenges that result in a downward spiral that continues into high school.

The Milwaukee Study and Cumulation of Change Theory

School adjustment during adolescence was brought to the research foreground by Ruth Simmons and Dale Blyth who conducted a landmark longitudinal study in Milwaukee schools between 1974 and 1979. This study initiated twenty years of research examining how schoolchildren fared when they transitioned to the middle grades. To date, transition to middle grades in rural areas and outcome comparisons by social class have remained largely unexamined. Researchers, even those who hypothesized that the school environment is a key factor in school adjustment, have failed to study and describe community and school environments. However, the Milwaukee study, and those that followed, contributed important new insights into the way early adolescents experience school transitions.

Simmons and Blyth (1987) examined the impact of age, gender, pubertal timing, and timing of school transition in a sample of 621 white students in 18 Milwaukee schools.[1] Participation, peer relations, grade point average (GPA), self-esteem, plans for the future, and independence were assessed in two major cohorts. One group remained in the same school all the way through eighth grade, the other group transitioned to junior high school in grade seven. There were data collection points in grades six and seven and again during the transition to high school in grades nine and ten.

Simmons and Blyth predicted, "The first major movement into a large scale organizational context may cause difficulty for the child, as may the dramatic changes of puberty" (p. 17). They wondered if the effects of such a transition could have consequences for some children even into high school, and they wondered who would be most at risk of having a hard time during and after the transition. A number of findings were significant and have relevance to my study.

The cluster of variables related to self-image and gender produced findings that indicated girls were at greater risk than boys in both K–6 and K–8 schools, *especially* when they transitioned to a junior high school in grade seven. Simmons and Blyth reported, ". . . females scored significantly more negatively than males in all four years. They score lower in self-esteem, lower in sense of self-stability, and higher in self-consciousness" (p. 63). But girls who stayed in the same school in grade seven did not show a drop in self-esteem and maintained higher self-esteem scores in grades nine and ten than their female classmates who did make a junior high transition (pp. 219–222). Positive peer evaluation resulted in positive self-evaluation for both boys and girls and victimization by peers was shown to contribute to lower self-esteem (p. 322).

Future aspirations to go to college were voiced more often by girls than by boys, but girls were less likely to see themselves having a life-long career (p. 79). In all four years, boys were more likely to be in trouble at school than girls (except for grade nine truancy), and boys reported being both victims and perpetrators of peer teasing more often than girls

(p. 81). Other changes noted included more feelings of anonymity in their new schools, higher expectations for autonomy and independence, and lower participation rates in school activities.

Simmons and Blyth concluded,

> . . . seventh grade children in the junior high school demonstrated several disadvantages that they did not exhibit the year before. Compared to the K–8 students, they show less favorable attitudes toward school, lower self-esteem for the girls, lower grade point averages, less participation and less leadership in extracurricular activities, and greater victimization especially among boys (p. 243).

Disadvantages persisted in high school: the junior high school cohort reported more feelings of anonymity, lower participation rates in extracurricular activities, and again, lower self-esteem in girls. Transition effects exceeded age and grade effects.

Simmons and Blyth discussed three possible theories for why children may be at greater risk for poor adjustment during the transition to grade seven. First, they proposed that the cumulation of change in a student's life made a difference: more changes resulted in more negative outcomes in GPA, extracurricular participation, and self-esteem, and the latter is true especially in boys (p. 294). Besides school change, they also considered pubertal changes, dating behavior, geographic mobility, and major family disruptions, such as death, divorce, and remarriage. Many children today experience major life disruptions more than once in their primary and secondary school years. Family disruption was very salient to my research participants and offered one explanation for difficult adjustment to seventh grade for some boys. The toll that disturbance in the family system takes on otherwise stable and resilient children is cause for concern for educators, parents, and policymakers.

In the discussion of their findings, Simmons and Blyth wondered if they would get different results in rural schools where children are less likely to encounter strangers in their new school. Though Simmons and Blyth speculated that "homogeneity among classmates might be protective," causing children to feel more comfortable (p. 308), in my study, economic and town heterogeneity turned out to be a vital *positive* force in the adjustment to seventh grade.

The second point made by Simmons and Blyth concerning critical conditions that influence adjustment to middle school is how student's experienced school in earlier years. Previous positive self-esteem and peer relations were beneficial to students during the transition, Simmons and Blyth reported; students who had poor sixth grade self-esteem and peer relations were at higher risk for poor adjustment in junior high school. My own study group was selected by a criterion-based sampling method that requested teachers to remove the names of sixth grade students who faced serious struggles academically or socially. By using these selection criteria, I was better able to understand the effects of social class and town of residence in a group of students who had experienced some success in school.

Third, Simmons and Blyth noted that for early adolescents, this is a time for shifting the focus from a primary (family-oriented) context to secondary (school, peer, and community-oriented) contexts. The transition to seventh grade accelerates this shift, and for some students, this can be problematic. Optimal development is possible when children are challenged enough during this process to find resources within themselves to cope and master new tasks (p. 352). To be successful, they argued, children need to recognize in their new environments some of the features of their old environment:

> It is understandable that youngsters are less able to cope if at one and the same time they are uncomfortable with their bodies, due to physical changes; with their family, due to changes in family constellation; with home, because of a move; with school, due to great discontinuity in the nature of the school environment; with peers, because of the new importance of opposite sex relationships and because of disruption of prior peer networks in a new school and the changes in peer expectations and peer evaluation criteria. There needs to be some arena of life or some set of role relationships with which the individual can feel relaxed and comfortable, to which he or she can withdraw and become invigorated (pp. 351–352).

An arena of comfort must exist somewhere in a child's life—at home, at school, in the home of neighbors or relatives—in order to successfully negotiate the transition to a new and more challenging environment. In the chapters that follow, I show that three factors interacted to provide an arena of comfort for most of the research participants: positive classroom environments, the encouragement of parents, and the coping strategies employed by the students themselves.

The results of this extensive comparative transition study are striking, yet without more information about the school environments, we are left with many questions. Are GPAs higher in the K–8 school because

grading practices are more lenient? Are the different schools in comparable neighborhoods with equivalent instructional and administrative
quality? Are the junior high schools traditional or innovative? Are the
racial and social class composition of the two types of schools the same?
In my study, distinct community cultures, economic diversity, and the
middle school environment have proven to be vital forces in understanding the transition to grade seven.

The Michigan Study and Stage-Environment Fit Theory

Following the Milwaukee study, a team of researchers examined
the effects of the transition to the middle grades in a study sample of
2,500 students from twelve school districts in middle-income communities of southeastern Michigan.[2] The students transitioned from grade
six in an elementary school to grade seven in a junior high school. The
two-year, four-wave Michigan study examined how changes in the
school environment during the middle grades affected self-esteem and
achievement-related beliefs and values in a student population that was
95% white. From Lewin's concept of person-environment fit, Eccles
and her colleagues (1993a, 1993b) developed the notion of "stage-environment fit" and postulated that there was a ". . . mismatch between
the needs of developing adolescents and the opportunities afforded
them by their school environments" (1993a: p. 90). The authors concluded that the developmental needs of adolescents—desire for
greater autonomy and self-determination, peer group identification,
and capacity for higher level cognitive work—were not adequately met
by middle grades schools. Eccles and her colleagues (1993a, 1993b)
outlined what they and other researchers found to be problematic disconnections between middle school environments and the developmental needs of their students.

First, the seventh grade students in their study placed higher value on
making their own decisions, but believed they had fewer opportunities for
decision-making in their new school environments. Some researchers
found a greater level of teacher control and discipline and fewer opportunities for students to be involved in decision-making and self-
management in the middle grades (Brophy and Evertson, 1976; Midgely
and Feldlaufer, 1987; Midgely, Feldlaufer, Eccles. 1988; Moos, 1979).

Second, middle grades schools generally have more students per
grade perhaps leading to less personal and positive relationships with
teachers. Instructional strategies seemed to exacerbate negative self-
evaluation and the lack of positive connection with school adults. In

most classrooms they found that lessons were taught using whole class task organization, there was an increase in between-class ability grouping, and students were called on to display what they know and to be evaluated publicly.

Third, middle grades teachers faced a greater emphasis on subject matter mastery and they reported feeling less effective as teachers especially with students of lower abilities (Midgely, Feldlaufer, and Eccles, 1989). Ironically, Eccles' research team found evidence that seventh grade classroom work required *lower* level cognitive skills than at the elementary school (1993a, p. 94). Like some of the students in my study, the Michigan students perceived a *decrease* in intellectually challenging work. At the same time, there is evidence that some junior high and middle schools set a higher standard for judging student performance, resulting in lower grades for many students, even when the work seemed easier to them (ibid.).

Students who transition to a new school in seventh grade may experience declines in grades, peer acceptance, school participation, decision-making opportunities, meaningful connection with adults, mastery of challenging subject matter, and self-concept (Eccles, Midgley, and Adler, 1984; Harter, 1982; Simmons, Blyth, Van Cleave, and Bush, 1979). These declines may initiate a downward spiral and the magnitude of the decline is predictive of future failure in school (Simmons and Blyth, op. cit.).

It is not just the turbulence of early adolescence that accounts for downturns in school attitudes, self-image, and performance; rather, it is the poor match between the early adolescent and the middle school environment. The findings of Eccles and her colleges (1993b) led them to these conclusions:

> We believe that the mismatch between the adolescents' needs and traditional middle grade schools and classroom environments results in a deterioration in academic motivation and performance of these early adolescents. More specifically, the environmental changes often associated with transition to traditional middle grade schools are likely to be especially harmful since they emphasize competition, social comparison, and ability self-assessment at a time of heightened self-focus; they decrease decision-making and choice at a time when the desire for autonomy is growing; they emphasize lower level cognitive strategies at a time when the ability to use higher-level strategies is increasing; and they disrupt social networks and decrease the opportunity for close adult child relationships (pp. 559–560).

The challenge to middle grades schools, then, is to provide the structure children need to give safety and support at their current developmental level, and also to provide an environment that is sufficiently challenging to move students toward higher levels of cognitive and social maturity (Eccles et al., 1993a).

Differentiating Results in Diverse Populations

Some researchers have found that students maintain or *improve* across the transition (Greene, 1985; Nottelman, 1987; Schulenburg, Asp, and Peterson, 1984). Noting that the effects of school transition on self-esteem and attitudes toward school had shown inconsistent results in a variety of studies, Simmons and Blyth (op. cit.) suggested that the racial makeup of the student body and the size and location (urban or suburban) of the school made a significant difference. Fenzel (1989), for example, found that suburban, white children who transitioned to a middle school with a team-teaching structure, did not show the same declines in peer relationships and school attitudes.

Seidman, Allen, Aber, Mitchell, and Feinman (1994) noted that authors had rarely distinguished characteristics of the sample by race, social class, and urban vs. suburban, so they clarified these characteristics and offered comparative information focusing on multiracial, poor, inner-city schools. They hypothesized that for these youth, the stresses of poverty and urban environment would result in an even greater developmental mismatch between children and their middle schools.

Seventy-six percent of the 580 youth in the Seidman study were from New York City and the remaining 24% were from Baltimore and Washington DC. The research participants lived in neighborhoods with high levels of poverty. Twenty-eight percent were black (African and Caribbean), 25% were white (Greek and Italian), and 47% were Latino (Puerto Rican and Dominican). The students transitioned from elementary schools to either 6–8 or 7–9 middle and junior high schools.

Along with self-esteem, GPA, and peer interactions, this research team also examined the impact of the school transition on perceived social and academic competence, a question that had been infrequently studied. They again found declines in GPA across the school transition, but they also found that academic and social efficacy increased and these results were strong across gender and racial lines. The youth in these schools believed that they *could* master difficult academic work, even when they reported lower GPAs. They held the self-protective belief that schools, and not their own lack of competence, were responsible for their academic declines. Unlike Simmons et al. (1978) who found that GPAs of black youth plummeted compared to those of white youth, Seidman et al. (1944) found that the GPAs of black and white youth declined equally, and more than the GPAs of Latino youth (p. 519).

These authors found that students reported an increase in "daily hassles" with school authority figures, but not with their peers: "Transactions with the school microsystem deteriorated after transition to a new school: youth reported increased daily hassles and decreased social support and involvement with school. On the other hand, daily hassles with peers decreased, and peer values became more non-conforming" (p. 516). The authors also noted that ". . . the more intensely youth experienced daily hassles with the transition to a new school, the lower their expectations of academic efficacy, the less they prepared for class, and the poorer their grades" (p. 520). When they found a relationship between achievement and alienation, it was related to reading and math achievement in the eighth grade, just at the time when grouping by ability became more prominent. The deleterious effects of ability grouping on middle grades students were noted in all three of these major studies and, in chapter 11, I will discuss the effects of ability grouping on the students in my study.

The Seidman study found declines in self-esteem across the transition but did not find gender or race differences. They also found that lower socioeconomic status was consistently related to *lower* levels of alienation, causing me to wonder if the increased peer group values that the authors also noted were protective for students who may have otherwise experienced higher levels of alienation. My own findings suggest a similar trend. Hillside students were generally more interested in friendship than popularity in the seventh grade. They were buffered by their ability to maintain close friendships, create a sense of community during the school day, deal with disappointment hopefully, and develop relationships with adults who encouraged them in school.

Although these authors failed to find generally negative trends across the school transition, they argued, "Developmentally, early adolescence is an inopportune time to leave the familiarity of one's school peers for a new group of peers, many of whom are older and who are perceived as having more anti-social values" (p. 519). They concluded that the development mismatch hypothesis, and not the problems associated with early adolescence, is still the most compelling explanation for understanding the effects of transition to middle school. They pointed to the need for further research in different populations and for the inclusion of family, neighborhood, and community factors.

Community-School Fit

All three of these major studies argued that school environments
fall short of meeting the needs of students. My research led me to believe that along with examining developmental stage and school environment interactions, we also need to understand home-school and
community-school interactions if we are to gain clarity on adjustment
during school transitions. I propose that the fit between the community
and the school is as important to consider as the fit between the person
and the environment. This work attempts to bring to light some of the
issues connected to the fit between the community and the school.

Moll, Amanti, Neff, and Gonzalez (1992) reported on a collaborative project involving classroom teachers as participant researchers, uni-
versity-based researchers, and Mexican American families connected to
the schools. The working-class, rural families involved in this study share
some similarities with the Hillside-Two Rivers families in my study. The
authors argued that children come to school holding tremendous
knowledge garnered from their families' historic and cultural resources,
yet this knowledge seldom finds its way into classrooms. Moll et al.,
called this information asset, "funds of knowledge," defined as "historically accumulated and culturally developed bodies of knowledge and
skills (p. 133)." They found that though children were often not able to
employ these skills in their regulated school interactions, they frequently and successfully used these skills outside of school. When teachers came to families with sincere interest and respect, they found parents
and students eager to share their knowledge with others, and when cultural knowledge was integrated into classrooms, students and teachers
found reciprocal benefits: enhanced learning for children and improved
sense of competence for teachers. Educators can use the funds of knowledge concept to incorporate diverse life skills, ways of viewing the world,
and cultural and historical understanding.

The "funds of knowledge" concept developed by these authors is a
useful way for educators to understand the well-developed repertoire of
skills students employ during the school day during both structured and
unstructured time. I noticed, for example, highly adaptive strategies on
the part of students during less structured times of the day that reflected
the styles of interaction that were encouraged by the communities
where the children resided. These strategies are described in chapter 8.

The transition to middle school represents both opportunity and
disruption in the lives of students and their families. As students adjust to
their new environment, they must also re-assess self-perceptions and
roles. For many students nationwide, this transition represents changes

such as new friends, a longer bus ride, an earlier school day, exclusive and competitive inter-scholastic sports, greater peer diversity, more institutional complexity, new choices, and more school adults to deal with each day. Transition researchers have pointed out that students do not show the same declines in schools that are supportive and developmentally appropriate (Eccles & Midgley, 1989; Carnegie Council on Early Adolescent Development, 1989). Mountainview Middle School students experience these changes in a relatively well funded school that has seriously considered and implemented many of the recommendations made by the Carnegie Council on Early Adolescent Development (1989): team teaching, health and civic education, flexible scheduling, parent involvement, and small group advisory periods. (For a more detailed summary of these recommendations, see Appendix 2.)

The following five chapters move from a description of the middle school environment as the context for students' experiences, to listening to how students anticipate this new environment and how teachers and administrators structure the transition, to a variety of classroom settings, to peer interactions during less-structured times of the day, and finally to how individuals, at the end of the school year, evaluate some of their seventh grade experiences.

CHAPTER 4

Mountainview Middle School

Rural, Regional, and Economically Diverse

Mountainview Regional School District (MRSD) was established in 1964 with the opening of a four-year high school located in Lakeview. Sixty-five miles from one end to the other, the school district serves six rural communities, each with a year-round population of between 500 and 5,000 residents. A regional junior high school (grades seven and eight) was established in the mid-sixties to alleviate overcrowding in the elementary schools located in each town. It was located on a second floor wing of the high school. Today, the sixty-acre campus contains the high school, middle school, vocational center, and a 4–6 elementary school.

Every year at the annual school district meeting, organized groups of parents request improvements to areas thought to be inadequate, such as the music and arts program, guidance and counseling services, and the aging high school building. Throughout this school district's thirty-five year history, building projects, and salary increases for teachers and administrators have been contested and sometimes defeated by voters who currently pay some of the highest property tax rates in the United States. A few days after the 1999 school district meeting, the front page of the local newspaper reported that the school budget had been "torpedoed" by citizens who voted down everything proposed except for raises to the grossly underpaid bus drivers. The 2000–2001 school district budget was over $24.5 million, requiring more than 60% of every tax dollar.

Mountainview Regional School District spends more per pupil than the state average. In the five-year period from 1993 to 1998, MRSD spent an average of $6,200 per student, equivalent to other school districts in the immediate area. In the same time period, the state average for per pupil spending was $5,400.[1] Free and reduced lunch numbers in school-year 1999–2000 varied from school to school (18.6% in Lakeview and 49.7% in Hillside), but overall, 29.4% of the students of this school district received free or reduced lunch compared to 72.25% in the nearest

metropolitan area during the same school year.[2] Several local teachers I
spoke with speculated that a fair number of eligible families do not enroll their children in this program because they do not wish to be the
beneficiaries of a government-sponsored program.

The school buildings in this district are considered safe places; no
metal detectors or police officers greet students at the door and when
there is a search for drugs or weapons in student lockers, the news is rare
enough to warrant a front page story in the weekly paper. Teachers often
leave their doors open, suggesting that what goes on in their classrooms
can comfortably be heard by administrators, colleagues, and visitors.
With funding that is a little better than average compared to other districts in the state, this school district offers students good facilities and
educational opportunities and, many people would say, a better than
average education.

More Than Basic, Less Than Elaborate

For nearly twenty years, seventh and eighth graders went to school
in a second floor wing of the high school. In her 1983 report, the principal wrote: "This junior high has proven itself time and again to be a
showpiece of good education for children. It deserves a basic home of
its own. Not fancy, not elaborate, just basic, flexible space." A building
bond was approved and, in 1984, a separate junior high school building
was completed and the wish for basic, flexible space was met. The building committee, comprised of parents, teachers, administrators, and
school board members, spent two years in design, contract, and public
relations efforts. The end result was a good, practical building that, despite some frayed carpeting and ruined ceiling tiles, still looks new to
this day.

From its inception, the middle grades teaching staff, with strong administrative leadership, embraced a middle school philosophy and implemented team teaching, flexible scheduling, heterogeneous grouping,
and interdisciplinary units. In 1991, the school board officially changed
the name from junior high school to middle school.

Mountainview Middle School is a two-story redbrick building behind the high school and connected to it by an indoor walkway. Large
windows in almost every classroom reduce the need for electric lights,
provide teachers an ideal location for hanging plants, and allow students to be connected to the outside world all day long. On one of my
observation days, the first blizzard of the year began to pick up steam
early in the morning and by 10:00 a.m. several inches of snow had

fallen. Excitement filled the air as students appraised the situation outside and anticipated an early release, long before it was announced by the administration.

In the spring, daffodils bloom along the sunny brick wall and the scraggly quince bushes lining the front walkway spawn a few pink blossoms. Posted on the glass doors at the entrance is the message, "Visitors: We love our students and we care for their safety. Please report to the office so we will know who our guests are." Just inside the entrance is a small school store where students sell refreshments during break and at dismissal time. Also on the first floor are the gym, music room, cafeteria-auditorium, and all the unified arts classrooms: art, foreign language, technology, computers, and family and consumer science.

The linoleum floors in the first and second floor hallways are kept shiny by custodians who have been working for the district for many years. The offices, music room, and second floor classrooms are carpeted, substantially reducing the noise level. Most of the core classes take place on the second floor, but one seventh grade team meets in four modular classrooms in back of the middle school, an indication that the middle school has already outgrown its capacity. The library and special education classrooms are also on the second floor. There are moveable partitions between some rooms making it possible to fit a whole team of eighty to one hundred students in one large space.

Pale green lockers line the halls on both floors. They are often shared by two students who stuff them with book bags, jackets, gym clothes, walkmans, CDs, comic books, and sports magazines. Sometimes mirrors, small plastic figures, and pictures of friends and favorite celebrities are taped to the inside of the door. Most walls in the school are off-white cinder block, but the back stairwell has a bright mural painted by students on salmon colored walls. Artwork is displayed along the corridors and some of the ceiling panels have been painted by students.

A few computers are available to students for schoolwork, Internet use, and to check e-mail. The library has ten computers, and is comfortably furnished with soft chairs, small wooden tables, and a couple of couches near the windows. Students are allowed to use the library copy machine to make copies for class projects. Every classroom is equipped with a public address system, a telephone for communicating with the office, a blackboard, trapezoid tables, more than enough chairs, teacher's desk, computer, file cabinets, book shelves, and many have a television and VCR.

Bathrooms are clean, most of the stall doors lock, and there are toilet paper, paper towels, and warm water. In this well-maintained comfortable building, custodians are appreciated and respected by students, administrators, and teachers. In fact, custodians have sometimes played a key role in providing students with support and guidance. In the mid-1980s, graduating high school seniors asked that two popular custodians deliver their commencement speech, a request that was denied by the school board.

The Office and Teachers Room

Just inside the front entrance, enclosed behind big windows, is the large open office with no counters to separate the school staff from students and visitors. In any school, the atmosphere in the office tells a lot about overall climate, power relationships, and respect for students and their parents. At Mountainview Middle School, two secretaries provide administrative support to the principal, assistant principal, guidance counselor, and special education staff. Mrs. Campbell has been employed as the head secretary for over twenty years—longer than just about anyone. She is a young looking fifty-something—petite, fabulous smile, and fiery red hair that some say matches her temperament. Her desk is located in the center of the large middle school office. She is a grandmother to nine children, and their pictures occupy a good portion of her desk. As a Hillside resident, she knows many of the families of Hillside and Two Rivers students.

Both women are busy, interrupted constantly by a steady barrage of requests. Between them, they know every piece of equipment, every source of information, and every system connected to school administration. In this hectic space, there are always students, some sent down from class because of an infraction, some sent by teachers to do errands, some to use the phone or see the nurse, and some to help out. This is a place where students with learning disabilities are welcome helpers and where parents and visitors are treated with consideration.

The principal often sits with one of the secretaries to catch up on both school and personal business. Her style seems to be to lead quietly, behind the scenes, with a soft voice, few words, and deep respect for the work going on in the classroom. She was once a teacher and she knows well that teachers must be committed to the school and to the communities they serve and, at the same time, have flexibility and autonomy to teach their students the way they feel they must.

Behind Mrs. Campbell's desk are teacher mailboxes that serve as a divider between the main office and the teacher's room set off in one corner. In this school, many teachers eat lunch with colleagues in their own classrooms, so there are seldom more than five or six people in the teacher's room at one time and they all sit together around a cluster of tables in the center of the room. The conversation is pleasant and relaxed; good-natured teasing of each other is common. Unlike many teachers' rooms where daily irritations are vented with unrestrained cynicism, this teacher's room has a positive and friendly atmosphere. The teachers of this school seem to like each other, or, at the very least, are generously tolerant of each other's idiosyncrasies.

Middle School Hallmarks: Teaming, Advisory, and Flexible Scheduling

In the 1999–2000 school year, 453 students attended Mountainview Middle School: 174 from Lakeview, 120 from Hillside, 64 from Deer Run, 49 from Farm Crossing, 38 from Two Rivers, and 8 from Meadow. This sizeable student population makes Mountainview Middle School larger than 75% of rural schools nationwide (Stern, 1994). Lakeview and Meadow students attended the same elementary school in grades K–6 and Hillside and Two Rivers students went to elementary school together in grades 4–6. There are about 50 staff members—administrators, teachers, teaching assistants, custodians, cafeteria workers, secretaries, and the school nurse.

Students are distributed between two seventh grade teams, two eighth grade teams, and one seven-eight team. English, math, social studies, science teachers, and special education assistants comprise each instructional team and they meet daily to coordinate special activities, see parents, and discuss the academic, behavioral, and emotional issues of their students. Team placements of students are made with an effort to maintain heterogeneity by town, ability, and gender.

The school day begins at 7:25 and ends at 2:25. Students take four core subjects and two unified arts courses a day, taught in fifty-minute periods, leaving one period for study hall, extra help, or enrichment activities. Teaching teams develop their own pedagogical styles and team culture; each of the middle school teams has a distinct character. Teachers can rearrange the schedule as the need arises, develop interdisciplinary units, and combine classes for movies and discussions. Students at the beginning of seventh grade often commented that the frequent schedule changes made it confusing and anxiety provoking, but they eventually learned to deal with it. Some things remain the same: the morning Pledge of Allegiance, announcements and a daily reading, the fifteen-minute all-school break, and a twenty-minute lunch. Almost every adult and child in the building spends part of almost every day doing silent reading. There are no bells; teachers tell students or students signal teachers when it is time to change classes.

There is a brief first period session known as advisory: a home base to encourage relationship building and guidance in a small group. Teachers, administrators, and teaching assistants all have responsibility for ten to fifteen students who meet in an advisory all year long. Once a week there is an extended advisory period thirty-minutes long, allowing time for team-building and personal development exercises that get mixed reviews from students.

The use of advisories and team-teaching encourages a shared sense of responsibility toward students. Some students name non-instructional staff members (custodians, secretaries, and coaches) as part of their support network at school. The adults in the building, regardless of position, are addressed using Mr., Mrs., or Ms. and last names, and teachers refer to each other this way when students are present.

Participation in extracurricular activities is encouraged and comparisons of participation by town will be explored in chapter 10. There are twenty after-school activities offered during the school year, including a very popular intramural sports program. Athletic teams include inter-scholastic football, soccer, field hockey, basketball, skiing, baseball, softball, cross-country, and track. Sports and drama meet daily and other activities, including art club, family and consumer science, photography, jazz band, math team, mock trial, student council, and yearbook, meet weekly or biweekly.

A Middle School Attitude with Junior High Academic Goals

A one-page informational handout explains how Mountainview Middle School tries to blend the best of the junior high school model and the middle school model. Junior high schools tend to emphasize subject-centered education, cognitive development, and mastery in separate disciplines through lecture and text-book methods of instruction, and middle schools are more inclined to emphasize student-centered education and social and emotional development through inter-disciplinary, project-oriented, experiential methods of instruction.[3] The effort to combine subject-centered aspects of the junior high school model and student-centered aspects of the middle school model was evident in the wide range of styles I observed. During my visits I noticed efforts to balance individual and aggregate needs, the student's need for belonging and connection and their need for autonomy and independence, and cognitive and social development.

Over the years, the middle school has come under fire for not being academically rigorous enough. Heterogeneous grouping is met with more and more criticism from some parents who want options for a more accelerated program. Even though the stated policy of the school is to provide instruction in heterogeneously grouped classrooms, teaching teams have flexibility in arranging and scheduling their group of about one hundred students, and they group by ability to some degree. This is especially true in math. Because there is an eighth grade algebra class, some seventh grade students are selected to take an algebra-prep math course. Several teachers and administrators told me that the drive toward higher level courses and ability grouping is coming from a small group of vocal parents, primarily from Lakeview, who are concerned that their children may not be intellectually challenged and may be held back by less capable or unmotivated classmates.

Student rights and responsibilities are outlined in a spiral bound handbook that also serves as a weekly planner for students who have learned the value of writing down assignments, deadlines, and reminders. It includes policies on promotion, grading, special education, accessibility for handicapped students, educational equity, technology, school dances, conduct, discipline procedures, and dress code. The dress code forbids, "apparel which depicts: vulgarity, rudeness, violence, unsafe or illegal acts, sexual, drug or alcohol-related messages; immodest clothing showing: spaghetti straps, undergarments, or midriffs; hats, sunglasses, hooded sweatshirts, and outdoor coats."[4] A new policy, enacted in the 2000–2001 school year, added big-legged elephant pants, chains, short skirts, and platform shoes to this policy. The dress code is very controversial, especially when it inhibits certain styles that signify group identity or culture, like hats, hooded sweatshirts, and big-legged pants. Noticeably absent in the student handbook are school policies concerning sexual and other forms of harassment, and statements about diversity.

All classrooms display a poster of the school's Standards for Success:

Be on Time for School and All Classes

Be Prepared with Materials for Each Class

Dress Appropriately for Success

Be an Active and Positive Participant in Your Education

Demonstrate Respect, Responsibility and Honesty to Yourself, Peers, and Adults

Demonstrate Respect for Your Property, School Property, and the Property of Others

Use Appropriate Language

Settle Conflicts Appropriately

Display Affection Appropriate for a Public School Setting

Demonstrate Good Behavior

Accept People for Who They Are

Challenge Yourself Daily

Parents and students can call an information line at any time to get a recorded message on school events, cancellations, and homework assignments. Make Up Study Time (MUST) is assigned to students who are behind in their schoolwork, giving them two hours after school with a teacher. All teachers have extra duties that include supervising MUST, monitoring the halls before and after school, and lunchroom duty. This is a school where a fair number of teachers come early and stay late; a practice that is widely accepted despite the occasional challenge by teachers who are active in the union. Middle schoolers are consistent about coming to school; daily attendance averages 94% (the high school daily attendance average is just over 90%).[5]

Experienced Instructional Staff

Thirteen out of the thirty-five (37%) instructional staff have been at Mountainview Middle School for more than fifteen years. In the 1999–2000 school year, there were twenty-three women (66%) and twelve men (34%) in classrooms, fifteen of them (43%) had graduate degrees. Six of the thirty-five were special education and reading teachers. Most middle school teachers live in Lakeview or in towns outside the district. In the 1999–2000 school year, fifteen teachers lived in Lakeview, fourteen lived out of district, and three were from Farm Crossing. Deer Run, Meadow, and Hillside each had only one middle school teacher residing there.[6]

In the 2000–2001 school year, salaries ranged from $24,987 for an entry-level teacher with a bachelor's degree, to $46,226 for a teacher with sixteen years of experience and thirty credits beyond a master's degree. Many teachers supplement this income with coaching and summer employment.

Classroom decor reflects the subject matter and personal styles of the teacher and there were colorful and interesting displays in almost every seventh grade classroom I visited. Posters of dolphins, wolves, and whales decorate the walls of many classrooms. Compared to the urban schools I visit, signs and symbols of diversity and social-political issues are noticeably scarce. Many teachers have family pictures and other personal items on and around their desks. It is evident that the teachers of this school put some effort, time, and personal resources into making their classrooms interesting, lively, friendly, and instructive.

Mountainview Middle School is a comfortable, safe, and well-maintained facility with more than adequate resources. An experienced teaching staff attempts to bridge distinct educational philosophies and to provide their students with a better than basic education. Seventh grade students operate in several arenas over the course of one day and are exposed to a much wider range of experiences and opportunities than sixth graders. From the moment they get on the bus before 7:00 a.m., and throughout the day during advisory, break, lunch, core classes, unified arts, and after school activities, until they get home in the evening, students must interact with a large and diverse group of people, navigate in a wide variety of settings, and utilize multiple skills.

CHAPTER 5

Sixth Grade Hopes,
Seventh Grade Discoveries

The students in my study perceived the transition to Mountainview Middle School as a challenge and as an opportunity. The task before them seemed both scary and exciting, offering new experiences, friends, and teachers. Their answers to my questions when they were in the sixth grade indicated that they felt the stakes were high, particularly the social stakes; fitting in, being liked, and feeling valued mattered to them more than anything.

Transition to a different school is an emotionally charged task. Several students from both communities expressed that they expected to feel nervous and scared in the first few days of school. Students expressed feeling anxious about having several teachers instead of one, learning to use their lockers, finding their classrooms in a new building, staying organized and on time, and being able to remember their homework assignments. They hoped the nervous, scared feeling would be a temporary phase in their adjustment to their new environment.

Being able to successfully accomplish a task that is perceived to have a high level of challenge and the possibility of failure promotes a sense of competence and confidence (Bandura, 1977). Likewise, to fail at the primary tasks of early adolescence may set the stage for increased alienation from school and peers (Finn, 1989). In this case, being able to master the middle school environment and the social, cognitive, and practical challenges it poses comes at a time when adolescents are also moving toward greater autonomy. The combination of perceived risk while simultaneously being more independent makes this a particularly loaded period of development, laden with potential for both disappointment and accomplishment. Much is learned about self-efficacy as students come to this new environment and succeed or fail. There is perhaps no other period of development where so much is learned, accurate or not, about the self and others.

As the research participants approached the end of their sixth grade year, I wanted to know how they were thinking and feeling about going to the middle school. I asked each of the thirty-two students in the study to complete sentences on a questionnaire about their hopes, worries, feelings, and interests. (A sample of the questionnaire is in Appendix 4. Thirty-two students were involved in the study in grade six but over the summer two students moved out of the district leaving a research group of thirty in grade seven.) From their answers, it became evident that as sixth graders imagined themselves at their new school, they were most excited by the prospect of making new friends and most worried that they would fail at that essential task. All thirty-two sixth grade students seemed able to visualize themselves in their new school, naming situations that they expected to encounter, like new teachers, more homework, and a new building where they would need to find their way. Their ability to anticipate concrete aspects of their new environment indicates that these students were preparing themselves psychologically for this transition and for the challenges and opportunities their new environment would offer them. In almost every case, going to a new school with many dozens of new classmates was named as something to be excited about *and* something to be worried about. As they moved toward seventh grade, social acceptance was their primary concern and meeting new academic challenges was a close secondary concern.

I studied the written sentence completions for common themes and categorized the answers in the following domains: social, cognitive, physical, affective, and development toward independence. Social comments included references to making new friends, keeping old friends, being liked by others, and being a good friend to others. Comments in the cognitive domain, included statements about getting good grades, trying hard, doing well in particular subject areas, getting work done on time, and having more class work and homework. Physical responses included comments about sports and physical ability. Affective responses revealed how students felt about going to the middle school and the way they wanted others to feel about them. Statements about having more responsibility and more privileges, being treated as an adult, and feeling older were categorized in the "development toward independence" domain.

Students from both communities made social and cognitive comments three times more often than physical, affective, or developmental comments combined. Lakeview children had about a third more cognitive responses than Hillside-Two Rivers children (28 responses from Lakeview students, 18 responses from Hillside-Two Rivers students). In the affective, physical, and developmental domains, responses from Lakeview and Hillside-Two Rivers were about equally divided.

Doing Well Means Making New Friends and Keeping Old Ones

Getting along with others and doing well in school seemed to be the most compelling concern for students from both communities. As these thirty-two sixth graders looked toward seventh grade, they anticipated opportunities to "make new friends," "become a better friend," "meet people from other schools," and "have more friends." But almost all students harbored some fears that they would not be successful at this self-identified imperative. When asked to complete the sentence, "Next year, I will be in a school with students from six different towns and I am worried about . . . ," almost all students finished the sentence expressing concerns like these:

> new people making fun of me, stealing my friends, and doing better than me at everything (Lakeview boy);

> people from other towns not knowing how smart and athletic I am (Lakeview boy);

> not being as popular as anyone else (Hillside boy);

> not getting to know people from other schools (Hillside boy);

> not making a good impression when I meet them (Hillside boy);

> making new friends and coping with so many new people at once (Lakeview girl);

> what they will think of me (Lakeview girl);

> losing some of my friends to other kids; and losing my friends I have now (Two Rivers girl and Lakeview girl);

> not having as much friends as I have here (Hillside girl).

Several of these comments indicate that students from both communities fear that something will be lost in the transition, such as friends, high positive regard for being smart or athletic, and social or academic standing. The most common response was, "them not liking me," written by three Lakeview students and four Hillside students, one of whom actually wrote "everyone hating me." Two students went a step further in anticipating possible disconnections with their peers, and wrote that they were worried about "kids being mean to me" and "them making fun of me."

However, when asked to complete the sentence, "Next year, I will be in a school with students from six different towns and I am excited about . . . ," *all* students wrote about meeting new people and making new friends. Although many students feared something of value could be lost in the transition, these resilient students were also able to anticipate hopeful gains in the transition—new friends and more friends.

The students in this study had been successful socially at their elementary schools. When they imagined themselves in classrooms and in the lunchroom with new people, they were able to draw their expectations and hopes from a history of success. They wanted to make a good impression on their new classmates and teachers; they knew they had been able to do that in the past but they wondered if their success would continue when so many more students would be available for comparison.

If these students who are at low risk of social failure experience a good deal of anxiousness about how they will be perceived and received by their peers and teachers in grade seven, imagine how much greater the anxiety must be for students whose foundation of self-knowledge is based on a history of social isolation and failure. There is evidence that the experience of social acceptance and rejection remain stable over time—accepted children continue to be accepted and rejected children continue to be rejected (e.g., Coie and Dodge, 1983). Social experiences and self-concept are mutually reinforced and cumulative.

However, it is not only what happens among peers that reinforce the same patterns of social interaction and isolation. By the middle grades, dozens of subtle structural reinforcements also work to reproduce positive and negative social experiences. It is important for educators to know how structural conditions like ability grouping, access to transportation, competitive and selective sports teams, and self-contained special education classrooms, interact with peer relationships, parental influences, and individual temperament to produce social and academic success and failure.

Students Anticipate Harder Work and Being Smarter

Responses about schoolwork were almost as common as responses about friends. Lakeview students made twenty-eight references and Hillside-Two Rivers students made eighteen references to expectations related to learning. Students said they expected to be "a good student or learner," "more responsible for my work," "on the honor roll," "a hard worker," "able to understand the work," and "smart." They expected to have "better grades," "a lot of homework," "good teachers," "cool teachers," "a good education," and "a fun learning experience."

Although students from both communities had comparable grades in the sixth grade and had been successful academically, Hillside-Two Rivers students seemed less certain about their academic performance at the middle school. Lakeview students not only had more learning-related responses, but they qualified their anticipated academic achievement with words like "good," "smart," and "better" twice as often as Hillside students.

Students coming to the middle school from Hillside Elementary School, navigate this experience with their imaginations and expectations at least somewhat influenced by factors that Lakeview students do not need to think about: the middle school is in a different community, they will need to take a long bus ride to get there, they are unfamiliar with the middle school building, and their peers from Lakeview have very little first hand knowledge about their town. Students and parents are also aware of the wide gap in average standardized test scores between Lakeview and Hillside, a topic discussed in chapter 11.

Understanding this, one sixth grade Hillside teacher I interviewed told me that she tells her sixth graders all year long that they are good students capable of doing very well at the middle school. She gives them examples of other Hillside students who have thrived there, and she encourages them to "go to the middle school and show them what you've got."

They thought they would be smarter and they were. Advances in cognitive skills were noticeable when I met with students in the fall of seventh grade. In the short six months since our sixth grade interviews, these students seemed to have developed higher-level analytic skills and an increased ability to articulate their perceptions clearly. In general, students from both towns seemed more confident and they were able to engage in conversations about abstract concepts. They were ready for more intellectually challenging work.

Choice, Privilege, Freedom, and Feeling Older

When students anticipated seventh grade in the spring of their sixth grade year, they also imagined that they would have an "older feeling" accompanied by "more responsibility" and "more freedom." These sentiments are consistent with the developmental needs Eccles and her colleagues (1993a, b) found in their research groups. Nine students from Lakeview and seven students from Hillside made comments that demonstrated development toward independence and more responsibility. Completing the sentence, "In seventh grade, I expect to be (or have) . . . ," students wrote, for example, a lot older feeling than I do now (Lakeview girl);

treated more like an adult (Lakeview boy);

responsible (Hillside girl);

more choices than I do now (Lakeview girl);

more privileges (Lakeview boy and Two Rivers girl).

These comments, together with the many sentiments expressed by students that seventh grade would be a time to make new friends, portray development at this critical transition as a time for widening social circles, experiencing more diversity among peers, negotiating possible shifts in close friendships, and anticipating a giant step toward autonomy with its associated responsibilities and privileges.

Research participants from both communities were equally active in sports and other extracurricular activities in the sixth grade. Seven of them, four from Hillside-Two Rivers and three from Lakeview mentioned their desire to play on sports teams in the middle school. For example, research participants anticipated opportunities to be "very good at sports," "on the soccer team," "a basketball player," and "good at athletics." Extracurricular participation will be explored in chapter 10.

Own-Town and Cross-Town Perceptions

In this regional school district, and in many others like it, social acceptance is influenced to some degree by the preconceived notions children bring with them about their classmates from other towns. How do Lakeview and Hillside students think about their own town and each other's town before and after the transition? In the spring of their sixth grade year (time 1) and again in the fall of their seventh grade year (time 2), I asked students to write what came to mind on encountering the words Lakeview and Hillside. At time 1, Lakeview students wrote these phrases next to the name of their town:

I really like Lakeview;

people are mostly nice people;

is a wonderful place and I'm glad I don't have to go to a different town in seventh grade;

fun and small;

beautiful town;

a lot of friendly kids, good schools;

home, family, school, fun;

good kids, don't do really bad things, nice town.

At time 2, Lakeview students wrote:

is rich;

a good town with mostly nice people in it;

is a cool town, I like it;

good friends, fun, good schools;

kind of a cozy friendly town—like *Cheers*—everyone knows your name.

Lakeview students' perceptions of Hillside reflect the fact that many of them are unfamiliar with that town. At time 1 and time 2, several students wrote, "don't know much about it," but importantly, five Lakeview students indicated they had "new friends" from Hillside in the fall of seventh grade.

Negative perceptions of Hillside were also evident. The Lakeview student who wrote, "people are mostly nice people" (grade 6) and "is rich" (grade 7) following the word Lakeview, wrote, "people might act differently or act stupidly" (grade 6) and "is poor" (grade 7) following the word Hillside. One sixth grade Lakeview girl wrote, "I've heard very bad things that I am not going to write," and when I pursued this with her, she put down on the paper, "incest, greaseballs, mentally challenged." Handing it back to me she said, "I want you to know I don't believe these things, but that's what I hear."

These stereotypes come as no surprise to Hillside and Two Rivers adults, but their children seemed to adamantly guard themselves against the realization that these perceptions exist. It was the *Lakeview* students, not the Hillside-Two Rivers students, who were more likely to bring these ways of thinking to my attention. Many teachers who have been in the school district for a long time feel that while these perceptions persist, they are more common in the older generation than in the younger generation. In my own experience, I frequently hear over-generalizations and distortions of Hillside's poverty, lack of education, pregnancy rates, drug use, crime, and sexual behavior. There have been efforts on the part of some teachers to address and change negative perceptions but there is also a strong sentiment, expressed by some teachers and administrators, that these issues are better left unspoken, to "not open a can of worms." I believe that an honest appraisal of these issues, not silence, is the key to increased understanding across towns.

While Hillside and Two Rivers parents sometimes privately and tentatively expressed their concern to me that their children might be judged in a biased way or not treated fairly, every single Hillside-Two Rivers parent gave lots of positive encouragement to their children. For example, while I was visiting a Two Rivers student and her mother at their home, the student told me she did not want to go to the middle school. Her sister had a hard time at the middle school and told her that kids from other towns were not as accepting of Hillside-Two Rivers students. Her mother encouraged her by saying, "Everyone is different, and you will go there and probably have a completely different experience than your sister." Her mother was right; this student *did* have a different and more positive experience than her sister.

Although Lakeview students sometimes mentioned stereotyped ways of thinking about Hillside-Two Rivers students, the Hillside-Two Rivers students seldom indicated that they believed they would be treated differently. Their demeanor was self-protective and hopeful. They were determined to go to their new school unencumbered by what they have heard from others, even when it came from trusted family members. Most of these students approached the middle school with confidence that they would be successful, and their teachers and parents supported this perception.

Hillside-Two Rivers students view Hillside positively, but less positively than Lakeview students view their town. Two students from Two Rivers viewed their town more negatively at time 2 than at time 1. I wondered if exposure to another town encouraged comparisons that resulted in these students judging their own community less favorably. Hillside-Two Rivers students wrote about Hillside in this way at time 1:

> a really beautiful town with an extremely good community;
>
> small and calm;
>
> a small but nice town;
>
> hometown, relaxed;
>
> a cool town;
>
> a lot of great people and businesses.

At time 2, Hillside-Two Rivers students wrote:

I have a ton of friends there;

safe, home, trusting;

an awesome school;

is the best place to grow up and live.

Several Hillside-Two Rivers students described negative aspects of their communities. "[a] town with nothing too good," "the sticks," and "someplace I moved to two years ago, but I don't like it," were noted at time 1. At time 2, three students characterized their town as "a very boring place." The lack of things to do in this rural community becomes an issue in early adolescence when socializing with friends becomes more important.

Many Hillside-Two Rivers students had been to Lakeview and their favorable responses at both data collection points focused on their viewpoint that there are "more things to do" there. For some Hillside-Two Rivers students, Lakeview is a:

cooler place to live;

big tourist town with lots to do;

[place where] people accept me differently and are more kind;

big town with lots of stores;

[place with] more things to do.

One Hillside student wrote, "[Lakeview] is a little harder, more gangs" in the sixth grade, and "is a tough town" in the seventh grade. One Two Rivers student changed her mind about Lakeview. In grade six she wrote, Lakeview "is weird" and in grade seven she wrote that it "has a lot of nice people." I expected to find the counter-stereotype for Lakeview reflected in the responses of Hillside-Two Rivers students—that Lakeview students are snobby. But comments like these were not made by Hillside-Two Rivers students on the questionnaires.

Another perception was revealed in students' responses: students from both towns commented that there were not many kids from Hillside in the middle school. There were, in fact, more students from Lakeview than Hillside-Two Rivers: ninety-one students from Lakeview and seventy-six students from Hillside-Two Rivers. When I told students the actual numbers were not that far apart, they were surprised. The actual numbers were not in line with their perception that Lakeview students outnumbered Hillside students. This distortion may be an indication of the way the school "feels" to students, and it "feels" as though there are a lot more students from Lakeview than from Hillside and Two Rivers. This perception reveals a subtle, subconscious awareness of whose presence is felt more powerfully in the middle school—who is noticed, who has influence, whose voices are heard.

Finding Common Ground

A couple of months after students came together at the middle school, I asked them to complete the sentence, "Now I go to school with students from six different towns and I have discovered . . ." Many of them were happy to find nice people, new friends, a "wider range," and classmates with whom they shared common ground:

> there are a lot of really neat people out there, a lot just like me;
>
> that I have friends there and that we are all pretty much the same;
>
> how many good friends you can make and what a wide range you can have.
>
> they are a lot like me;
>
> that I can make new friends from six other towns;
>
> they are all very nice no matter where they come from.

Some students noticed differences:

> there are many cool people from different towns with different characteristics (Lakeview boy);
>
> how different I am (Lakeview boy);
>
> that we all act different ways than people in our town (Hillside girl);
>
> people have many different learning abilities (Hillside girl).

One Lakeview girl was able to see both differences and similarities at the same time. She wrote, ". . . most of them are very different in many ways but are also the same in many ways as the other kids I have lived with." What becomes clear in these comments is that students are well aware of the diversity in their school. They actively sort out what diversity means in their daily interactions, they are increasingly conscious of their own self-identity based on comparisons with others, and they have language to explain what they observe. Seeing diversity as positive and being able to find common ground with others are important steps in social development.

Sometimes social comparisons lead to weaker self-concept. A Lakeview boy wrote, "there's more people and I am not as popular." Three of the fourteen students from Hillside and Two Rivers evaluated students from other communities more positively than students from their own town. They wrote:

> my Lakeview friends are more fun, free spirited, and nicer;
>
> people from other towns are sometimes smarter than people from our town;
>
> there are nicer people in other towns.

These sentiments, expressed in the fall of their seventh grade year, are important reminders of the struggle some students face when they try to maintain a positive self-concept in light of social comparisons that are at least partially based on stereotypes. By and large, the early impressions of most students from both towns reveal a positive regard for their classmates and a sense of relief that other kids are "a lot like me." As Eccles and her colleagues suggested, early adolescents are interested in greater autonomy and opportunities to be challenged intellectually. However, it appears that for these research participants, expanding and deepening peer connections are equally important to them, indicating that the stage-environment fit researchers may have over-emphasized autonomy and failed to articulate the potential benefits to adolescents when they transition to a more diverse school environment.

The passage to middle school is an opportunity for exposure to diversity at a time when students are developmentally ready for more reciprocity in their peer relationships and a wider social range. Social perspective-taking abilities can be enhanced through interactions with classmates from different backgrounds. However, as the responses above indicate, social comparisons can also serve to confirm preconceived biases and lead students to more negative appraisals of their classmates, themselves, or the communities they come from.

Teachers, families, and communities seem to speak in one voice to students about cooperative social behavior and actively guide social learning in the early grades. But, as students progress through the grades, social interactions are less frequently guided and there is less consensus about social behavior as academic and athletic achievement become more important goals and competitive attitudes become more acceptable, even encouraged.

The student answers in this section confirm that this transition is a critical moment requiring thoughtful support and active guidance from educators, parents, and community members. The students in my study had that kind of support. Sixth grade teachers and parents can assist students who are less able to imagine themselves as successful seventh graders by helping them to articulate their hopes, expectations, and concerns. In the following chapter, I will describe how Mountainview Middle School structures the transition process, and how this process responds to the social, academic, affective, and developmental concerns described in this section.

CHAPTER 6

A Transition for Parents and Teachers

Structuring Successful Transition

At the end of the 1999–2000 school year, I visited the middle school to see some of the research participants who were now nearly at the end of their seventh grade year. As I walked into the middle school, I saw several research participants, now experienced seventh graders, conducting orientation sessions with small groups of curious sixth graders. My students and I beamed at each other; the transition process had come full circle.

For soon-to-be seventh graders, an important part of the transition process is the unofficial and often invisible orientation they seek and receive from older siblings, relatives, and friends. Most of the students in this study identified other students as important sources of information as they prepared themselves for the transition. These slightly older peers and family members answered questions not answered by other sources: Are the teachers nice? What are the dances like? What if you forget your homework (or text book, or gym clothes, or agenda books)? How easy is it to get lost in that building? Will the kids from the other towns like me? Do the kids date? Do drugs? Fight? Not only did I consistently find students using other students to fill in the gaps in the information they were given, I found that the information students received from each other was usually reliable and encouraging.

The transition process for sixth graders begins early in the sixth grade year, and continues well into the first semester of the seventh grade year. In this school district, it is a process that directly involves sixth and seventh grade teachers and guidance counselors, elementary and middle school administrators, sixth grade students and their parents or guardians, and seventh grade students. The middle school guidance counselor, Ms. Young, coordinates the well-defined transition process. This chapter will describe this framework and will demonstrate that students are not the

135

only ones with hopes and worries during this process; parents also antici-pate this transition with a degree of consternation.

When asked if they felt prepared for seventh grade, most students from both communities said they did. They said that as sixth grade stu-dents, their teachers frequently interspersed lessons with advice and hints. "Next year at the middle school . . ." the forewarning would begin, and then end with information about homework, being prepared and organized for classes, higher expectations for personal responsibility, opportunities to make new friends, and so on.

Sixth grade teachers complete student and class profile sheets, de-signed by Ms. Young, and send them to the middle school by the end of March to assist with team composition and curriculum development. The class profile summarizes instructional highlights, field trips, assigned novels, topics covered in each of the four core subjects, and special pro-grams. Individual student profiles, completed for all two hundred and fifty plus sixth graders, provide information about academic ability, per-formance, motivation and preparedness in each subject area, along with information about the student's interests, talents, behavior, and obstacles to learning. These profiles provide useful social information for team composition that is made in the interests of diversity and student success.

At the beginning of March, a packet is sent to each sixth grader's home. It includes information about the team concept, band, and the world language program. Parents are encouraged to think flexibly about their child's team placement and the transition to seventh grade is framed as an opportunity for students to "move beyond their narrow el-ementary school experiences to have the opportunity of finding other students of similar abilities, interests and goals."[1]

A Parent Survey Sheet requests that parents give their preferences for team placement, language, and band, and it gives parents an oppor-tunity to share concerns and information about their child. Combined with information sent on each student by teachers, this information can provide a comprehensive and valuable profile for each student. The de-gree to which parents influence placement decisions is unclear, but an-ecdotal information suggests that while most parents respect the process recommended by the school, a handful of influential parents *do* have the last say in their child's team placement. And while some parents have too much influence, others who cannot or do not read the information and respond to the survey may not be able to learn about the middle school program or provide valuable information about their child.

A small booklet is given to all sixth grade students and another is sent to parents in April. The student booklet describes what will be dif-ferent in seventh grade: "You will have up to seven teachers a day; you will have a locker; there are no bells; the day begins and ends earlier." Students are introduced to extracurricular activities, the team concept, and unified arts choices and they are given cues about "what's hot" (new friends, dances, field trips, more freedom and choices, and being able to make a new start) and "what's not" (no recess, waking up earlier, more homework, new rules, missing younger friends). The brochure for parents offers similar information about activities and course selections, and also frames the middle school experience as a time when there will be "new academic demands . . . and greater demands for support at home." Parents are called upon to encourage consistent school attendance, to know about school policies regarding dress and homework, and to structure time in order to support their child's academic work.

Several seventh grade students go back to their elementary schools to speak to sixth graders about the middle school, and in June, sixth grade classes from each elementary school visit the middle school. Finally, seventh graders arrive at the middle school and within the first few weeks of school, they go on an overnight camping trip with all members of their team. The goal of this trip is to build a sense of community among the students as they come together from six towns for the first time.

Parents and Adolescents on the Threshold

One evening in early April 1999, I attended the Parent Information Night at the middle school to listen to presentations to parents of sixth graders by school staff members. About one hundred mothers and fathers, and perhaps thirty children, spaced themselves out in the middle school cafetorium. In all, about seventy-five of the approximately two hundred and fifty families of sixth graders were there.

The middle school teachers leaned against the back wall, some looking weary after a full day of school, most looking around the room with interest, sizing up what the next school year will bring. The principal, a fit woman of forty-something, welcomed everyone in a soft, calm voice, and explained the structure and purpose of the evening. From their questions it became clear that parents are mindful of the weighty symbolic meaning of the coming year: a giant step toward mid-adolescence with all its real life challenges, folklore, and myth. Middle school staff must alleviate fears early in the school year, encourage enthusiasm about new opportunities, and balance their teaching to respond to a variety of interests and concerns.

The audience of parents and students sat on benches that were set up in three sections of fifteen rows. Two families caught my eye, both involved in this study. As I took in the way these two families were present at this event, I was struck by the breathtaking meaning of this transition for parents and their children, regardless of social class background, and for the teachers who lined the back of the room.

One family—mother, father, sixth grade girl, and younger brother— sat in a tight group. The whole family was out for the evening to learn more about the elder child's new school. The mother, a large woman with an easy smile, and thick, wiry brown hair, looked comfortable wearing shorts and a T-shirt. Everything about her demeanor was open and generous, pleasant and relaxed. Her son, a cute, stocky, fifth grader, also wearing shorts and a T-shirt, leaned against her with both feet on the bench and his knees drawn toward his chest. During the talk, he was looking at a comic book and appeared at home and happy. His mother had her arm around him and gently rested her hand on his round belly as he slouched comfortably into her.

When I visited this family a few weeks prior to the Parent Information Night, this boy was skidding his way around the yard on a loud four-wheeler, in snow and mud, even then wearing a T-shirt and shorts, though the temperature was in the low 50s. Later that spring, chickens ran around the yard and flowers bloomed along the walkway. This family works together to care for the animals, plant flowers, and renovate their mobile home.

The sixth grade girl who had recently agreed to be a research participant in this study, sat up straight on the other side of her mother, close enough so that legs and arms were touching, but with much more decorum than her younger brother. A foot or two on her other side sat her father; they both listened intently to the speaker.

On the other side of the room, in the same lateral row of benches, sat another family. When I visited this family in their hilltop Lakeview home overlooking dozens of acres of open horse fields, beautifully landscaped yard, and a view of the lakes and mountains, I was served tea in the parlor, a room filled with antiques and artifacts from around the world. Now at the open house event, in a room of people from a broad range of economic and educational backgrounds, these parents listened carefully. Their sixth grade daughter and only child sat in a distant front row with a group of friends. She was clearly enjoying being with her peers. Everything about her demeanor conjured a sense that this twelve-year-old was running enthusiastically with outstretched arms toward her new environment: lockers, new teachers, lots of new friends from other towns, and most importantly, more independence from her parents. While the sixth grader from Hillside sat near her parents uncertain and perhaps a little fearful about what her new environment might bring, the sixth grader from Lakeview was, in many ways, already full stride into the transition.

I know from my conversation with these two Lakeview parents that they were deeply concerned that the middle school might overemphasize social development and fail to provide the academic rigor and discipline they wanted their daughter to have. They worried that the middle school philosophy might place their daughter's future academic options at risk. They also wondered how she would fit in: "We are an unusual family here . . . we both have excellent private school educations. She is afraid she is going to stick out like a sore thumb, and she wants desperately to fit in." Indeed, their fears were understandable. Their daughter was already grasping for all that her new school represented: friends from families with very different values, more opportunities to be social, and less adult supervision.

Like the parents of Seeley's *Crestwood Heights* (1956), these Lakeview parents have goals for their daughter that include a good education, a nice career, and, importantly, friends who will support and encourage the lifestyle and values that are important to them. This family wants the school to join them in promoting a sense of responsibility, self-discipline, healthy competition, and future orientation. They do not believe in heterogeneous grouping because they believe it stifles creativity and ambition and holds back students who could be progressing more quickly. They expect the school to restrain their daughter's blooming social desires and her drive to experience things that contradict their values. School, they believe, is where you go to learn and to be prepared for a career and not a place for "touchy-feely" classroom experiences that emphasize social interactions.

The Hillside family, on the other hand, represents a different orientation to this experience. Like the families in *Urban Villagers* (Gans, 1962), they seem to hold on tight to the love and the closeness they share. This mother knows that there is no way any teacher is going to nurture and love her kids the way she does. The values these parents want the school to encourage are values that do not interfere with close family bonds. Like other Hillside families, they feel they have *much* to lose in terms of family and community identity when their children go off to a school in a different community—a community that is unfamiliar with Hillside. The parents of Hillside wonder if their children will be *seen*, encouraged, and instructed in a way that acknowledges the talent, history, lifestyles and values their children bring with them.

This example also illustrates how people from diverse backgrounds may shape their environment, seeking to make it more familiar. Over and over I witnessed students and their families not only adjusting to new environments but also changing them in ways that would accommodate their needs. On the school bus, in their classroom interactions, in the lunchroom, and during break, students sought to bring their resources from home with them. Amber's mom brought home to the middle school cafetorium. Undaunted by this new environment, her demeanor laid claim for her family a sense of safety, confidence, and connection.

"We Are a Melting Pot Right Here"

This general session was followed by small group sessions, conducted in seventh grade classrooms by seventh grade teachers. I followed a group out to one of the modular classrooms where Mr. Jordan, an English teacher and twenty-year employee of the school district, facilitated a discussion. He started, "How many of you have a sense of humor?" Most of the fifteen people in the room put up a reluctant hand. "You're going to need it. Life's going to change in the next year." He spoke briefly about the developmental aspects of the middle school years. During my home visits, a few parents expressed the feeling that the middle school structure exacerbates developmental problems and encourages a premature preoccupation with socializing. Some parents seem to appreciate the idea that the teachers and they are "in this together," but others resent the implicit message that all adolescents go through pretty much the same thing, and that teachers know more about their child, and the year to come, than the parents themselves. Half of the parents in the room had questions, most of them focusing on safety issues and how they can continue to be involved in their child's education.

Mr. Jordan's presentation was relaxed and reflected his years of teaching experience and his appreciation for middle school children. He addressed many of the concerns I heard during my home visits: an earlier start and end to the day, a long bus ride, and a much larger and more economically diverse student body. "By the end of the second week, they are all done wishing they were back in their elementary schools," he said, and six months later I found this statement to be accurate for all but one of the thirty research participants.

He suggested that this transition, and the developmental step it represents for children, is also a powerful developmental moment in the lives of parents. As a parent who had already experienced watching his own children grow into their teen years, he said, "This is going to be harder for some of you than it will be for your kids." Parents worry that they will "lose" their children to peer pressure and to the influences of other adults. They fear their children will not perceive risk and danger in the way they want them to. In the room, there was almost a sense of dread and the unspoken recognition that an awful lot can go wrong during the next few years.

Mr. Jordan spoke directly to the issues underlying my study when he said: "We are a melting pot right here. Our job is to get these kids together." Town differences are so salient that everyone knew exactly what he meant though he never spoke directly about town or economic differences. Frequently, during interviews, observations, and home visits, I heard the language of integration and assimilation used to describe the middle school transition experience. The long bus ride is sometimes referred to as "forced busing" by parents who resent having to send their children out of town to go to school. Teachers speak of the integration of a diverse group of students as being like a melting pot. Some worry that certain policies and practices segregate certain students. The framework of interpretation that many people take to this experience, revealed by the language that is used, is a framework of diversity. However, I found conscious, deliberate efforts to address this diversity on a day-to-day basis to be inconsistent—a person-by-person preference or skill rather than a school-wide goal.

Mr. Jordan assured parents that his teaching team had considered these issues:

> If you live out of town, your child might be getting on a bus at 6:00 in the morning. It is an amazing adjustment for parents as much as children. It is very difficult when you live out of town, to get your kids to sports and other activities. It will not be as easy for you to come to school as it was when your child was at the elementary school. But, if things are not going well in two or three weeks, we need to get together. And if you're driving twenty miles to get here, we aren't going to meet for just five minutes, it's going to be forty minutes and you will meet with all four of us on the team.

But, recognizing that students need to have an opportunity to master their new environment on their own, he emphasized, "Give your kids a week or two to adjust. Don't come in here the first week saying that things aren't going well. Give them a chance." Here, he carefully balanced the parent's need to protect their child, the child's need to independently experience and make sense of their new environment, and the teacher's need to establish the rules for engagement in the middle school domain. The message to parents was, "This is a time to let go a little. They *want* you to let go a little, or at least, to not show it as much."

With this advice, Mr. Jordan confidently and, I think, consciously, entered the treacherous territory where the particular, intimate, subjective knowledge of parents, and the collective, developmental, and less personal knowledge of teachers, coincide in a precarious balance. Parents are at this moment being asked to give up a large amount of control to teachers whom they do not know, and to a school that may be far from home, and they worry, as they must, about how their children will be treated and cared for when they get to grade seven. Teachers walk a fine line when they assert their developmental knowledge of adolescents to worried parents.

Lawrence-Lightfoot's analysis of the disjuncture between parents and teachers is as contemporary and meaningful today as it was when it was written in 1978. She argues that differences in perspectives result from the "*particularistic* expectations that parents have for their children and the *universalistic* expectations of teachers" (p. 22). With different duties and goals, parents and teachers are at odds about many aspects of schooling and, as children progress through the grades, parents feel more and more excluded from their child's education, a situation that may deepen the negative stereotypes on both sides (p. 26–27). However, Lawrence-Lightfoot argued, the differences represent a necessary and functional shift for children who are moving toward integrating new ideas, values, and expectations that are acquired from people outside their family system. Still, she maintained that, "Discontinuities between families and schools become dysfunctional when they reflect differences in power and status in this society" (p. 41). There is evidence in my research that parents from different communities hold different expectations for schools and there is evidence that parents do indeed perceive differences in power and status. An essential task for these middle school educators, therefore, is to accurately assess power differences and to respond appropriately. Teachers who are tuned in to the power differences among parents will seek information from parents with less power and will provide equitable access to participation and decision-making opportunities.

The overall message was clear, "You are welcome here. We look forward to your arrival. Most kids really like it. We will do everything we can to build good relationships among students. Don't be afraid to contact us if you have concerns." Finally, Mr. Jordan emphasized that his goal is to build relationships that will last the next six years. "I guarantee you that by the end of the second week, your son or daughter will have a lot of new friends," but, he cautioned, "If your child doesn't want to come to school, doesn't feel that he or she has friends, something is wrong. You've got to come to see us as quickly as possible." These words, spoken by Mr. Jordan just days before the tragic deaths of students in Columbine, Colorado, were particularly meaningful to parents.

CHAPTER 7

Classrooms, Teams, and Teaching Styles

The Classroom as the Context for Socialization

United States society views schools as the principal institution charged with the responsibility of socializing children and preparing them for the future (Dreeben, 1968; Parsons, 1959; Seeley et al., 1956). Parents entrust the school with preparing their children for life—intellectually, socially, and morally—but not without considerable concern about the content of the curriculum, the pace and style of instruction, the tone and atmosphere in the classroom, and the relationship between their child and the school community. As an institution whose primary objective it is to mediate development, schools represent "a link not only between successive phases of the life cycle but between the private realm of the family and the larger public domain" (Dreeben, 1968: p. 2). However, exactly how this is done, and toward what end, are by no means matters that have widespread consensus. Communities and the families in them differ in their expectations for schools, and opinions are brought to bear on school policy and practice.

Noting that schools must respond to the diverse needs of students and competing community views about schooling, Waller (1932), described schools as being a "despotism in a state of perilous equilibrium . . . threatened from within and exposed to regulation and interference from without" (p. 10). Schooling is contentious because its role is so essential. Schools are the center of "cultural diffusion," said Waller, engaged in "the transmission of a vast body of culture which is passed on from the old to the young" through rituals, symbols, rules, patterns of interaction, and instruction (pp. 103–104).

But while some described the school's enculturation function as a benign truth, others, like Bowles and Gintis (1976), argued that the "vast body of culture" that is being passed on through education is carefully tailored to reproduce a hierarchical class structure that prepares students for unequal positions and roles in the labor force. "The educational

143

system . . . is best understood as an institution which serves to perpetuate the social relationships of economic life," these authors argued (p. 11) and these relationships maintain rigid class boundaries and an inequitable distribution of power, roles, and authority.

At Mountainview Regional Middle School, I witnessed a wide range of instructional styles that emphasized diverse values and skills. I watched and listened for evidence of inequality based on social class, and I paid attention to the way the students themselves interpreted their experiences. Students arrived at the middle school with vast differences in access to resources. Structures and practices that reinforce the unequal opportunities and experiences that students arrive with, setting them farther apart, *do* exist, such as ability grouping and irregular accessibility of after-school activities. However, my observations, interviews, and student focus-group sessions revealed much more than a process of pernicious enculturation carried out by active agents (teachers) and imposed on passive recipients (students). Time and time again I witnessed *students* as active agents of cultural transmission, passing onto their peers values, styles, and ways of thinking, and I saw students as active resisters to enculturation that was in opposition to the lifestyles and values of their communities and families.

It also became clear that students not only learned from their teachers, they studied them. In middle grades schools, teachers often become the first important non-familial mentors to students. My conversations with students revealed that they knew a lot about their teachers, took their words seriously, wanted to do good work to please them, and thrived in the feeling of being in their teacher's good favor. Sheer numbers prevent teachers from knowing as much about their students as their students know about them and I found some students would solicit their teacher's attention and interest while other students were more reticent.

In this chapter, I examine the classroom interactions among students and between students and teachers. Seeley, Sim, and Loosely (1956) asserted that the "classroom is the most potent unit of interaction in the whole social system of the school" (p. 269). At the end of seventh grade, three students named losing a favorite teacher mid-year as their number one disappointment, and five students named "nice" or "cool" teachers as their number one surprise. Teacher-student relationships continue to be vitally important even as peer relationships gain ascendance in middle school.

Through most of my time at Mountainview Middle School, I marveled at the orderliness, engagement, and interest of the students. Most classes, fifty minutes in length, were on-task most of the time. Students were relaxed and friendly in the classes I observed. I was invited to join students at their lunch table, and always received thoughtful responses to my questions. Although my presence was treated with curiosity, interest, or indifference, there was never an unfriendly response from students or teachers. These things are indicative of overall positive relationships between adults and students in this school, and a high level of teacher confidence.

What follows are five snapshots from inside middle school classrooms that demonstrate a variety of styles, teaching challenges, classroom agendas, and teacher-student relationships: a highly structured math class with Ms. Streeter, an example of teaching geography in both a heterogeneously and homogeneously grouped class of students with Mr. Walden, the challenges of diversity in large group band instruction, the remarkable range of students in a physical education class, and an intimate language class experience with Ms. James.

Structured and Predictable: The Millennium Team

The two men and two women who teach Team Millenium students stress organizational skills, structure, and mastery of subject matter through individual work and subject-centered instruction. Students negotiate a wide variety of teaching styles that range from highly structured and predictable with firm boundaries establishing the teacher as the classroom authority, to styles that are flexible, relaxed, and personal.

During the first period advisory a group of boys and girls were hanging out on the comfortable couches and chairs in one corner of the room, bantering with each other and having fun. Several boys worked quietly and independently over on the other side of the classroom. Most school staff use this twenty-minute small group session as a relaxed introduction to the school day—a chance to get organized and say hello before the first academic class. A minute before students had to move to class, they were told about a change in the schedule. Immediately, there was a shuffling of books as they adjusted to this news. In January these experienced seventh graders seemed undaunted by this last-minute alteration but, earlier in the year, these sudden changes caused a great deal of confusion and anxiety. Students worried they would not have the right books and would not go to the right class at the right time.

We moved next door for Ms. Streeter's Algebra-prep math class, and though she was not there for the first ten minutes, students settled in immediately and began to work quietly on the problems written on the board. Some students took out reading books when they finished their work; others talked in hushed voices. On the walls, cartoon posters reminded students, "Keep up with your work. It's no fun playing catch up," "Step by step logic is more important than memorizing," and "Write calculations neatly and carefully."

Ms. Streeter arrived, and without a greeting, sat down at the front desk and began to take attendance. The quiet talking stopped immediately and each student replied "prepared" when his or her name was called. Ms. Streeter's manner was serious, direct, and on-task, as she quickly reviewed the problems on the board, calling on students with or without raised hands to give the answer. She stated each correct answer twice. The pace was quick, but students appeared to keep up, and by the end of class, every student had answered at least one question. Students with wrong answers were told they were wrong without sentimentality, students with correct answers were told they were correct without praise. Ms. Streeter walked around the room looking at each student's homework, as students took turns answering the assigned questions. After each set of corrected problems she asked for a public appraisal, "Who got 100% of those right?" Most hands went up.

The seventeen students were in assigned seats, boys and girls alternately, at three semi-circle rows of adjacent trapezoid desks. When Ms. Streeter wrote on the board, students copied her perfectly formed words into their notebooks. They were learning about common denominators, multiples, and factors. After several examples were worked out together, she gave them problems to do on their own. While students worked quietly on the new set of problems, Ms. Streeter sat next to a student to provide individual instruction. A few students went up to her desk for help and others who finished their work quickly pulled out their reading books and read silently.

With just three minutes to go, the last set of problems was corrected and homework was assigned. One student asked, "Is the homework always on the class notes?" In Ms. Streeter's class there is *always* an always. Students sit in the same seats, Ms. Streeter's instructional style and the pattern of each class is consistent and predictable. By 8:30 in the morning, these students had already done a substantial amount of work. As students left for their next class, some of them joked a little with their teacher, but with caution. This is a style that Ms. Streeter has refined over her twenty-year career as a math teacher.

Later, I asked a group of students who stayed after school with me about the variety of teaching styles I had observed, and especially about Ms. Streeter's class. "[Ms. Streeter] scares me, she really scares me. You can't even get up and sharpen your pencil during class," one student said. But some students seemed to appreciate the structured predictability. Importantly, they all felt they were really learning math. Students from Hillside and Two Rivers who arrived at the middle school fearing they were behind their classmates from other towns, seemed *especially* appreciative of Ms. Streeter's all-business attitude. Students consistently evaluated teachers on the basis of whether they felt they were really learning something. "Teachers can't just be friendly," students told me. "They have to be able to help me learn when I am having a hard time." But students also appreciate some flexibility. Students from both towns told me "good teachers let the small stuff go." They said they appreciate teachers who know when to come down hard and when to back off.

The Striders: Teaching for Different Learning Abilities

To get to the Striders, you have to go through the middle school, out the back door and across the service road to a set of four modular classrooms. On cold days, students without coats rush from classroom to classroom and teachers feel the extra fresh air does them good. Students and teachers like being in the modulars where they are separated from the main school, giving them a sense of greater freedom.

The team's administrative leader and English teacher, Mr. Jordan, signaled a welcome when I entered the room. During the brief advisory period, he sat on a table and leaned back comfortably, chatting with students. In the science room, the girls watered and fed the rats, fish, and turtle, while a group of boys kicked around a hacky-sack. There are three men and one woman on this teaching team and among them, they have nearly eighty years of classroom experience. Mr. Jordan and Mr. Walden have been teaching at the middle school together since the early eighties, and Mr. Walden, a former school administrator, is the most senior person on the entire staff. On this majority male team, sports analogies often clarified lessons and the tone was relaxed, fun, and fast-paced.

Mr. Jordan was animated, energetic, and provocative as he taught his English class using a short story by Guy de Maupassant and an article about the legend of King Arthur. He reassured and encouraged students frequently. Sharp reminders to his students to talk less and work more balanced his easy-going manner. He loves being on stage, knows he is a good teacher, and thrives in the admiration of his students and their parents. His room was tidy and homey with neatly shelved books, framed pictures on the walls of flowers, ducks, and barns, and behind his desk, pictures of his two teenage children.

All during Mr. Jordan's English lesson, a woman wearing a colorful sweater silently checked heads for lice. She made the rounds, standing for a minute or two behind each of the eighteen students seated at two rows of trapezoid tables, and fanned each head of hair through her fingers. Mr. Jordan taught, students participated, and no one seemed to make an issue out of it. In fact, it seemed that these twelve- and thirteen-year-old children were enjoying the gentle physical contact.

During the 1999–2000 school year, the Strider's teaching team, led by Mr. Jordan, agreed to deviate from the school's stated policy of heterogeneous grouping of students and decided to select one group of students of "higher ability" who would have an accelerated curriculum. This group was formed based on math scores, first-quarter classroom performance, and teacher recommendations. Once the eighteen students were selected, there were only a couple of changes for the rest of the school year and the group stayed together for all four core classes. (An analysis of this practice, particularly the social development implications of ability grouping, is in chapter 11.)

In math, Ms. Lyons made her accelerated students rise to the occasion. On the day I visited, her seventh graders were working on problems like these: 82.458/0.09, (482.7)(0.039), 11/15 of 850. She seemed proud of this group's abilities and achievements and she feels strongly that kids capable of this level of work must be challenged, and not held back by less capable students. She said persuasively, "There are students in my classes who are doing third grade math and students capable of high school math. I am just one person; I am only human. If I had an aide that would be different." This teacher, affectionately called Mother Superior by some of her colleagues, is bothered when students are not interested in what she has to teach them, and passionate in her drive to teach math to *all* children. Though I witnessed tense moments in her classroom that brought me back to the nuns of my youth, Ms. Lyons said she has a soft side. Colorful kites hang from the ceiling and her Valentine's Day bulletin board is decorated with satin red hearts, lacy doilies, and evocative words like "desire."

When I returned the next day to a heterogeneously grouped math class, Ms. Lyons was sitting at a table with a student and letting him have it right between the eyes: "Don't you *dare* say that to me [pounding the table for emphasis]. Don't you tell me you don't know. I wrote those instructions on the board each day and you *chose* not to do it. I do my job and I do it very well." The rest of the class was absolutely silent. Confrontations like these have earned Ms. Lyons her nickname. She was impassioned and demonstrative with both groups, but more stern and structured with this heterogeneous group. Another student raised her hand, but Ms. Lyons was not about to be interrupted. After making her point clear, she began to instruct the absent-minded student on the work he had missed.

Other students did not seem disturbed by their teacher's manner. As the class went on, she circulated to other students giving them individual attention. They were learning to add fractions. Students with calculators were allowed to use them but several students did not have calculators. She was insistent about precise answers and she did not try to soften her response to incorrect answers, she just said, "No, that's wrong." Yet most students had their hands up. They were willing to be wrong because everyone is from time to time—it's simply part of learning in this class. "Are some of you not getting this?" she asked, and several students raised their hands. She explained again quickly, but three or four students seemed completely out of the loop. In each of the classes I attended, there were several students who appeared to be lost.

There was an unmistakable difference in the way teachers taught to their different groups of students. Mr. Walden, a social studies teacher, also seemed to adjust his style with each group of students, while maintaining high standards. In the first geography class I attended, Mr. Walden sat on a stool in front of the room, while students brought their folders to him to review. "Start looking at the sheet of paper you just got and stop talking," he told them in a good-natured tone as he continued to check student work. Undaunted, most of them continued talking and did not look at the paper. Mr. Walden is a top-notch teacher, referred to as an intellectual by some of his students. He has thirty years of classroom experience and was entirely unflustered by my presence and by the continuing low-level drone of talking in the room. This is the Galaxy group, the students selected for accelerated learning. They seemed to understand that they had a special agreement with their teachers: they can get away with socializing with each other because, they told me, they "won't get out of hand" and they "still get their work done," unlike their peers in other classes.

Seven students were sent across to the middle school to work independently in the library, and everyone else was told "grab a book, sit at a table by yourself, and collect some information for your world religions projects." As they worked, Mr. Walden sat in the same place in front of the class and interacted almost constantly with his students as they worked, advising them on how to use an index, what kind of information they will find in the appendix, and so on. Dozens of small paper globes that students made bobbed up and down from the ceiling and flags from fifteen countries lined the top of the blackboard. Projects were graded by rating each of the following criteria from excellent to poor and these standards were the same for all students in all classes: strong introduction with thesis statement, supporting paragraphs with topic sentences, specific examples, statistics, and facts, strong conclusion, persuasive argument, organization of ideas, spelling, mechanics (punctuation, grammar, indentation, etc.), attention to guidelines, and bibliography.

Later, in the teacher's room, Mr. Walden told me, "I'm teaching them to be independent. That's my goal." The Striders are encouraged to be independent, responsible, organized, and thorough. There is a focus on the mastery of basic, foundational concepts in all four core subject areas.

The sharp contrast in teaching style and tone between the accelerated and regular group was noticeable as soon as the second geography class I observed began. In this heterogeneously grouped geography class, Mr. Walden was more direct, methodical, and firm. He was up the entire time, working with each student one-to-one at his or her desk. As they began to work on their projects Mr. Walden insisted on absolute silence. Some students appeared ready to go, others yawned and slowly rummaged through notebooks for their work. One student was warned, "If I see you talking again, you're after school," and I knew he meant it.

Compared to the relaxed peer and student-teacher interactions in Galaxy, the interactions in heterogeneously grouped classes were vigilantly controlled, giving me the impression that teachers felt there was a higher probability that some of these students would "not know when to stop" if given too much leeway. There were several hands in the air the entire time as students worked on different assignments, at their own pace. It became quiet and busy, as Mr. Walden worked with one student then another, and another. He was patient and respectful. Some students never asked for help, others seemed to have their hand up three or four times during the class period. When I hear teachers wonder how they can teach a wide range of abilities in a single classroom, I think of Mr. Walden, going calmly from student to student, working on a variety of skills, and with diverse learning styles, in one class period.

The teachers of Team Striders stressed independence and organization, using an active, fast-paced, teacher-centered, direct style of teaching. These veteran teachers hold strong opinions. They take bold stands on controversial issues, like ability grouping, and they freely criticize school administrators whom they feel do not know as much about the classroom as they do. Surprisingly, however, I saw many opportunities for critical thinking and dialogue among students go unused even in the accelerated class.

In an after-school student focus group, students were unequivocal about their respect for their teachers. Ms. Lyons was referred to as a "nuts-and-bolts kind of teacher." Students told me that she takes the time to explain things, she has a predictable style of teaching, and they know what to expect when they go to math. But her mood is not so predictable. One student said, "[She] yells one minute and the next minute is nice to you." They drew a sharp distinction between teachers who "yell" because they want you to do good work, and teachers who "yell" to make fun of you. The latter is something unanimously regarded by students as disrespectful and unnecessary. Either way, yelling can make you "not want to care," they said. But, overall, they said their teachers ". . . never really give up on trying to teach kids. They try to motivate you." Students were also observant of any sign of favoritism toward particular students and noticed that some teachers did have favorites. They were extraordinarily conscious of how their classroom's most cherished resource—teacher time and attention—was spent.

During my two-day visit with the Striders, I overheard a student make a negative comment about Hillside to a new student who had just moved there. The Hillside student responded, "I don't care, I'm not from there. I'm from Connecticut." I wanted to know what the students in my after-school focus-group thought of that interchange. They told me that their team teachers worked to bring students from different towns together. At the beginning of the school year, Mr. Jordan told students that being on the Striders meant they were in this together; they were not a divided group of students from six different towns. Students were deeply impressed by these sentiments boldly stated by an admired teacher. Students from Hillside-Two Rivers and Lakeview said that getting along with others regardless of their background is a core value of the Striders Team.

Inadequate Resources Constrain Good Teaching

"Come to Band, it's fun," Zoe encouraged me to follow them down the hall to the band room, a large, carpeted room, with music stands and instruments everywhere. Students quickly arranged themselves and soon the chaotic, dissonant sounds of seventy-three seventh graders tuning up on a variety of instruments—horns, drums, guitar and keyboard—filled the room. Their teacher, a woman who has been at the middle school for more than fifteen years, was in the pit and ready to go. "We are going to play for thirty-five minutes straight today," they were told. She raised her hand and the baton and there was silence: "Feet on the floor, sit up straight." They are familiar with these words and adjusted themselves immediately and then began their arduous practice without any sign of reluctance.

Seventh graders are enrolled in two quarter- or semester-long unified arts courses: physical education, band, technology, computers, and foreign language. By middle school, special education instruction in separate groups and classrooms may be a barrier to both social development *and* cognitive development (Krantz, 1993). Therefore, at Mountainview Middle School, students from accelerated classes and students with Individualized Education Plans (IEPs) are instructed together in unified arts. However, the principle of inclusionary education and the actual practice of it are quite far apart. In most classes, students with IEPs were easily distinguishable by where they sat in the classroom (in band they sat in the back row), by the assignments they were given, by the ways students interacted, and by the patterns of teacher-student contact.

Band is an elective and more than a quarter of the seventh grade students—seventy-three of them—take it. Ms. Jackson said that until Hillside improved their elementary school music program, her band class was half this size and made up primarily of Lakeview students. Now more students from all communities arrive at the middle school prepared to take band but without additional funding, Ms. Jackson meets this challenge without help.

Most students played throughout the class, but in the last row, eleven students—ten boys and one girl—waited patiently for their turn for almost thirty minutes. These students all played percussion instruments, but there were not as many percussion parts in the music I heard them practice, and there were not enough percussion instruments to go around, so students had to share them. Students who cannot provide their own instruments can get help paying for instruments if their families cannot afford them, but some families may not ask for this provision.

Ms. Jackson shouted instructions and corrections constantly as they played: "Sit up straight, breathe from the belly," "Horns, smooth it out, soft tongue," "No, that's wrong, go back and play it again." When the eleven students not playing in the back of the room began to talk to each other, they were firmly admonished by the teaching assistant who travels with a few of them to different classes. Ms. Jackson worked the piece of music over and over again, sometimes loudly clapping out a faster pace to get the dragging instruments back on measure. Students worked hard and they liked it—the movement, the fast-pace, and the thrill of getting it right. Finally, some of the percussion students got to play. At the end of the piece, there was a very strong percussion finish and I felt jubilant that the students in the back of the room got to be in the limelight for a moment.

Band *should* be where students who struggle in core classes might enjoy success and a chance to contribute fully to a peer group project. But in this case, the separate status, location, and inequitable distribution of resources (instruments and teacher attention) may actually deepen the sense of separation for students already separated from their peers in too many ways.

After class, when I asked Ms. Jackson about the students in the back of the room, she explained how the class had grown and that the resources had not kept up with the demand. She seemed frustrated by the situation, *and* with the percussion students. Experiential, artistic, and physical opportunities can level the playing field for students who struggle academically; but to Ms. Jackson, these students are an uncomfortable daily reminder that she can't do it all.

Judgments are made all the time about student maturity, ability, preparedness, and aptitude that influence the course of instruction a student will experience. Some students have strong parental advocacy on their side or convincing personalities; but I wondered, who is speaking for the students in the back of this classroom and countless others like them? Special education students were easily distinguished in every unified arts classroom and in the lunchroom—places where they were supposed to be mainstreamed. Opportunities for students to work together might be a more developmentally appropriate and socially acceptable way for students with special needs to learn new skills, but in classrooms and in the lunch room, I saw very little evidence of social and work-related interactions between mainstream and special needs students—a distinct loss for both groups.

What Students Bring to Us: The Challenge of Inclusion

When I arrived in the gym on the first day of the second semester, students were in the locker room. Once ready, the thirty-six students assembled along the end line of the basketball court. Like all unified arts classes, there is a broad range of diversity among the students in this class. A flustered student came out of the locker room last and told Ms. Olivier that he could not open his locker. This was treated as an expected and easily rectified occurrence but I am struck by the fact that, even in late January, seventh graders experience an ongoing sense of newness.

Ms. Olivier gave a brief introduction to the semester-long program, and then asked them to run laps to warm up. Most of the students took to this gleefully. Some dashed out as fast as they could, only to end up walking after a lap or two, others paced themselves and jogged steadily for ten minutes. Twelve- and thirteen-year-olds, large and small, awkward and graceful, amateurish and skilled, made their way around the gym.

In gym classes everywhere, some children will not or cannot change to different clothes for physical education. One plump child with red hair, round face, and pale complexion did not change and did not join the group. He was wearing a mustard yellow sweatshirt, brown corduroy pants and had on pack boots instead of sneakers; a dark green T-shirt under his sweatshirt went almost to his knees. He slowly made his way around the outer-most periphery of the gym, eyes down, talking to himself, as students rushed past without seeming to notice him. When he approached the bleachers where I was sitting, he looked up and I smiled. Without returning my smile, he came over and stood silently for a moment and then said, "I'm Henry. I hate this class. I have to figure out how to get out of this class."

I learned from Henry that he lives in Center Hillside with his mom and two teen-age brothers. His dad died suddenly of a heart attack a few years ago and his mom struggles to make ends meet. They live in a rented home in the center of town; in fact, in one of the homes that gave me thoughtful pause several months earlier, as I was collecting information for the Hillside chapter. Henry explained why there would be no consequences for not participating: "They can't call my mother because she's in New Jersey watching her boyfriend in a curling tournament."

The range of students in our care each day is breathtaking. The learning, emotional, physical, and social issues brought to any school are almost unfathomable. Henry lives with tragic loss and in poverty. In the days that followed, I saw Henry frequently, on the bus, in the lunchroom, and in class, always sitting separate from his peers. His classmates did not seem to tease him, indeed, they barely noticed him at all. I looked around the gym. Most other students were wearing gym clothes in styles acceptable to their peers but I wondered what other burdens these students might be carrying.

A few days later when I visited this class, I was happy to see most students, including Henry, playing volleyball. I felt enormously grateful to Ms. Olivier for bending school rules and allowing students to participate even without gym clothes or sneakers.

Trent, a student in my study, was wearing a T-shirt that proclaimed, "I was born ready." He demonstrated volleyball sets, and frequently answered questions asked by the teacher. I noted that the students who got the most play and who volunteered to demonstrate new skills to the rest of the class, were most often students I recognized from Team Strider's accelerated class. Physical ability and cognitive ability are not related, but the students who appeared most confident and engaged were academically successful students.

Trent and Henry negotiate lives that are worlds apart. After school, Trent will drive his new snowmobile back to his lakeside home where both parents will join him after a long day at work, and Henry will join his older brother and ride the bus back to a drafty home in Center Hill-side where there will be no adult tonight, or for the next few nights. How might these boys develop an empathic understanding of each other's lives? Without guidance, stereotypes about each other will be reinforced in many subtle ways, at school, at home, and in the community.

The announcements on the loudspeaker suddenly interrupted my reflection. Ironically, Mrs. Campbell's "words of wisdom" were about diversity and beating the odds. The story was about a Mexican American student from a family of migrant farm workers who went on to college and law school, but no one seemed to be listening. As soon as they got the signal, everyone ran for the locker room to change—it's break time! During break, the gym was packed with students shooting baskets. The play was exuberant, bordering on aggressive, but most of the boys and girls seemed to be having a good time.

Most students were preoccupied during break, but I struck up a conversation with one student, just hanging out. He eagerly told me that he doesn't like school, got two Fs on his report card, and said he will quit school as soon as he can: "No one in my family finished school; it's not my family tradition." "But these days, jobs will be harder to get," I argued. "I don't care. My uncle has a garage and that's where I'll work."

In my days at the middle school, I saw very little teaching about diversity. Public schools are the most diverse institution in the United States, yet purposeful discussion about diversity, starting from the actual lives of students, were noticeably absent in most classes. As more young lives are taken each year as a result of intergroup and interpersonal misunderstanding and intolerance, educational goals that include social awareness, compassion toward others, and multicultural education addressing race, class, religion, sexual orientation, ability, and gender have become necessary components in any school's curriculum. No one can claim to be educated in today's world without a grasp of these issues.

A Community of Active Learners Find Out About Other Cultures

Different teaching styles have as much to do with subject matter, class size, and student abilities, as it does personal temperament. Students seemed adaptable and forgiving when negotiating the complex variety of teaching styles and classroom cultures they encountered each day. It was only the third day of Spanish for the thirteen students in this class. Ms. James delighted students by addressing them with their chosen Spanish names, as they took turns practicing the date and the days of the week. When Ms. James described her experience as a foreign exchange student in Ecuador, she was careful to emphasize that when she spoke about different customs, she meant *different,* not better or worse.

They were taught basic questions and answers in Spanish, practicing in full chorus: *Como se llama? Como estas? Cuantos años tienes?* Correct answers or a good effort earned students little green tickets for candy. They tried these new phrases one by one, frequently making mistakes that were corrected with generous reassurance, "Don't worry about it, everyone does that at first." Unlike Mr. Jordan and Mr. Walden, the "cool" Striders teachers who banter playfully and keep a few steps ahead of their students, Ms. James does not try to be cool. She would fail "Middle School Humor 101" miserably, but her classroom feels like a safe community.

Arianna told me that in elementary school she was very afraid of speaking in front of the class. In Spanish, she raised her hand often. She seemed nervous, squinting her eyes and speaking very softly, but she was finally learning to participate and her risk-taking was met with success. The students were instructed to pair up and try out the new phrases in conversations with each other. They got up and moved around from one partner to another. There was lots of laughter and sincere efforts to imitate Ms. James' exaggerated accent. The students then sat back down to copy words neatly written on the blackboard. "Look, you already know all this and we have just begun!" Ms. James and her students were pleased. This well-planned class utilized a wide range of teaching styles, enabling students to work quietly on their own, interact with their peers, and interact with their teacher.

In the last few minutes, Ms. James had the students write and say the names of every country in Latin America. Then she put on a cassette tape and they *sang* the countries to the tune of La Cucaracha— one of the few Spanish songs familiar to many non-Hispanic students. "Feel free to bee-bop," she told them. A group of girls jumped up, jiving to the music; *everyone* was joyfully singing the lively tune. When they finished, she had "dulces" for everyone because, she said, "I think it is so sweet when you sing." They seemed unselfconsciously like the twelve- and thirteen-year-old children they were, experiencing something all too rare: a cooperative, respectful learning community, where they were involved in the action.

Suddenly, it was time to go, "Give me your folders as you go out. Adios!" It was the end of the school day and in the halls there was a distinct change in student demeanor. Some boys yelled loudly to each other as they left the building, a few couples held hands, and many of them moved toward the door with determined energy, finally able to wrestle out of the firm hold of the teachers. They know they are just seconds away from the school's domain, and they know their behavior will probably go unchallenged. As students left the building in high spirits on this snowy day, only a few had on hats and mittens, and some were wearing just T-shirts. Students told me that they are afraid to miss the bus so they just grab their stuff and go. I was constantly made aware of the mix of challenge and stress, exuberance and boredom, satisfaction and anxiety that characterize every school day and the multiple strands of meaning that lie beneath every interaction. Within minutes most students had cleared out of the building and I experienced that wonderful calm that envelops an empty school at the end of the day.

CHAPTER 8

————————

How Students Shape
Less-Structured Environments

Perhaps the most important time to observe students' peer interactions is during unstructured periods when students are together with less teacher supervision. The school bus, the halls during morning break, and the lunchroom quickly became important instructional venues for me. It is in these places and at these times that students are most free to structure their environments in their own way. Teachers often dread the more unstructured times of the day; it is during these periods when a teacher's tenuous hold on students' attention and behavior is most at-risk of being entirely undermined by a single well-timed comment or prank by a thirteen-year-old seeking to earn "points" with a group of peers as witnesses. Moments like these are difficult for the most seasoned and hardy teachers whose sense of competence is on the line when challenged in this public way. Some students also loathe these times of the day when their more influential peers set the tone and standards for acceptable behavior. The most valuable capital for students during these times of the day is peer acceptance and self-preservation. Everything else pales by comparison.

The Morning Break

Just before the break, a student's voice on the public address system signals everyone to stand for the pledge of allegiance. There is nearly a hundred percent participation in this ritual, but as announcements are read, student attention dwindles. Each day, Mrs. Campbell reads "words of wisdom"—stories about real people that encourage students to think about diversity, working through conflict, friendship, compassion, and being a good citizen. This type of character education was not evident in many classes during my observations at the middle

159

school, and unfortunately, students are itchy to get to their cherished break so they have a hard time concentrating on the brief lesson. On one morning, the reading was about love and began with a story from the Cuban revolution. Through the increasingly loud clamor of students talking with one another, I heard the words, "Love is the glue that holds us together, hate separates. Love creates, hate destroys . . ."

A walk through the halls during the morning break is a good way to become aware of the vast physical variations, temperaments, and styles of the twelve- to fourteen-year-old students. Some are as tall and as physically developed as full-grown adult men and women, and some are small enough to pass for much younger children. Some stride confidently, shouting to their friends down the hall, their manner just *daring* any adult in earshot to tell them to tone it down. Others shuffle quietly, eyes cast down, avoiding, perhaps even fearing, interactions with their peers. A few greet me with friendly smiles, most look past me. I am an unimportant occupant of this vibrant adolescent space but I also learn from students that it is *especially* during these times that many of them wish for a more vigilant teacher presence.

The fifteen-minute break is the only time during the entire school day when students can connect with friends on other teams; it is very valuable social time. It is also the time to grab a quick snack. The cafeteria serves a light breakfast and by 9:30 students who came to school without eating are hungry. When they completed questionnaires in the spring of their seventh grade year, ten of the thirty research participants said that break was their favorite time of day. The halls, cafeteria, and gym fill with seventh and eighth grade students; teachers are scarce and students command the tone, attitude, and manner of interacting. During my interview with the guidance counselor, she told me that accreditation visitors from other middle schools are surprised by the amount of freedom students have, particularly during this less-supervised break.

As a former middle school teacher, I remember walking down student-packed halls with the unsettling knowledge that adults are viewed by some students as antagonistic to their *real* purpose at school, which is to connect with their peers. But Middle school teachers know that they are important in the lives of students, so important, that students sometimes have to put a lot of energy into wrestling *out of* connection and identification with their teachers, in order to have healthy peer group relationships. The students' drive to interact and create a space for themselves is almost overpowering during this mid-morning free time.

Jeans and chinos seem to be worn by nearly everyone, with T-shirts or polo shirts, and sneakers or low-top hiking boots. Some girls wear skirts that are either long or short, but definitely not mid-length.

Research participants told me that, for some students, dress is very important. A fashion mistake can cause some students a full day of self-conscious anxiety. Students may try out a new piece of clothing and, if their peers don't like it, change into safer clothes that they brought from home, just in case. I noticed students wearing clothes from Nike, Abercrombie and Fitch, the Gap, and Old Navy; others attempt a unique appearance with *avant-garde* artistic flair. A handful of students dye their hair black, purple, green, or orange, wear chains on their pants, dog collars around their necks, and pierce their eyebrows, lips, noses, or tongues. In 2000, the new dress code outlawed some of these styles, and by the beginning of October, more than one hundred junior high and high school students had been given warnings and one student had been suspended for violating the controversial new rules.[1]

As students enjoy their freedom, there is some out-of-bounds behavior—a girl rides piggy back on another girl down the hall, a boy kicks his locker very hard, a boy and girl have a romantic moment in the stair well, there is some loud shouting—but mostly, the 453 students behave reasonably.

Where Are All These White Kids Sitting in the Cafeteria?

In her book, *Why Are All the Black Kids Sitting Together in the Cafeteria?* Beverly Tatum (1997) explores the answer to this question within the framework of adolescent identity development. Black youth not only struggle with the universal question, "Who am I?" but they must also think about, "Who am I racially and what does it mean to be Black?" (p. 52–53). Developing positive self-identity requires establishing bonds with others who have similar interests and backgrounds; "joining one's peers for support in the face of stress is a positive coping strategy" (p. 62). It would be incorrect to make uncritical connections between identity development in black youth and identity development in rural white youth, but I found many common themes. Nowhere else is social status grouping more evident than in the lunchroom, where an entire team of about one hundred students can sit wherever they want.

In the first chapter of this section, I reported that, in sixth grade, the research participants anticipated having the opportunity to make new friends and they came to the middle school excited about meeting peers from different communities. In the spring of their seventh grade year, they were asked to complete the sentence, "The best thing about seventh grade is that now I have . . ." Twenty-two out of thirty students finished the sentence, "more friends" or "lots of friends."

But how successful were Lakeview and Hillside-Two Rivers seventh graders in establishing connections with each other? At the end of the seventh grade I asked students to "put a check mark next to the towns where you have really good friends." They were asked to use a 0 to 4 scale to indicate how often they go to the homes of their friends. Six of the sixteen Lakeview students reported having one or two good friends from Hillside or Two Rivers, and seven of the fourteen Hillside-Two Rivers students reported having one or two good friends from Lakeview. However, I also found that students visit their friends from other communities never (0) or rarely (1). The friends they made from other communities were "school friends" whom they seldom saw outside of school.[2]

Through the first half of the seventh grade school year, students slowly and carefully began to adjust their expectations and perceptions. I witnessed students actively holding off disappointing realizations about their new environment. Most of the research participants remained positive throughout their seventh grade year and insisted, "We are all the same; it doesn't matter what town you are from." However, student experiences during this time often countered that perception. For example, halfway through the school year, Oceana, a student from Two Rivers, went to a friend's birthday party in Lakeview and was surprised to find that out of twenty guests, she was the only one from Hillside or Two Rivers. Ethan, from Hillside explained to me, "People think if you live in a trailer home you are nothing but trailer trash. And people from outside Hillside think that's how everyone in Hillside lives. The idea of being 'trash' expands to other kids in Hillside." This sad and insightful explanation of how a stereotype works goes a long way in explaining how students from Hillside may be interpreted by their peers, and why it becomes so important to identify oneself as being *not* from impoverished Center Hillside. Students from Lakeview also experienced stereotypes. Olivia, a Lakeview student from a family with a modest income, was astonished and hurt to find that some of her peers characterized her as a "preppy snob" because of the town she lived in.

Making friends from other communities and choosing where to sit in the cafeteria are decisions made in the context of social perceptions that have dizzying complexity and find resonance in broader cultural messages. So, when I visited the middle school lunchroom, it was not surprising that I found some of these sentiments evident in how students arranged themselves, despite the fact that I was told by teachers *and* students that everyone sits together.

In the middle school lunchroom, two tables in the back had twelve and sixteen students each, even though the rules say there can be only four students to a side, eight students in all. Accommodations like these, offered to some, but not all students, are not lost on adolescents who are vigilantly observant of uneven treatment. At these back tables the boys looked tougher, bigger, more physically mature; the girls were athletic-looking and well dressed. Three Lakeview girls who were research participants sometimes sat at the back tables.

At the opposite end of the lunchroom, near the lunch line exit, three girls occupied a table of their own. One of them had on a pink Winnie-the-Pooh sweatshirt; her smile revealed a mouthful of badly decayed teeth. I was invited by one of the girls to join her at this table. She seemed unselfconscious, talking enthusiastically, waving her hands, and smiling with a line of chocolate milk on her mouth. This is the sort of thing that irritates the heck out of the students sitting at the back tables.

In my after-school focus-group session, several research participants from both towns told me that most kids are "floaters" and sit in the middle. In the back are the popular tables. After asking for this explanation of seating arrangements over and over again, I learned that students gave consistent answers and that they did not mention the students at the front tables until I pursued it with them. This is a sad example of just how invisible low-status students become. Some students referred to this as the "loser" or "outcast" table.

When I asked about the students at the front table where I sat at lunch, a girl from Lakeview had a strong reaction, "They are very unpopular, extremely annoying, and wicked suck-ups. [They] don't know how to dress . . . and have bad complexions, and bad teeth," she said. As I listened to this reaction, I was stunned by the power of her response—a class-biased, gut-level, emotional response coming from a twelve-year-old speaking about her peers. These girls, who seem to not understand the rules for social acceptance, are an affront to some of their more status-conscious peers. To feel so strongly, to respond with such repulsion, says something about how anxious some early adolescent girls may be about appearance and peer acceptance—a vulnerability the clothing and cosmetic industries are eager to exploit. I ask what would happen if the girl with the Winnie-the-Pooh sweatshirt sat down at the back table. "Everyone would leave," was her matter-of-fact response.

Teachers and parents play an important role in helping students recognize these patterns and prejudices and helping them interpret what they mean. Ethan summed up our after-school discussion: "Let me put it this way, if you are popular, school's a breeze, but if you are an outcast, school is a living hell." We have to understand how the cruel rejection of some students puts all students at risk.

Over and over I asked students in the lunchroom, "Is there a popular table?" and over and over students answered consistently naming the same tables. The only students who had trouble with this designation were the students actually sitting at these tables. They said, "Everyone is popular" and "People sit wherever they want." At one point, when I asked this question of a boy sitting at one of the middle tables, he got up enthusiastically, "Yeah, I'll show you." He strode to the back of the crowded cafeteria, pointed at the table I had already picked out, and shouted down to me: "It's this one." Some adults may not want to address these issues in schools but the students experiencing the disconnections day to day have no trouble naming them.

Students also explained something I could not have guessed: they distinguished between a table of popular kids who are "nice" ("cool") and a table of popular kids who are "mean" ("snobby"). They told me that anyone could sit at the nice popular table but not at the snobby one. What is amazing is that three groups of students independently described this to me in almost exactly the same way.

Students also sort themselves out in the lunch line. Perhaps to avoid harassment, some students, often the same students who sit at the front tables, go to the back of the line and are left with precious little time to eat their lunch. I watched the student Henry from gym class get his hot lunch last, gulp his food quickly, and when the bell rang less than ten minutes later, throw the rest of it away.

Students told me that they sit with their friends and with kids they get along with. Sometimes they sort themselves by interest—skateboarding, snowboarding, and music tastes, for example—and often students sit at tables with their sports teammates. In all three seventh grade lunch periods, I found tables where there were students from all towns sitting together, and I found tables that were populated by students from only Hillside-Two Rivers or Lakeview. One Two Rivers boy proclaimed proudly, "I sit with my Hill-town home boys"—a comment that clearly calls to mind Tatum's point that students sit together to feel a positive sense of identity, sometimes defying the dominant group. I learned that when separations do exist between towns, the lines are drawn more dramatically between Lakeview and Hillside than between any other two towns in the district. Only one out of thirty students said that he often sat with different students; all other research participants reported that they usually or always sat with the same people at the same table every day.

During one lunch period, I sat in the back with the "popular" students and I asked where they were from. Most of them were from Lakeview and Deer Run. "Is anyone here from Hillside?" I asked, and one boy, a research participant from that town, covered his head and put it down on the table.

The School Bus as a Micro-Community

Every day of the school year, Mountainview Regional School District provides bus transportation to students over an astonishing 3,741 miles of hilly back roads and state highways.[3] Monday through Thursday a second after-school bus, the late bus, leaves at 4:45 to bring home middle and high school students who stay after school for activities or extra help. More students from Hillside and Two Rivers ride the bus than students from Lakeview who can rely on rides from parents or friends, or who have cars of their own. Only five out of sixteen research participants from Lakeview took the school bus regularly in grade seven while all fourteen of the Hillside-Two Rivers students relied on bus transportation. Many Hillside-Two Rivers students ride the bus all the way through high school.

On average, Hillside-Two Rivers students got up in the morning forty minutes earlier than Lakeview students (5:10 a.m. for Hillside residents, 5:50 for Lakeview residents) to ride the school bus for between thirty and sixty minutes, to arrive at school at about 7:15, for a school day that begins at 7:25. If Hillside-Two Rivers students stay after school and take the late bus, they arrive home an average of thirty minutes later, 5:30 to 6:00 p.m.[4] I rode three bus routes in Lakeview and three in Hillside-Two Rivers.

The Hillside-Two Rivers Buses

One February morning in the winter of 2000 I left my house at 5:40 to catch the school bus in Center Hillside. The temperature had finally risen above ten degrees, after a weeklong subzero cold spell. The light in the sky reminded me that many weeks had passed since I first started these school-day observations. A month ago, there was no sign of dawn at this time of the morning; now, daylight crept into the sky before 6:00. On my way to Center Hillside, I rode the ridge in North Lakeview in awe of the morning. The sky was a velvety, steel blue; a full moon above the distant hills to the west brightened the horse fields and glistened on the frozen lakes far below.

Back down in the valley, lights glowed in the apartment buildings I passed in Center Hillside on my way to the bus stop. At the junction, I asked permission to park alongside a four-unit apartment building that extended off a tired, old house. Several other homes cluster around this quiet, historic corner. A woman put her handicapped child on a special needs bus and offered to let me wait inside to stay warm. I declined, but after a few more minutes, I was wishing I had accepted. Soon a couple of teens joined me in the silent, cold dawn. They were not dressed in the warm winter coat, hat, and mittens that I was grateful for that morning, but had on light jackets or sweatshirts over T-shirts and bare hands and heads. A car or two from farther up the hill drove a few more students down to the corner. Bus stops come within a mile of students' homes and, on cold mornings, some parents give their children a ride to the stop and let them wait for the bus in the warm car.

Finally, out of the darkness, headlights and red safety lights glared at us as the yellow school bus, looking gigantic on the small country road, rambled closer. Vapor billowed from the exhaust and the sudden smell of diesel fuel invaded the crisp air. This is Bus #18—the infamous Center Hillside bus that even students say is a "bad" bus. Stories of questionable credibility are passed down through generations of middle school students: "They put a surveillance camera in this bus to monitor what is going on in the back seats because students were getting stoned on the way to school;" "The kids in the back once threw a bus seat out the window;" "What those kids do back there is so bad, I can't even tell you." Students seemed to derive great pleasure from the very thought of their classmates pulling off terrible things right there on the school bus.

Many people I spoke with said that student behavior in general is much worse now than fifteen years ago. There is also a perception that students from lower income families are more behaviorally challenging than students from higher income families. I failed to see much worse behavior in the students from Center Hillside, but I did see more defiance, alienation, and indifference from young people from families who are thought to "have everything going for them." If educators, policy makers, parents, and students fail to see and articulate this issue clearly, both Hillside *and* Lakeview students will be hurt by it.

As the bus approached, a dozen or so students came out from cars and houses. The bus driver was Norris, an older man, quiet, I was told, until he gets angry, but on the ride to and from school, I did not hear him angry, nor did I hear him say much of anything. Unlike all other school staff, students address Norris and most other bus drivers by their first names. In Hillside and Two Rivers, bus drivers not only know their students' names, they know their students' families as well. I was grateful that Norris was listening to the CB radio rather than playing the tabloid radio stations other bus drivers had on for their students. The young male and female DJs target a school-age audience with thinly restrained sexual talk ("Are you hot this morning?"), humor that encourages intolerance of others, and news stories that sensationalize violence. This was the first stop of the nearly one-hour-long bus route. We passed residences where I know middle and high school-age children live, but where no one got on that morning.

Like the other Hillside-Two Rivers buses, this bus became crowded; many seats held three students. As soon as a handful of students were riding, interactions became lively. One boy, a few seats behind me, loudly punctuated every sentence with "f___in' [this or that]." Some of the students around me seemed embarrassed by his lack of restraint in front of a stranger with white hair.

One boy got on and slid into the seat across from me. "Like my jacket?" he said, as he stroked the black leather, "My dad gave it to me when I went to see him this weekend." This fifteen-year-old boy was achingly sweet in his enthusiasm. He told me he is a good student and I asked, "What's your favorite subject?" He answered, "Phys. Ed." "Well, maybe you will be a Phys. Ed. teacher," I said and we continued to talk about future possibilities. Though he sounded unsure of his prospects, I sensed he was enjoying and appreciating the interaction. Another student in her junior year, told me she wants to go to nursing school, but does not know of any. I wondered how these students acquired information about higher education and the encouragement to pursue it. When a student does not cause any trouble and seems unsure about higher education, he or she may have precious little time with over-stretched guidance personnel. High school students told me that it is possible to never see a guidance counselor in a formal, individual session in their entire twelve years at school.

Most of the chatter was lively, friendly, and inclusive, covering topics like spectacular skiing wipeouts and snowmobiling over the weekend. A couple of girls exchanged cheap jewelry. One boy asked a student a few seats behind him, "Hey, how much was that cap?" referring to the nice new Nike baseball cap. "Twenty bucks," was the reply. "If I give you 20 bucks will you get one for me?" In this rural area there is no public transportation and many students do not frequently get to the popular department stores forty-five minutes away. A student I recognized from school was engaged in a lively, connected conversation with an older boy in back of him. I was surprised to see his energetic affect after having observed him as a quiet, shy, self-conscious, and inarticulate student in his special education classroom the previous day.

This is the loveliest of all bus routes. We rode up a steep, narrow, dirt road; large trees on both sides were weighted down with snow. Daybreak came and suddenly bright sunlight diffused through the frosted windows and glowed on student faces. Once we crossed the line into Lakeview, we no longer picked up students. We passed one house where a middle school student was clearing snow off his parent's car; he will get a ride to school with his mother or father. Lakeview and Hillside students do not ride the same buses.

The friendly, interactive atmosphere on this bus was similar to what I experienced on the other Hillside-Two Rivers buses. All three buses were crowded, but while Norris was more reserved, the two women bus drivers I rode with called their students by name and participated in the conversation. "Hey, Nate, I saw you got your snowmobile fixed. Out terrorizing the neighborhood again?" "Are those flowers for me, Sally?" "Got your homework done, Eddy?" The bus driver bantered with most students as they climbed on board. In West Hillside, I got on the bus at the second to last stop with a small crowd of students who came from the trailer park across the street and the apartments upstairs from the gas station-convenience store. Three students squeezed into each seat. I was quickly drawn into the conversation that was going on among all the students in the first few rows and the bus driver. Boys and girls, high school and middle school students, were all talking to one another, having a good time.

I shared a seat with a cute, impish seventh grade boy by the name of Tim who enjoyed being the topic of conversation for much of the ride. Students asked why I was taking the bus and I told them, "I am writing a book about middle school." Tim nearly jumped out of his seat, "Can I be in it? I want to be famous." The others around him teased, "Oh you'll be famous all right, Tim—probably one of 'America's most wanted criminals.'" "Tell her what you did a couple of weeks ago, Tim, maybe she'll write about that," suggested the student behind me. Tim gleefully told me he decided to pierce his lip on the ride to school. By the end of his morning bus ride, he was a little bloody and had a hole in his lip with an earring in it, but then, "the nurse made me take it out," he complained.

He and his peers were laughing about this, but I couldn't help think about the narrow window of time this twelve-year-old has to get away with this sort of thing. I wondered about what it meant for Tim to pierce his lip that morning. Was he motivated by the desire to make his peers laugh? A drive toward peer acceptance? Experimentation with an unusual fashion? But how long might it be before students begin to laugh *at* him rather than *with* him? There are substantial risks to students who try to fit in to their expanding peer group at the middle school even when it causes them harm. Students frequently told me that to be accepted, you can't look like you are trying too hard. Humor must be smooth, savvy, and well timed; awkward, ill-chosen attempts at being cool appear desperate and usually fail.

This back-and-forth with lots of laughter and participation from all around went on continuously for the forty-five minute ride. It was fun, affectionate, silly, and well accepted, never crossing the line into abusive or degrading harassment. Bus drivers provide an important transitional environment between home and school. The students on this bus had a positive experience to get them off on the right foot. By the time we got to school, I was feeling great.

Jaz walked with me to the school entrance. "I sit next to Shaun every day. He's like my older brother," she told me. Shaun is a tenth grader. This is an example of the kind of informal care taking that is so prevalent in the lives of many Hillside and Two Rivers students. Neighbors and friends become extended family for the purpose of providing companionship and, in this case, a sense of safety to Jaz and a gratifying mentoring role for Shaun. These relationships are essential in the lives of many Hillside-Two Rivers students, who seem to have internalized the norms of interdependence that helped their communities thrive for generations. I saw this sense of mutual reliance everywhere I went in Hillside: in students' homes, on the school bus, in the lunchroom, and at community meetings. Is there space for this value to be carried into the classroom during instructional time?

These Hillside children have had a good social start to the day, in the company of people who become like family. In the same way Amber's mom defined her family's space at the middle school open house, resilient students find ways to make their environments safe and familiar.

The Lakeview Buses

The light was just coming to the sky when I met my first Lakeview bus at 6:45. All along the thirty-minute bus route, students got on quietly and took an empty seat. Many either fell asleep or listened to music on earphones. Only a couple of pairs sat together. For a long time, only the low drone of the engine could be heard, but, as the light grew, a few quiet conversations broke the silence. There appeared to be no words exchanged between students and the bus driver. By the time we reached school at 7:15, the bus was about a third full, with most students spaced out in separate seats. Students were polite, but I was not drawn into conversations as I was on the Hillside-Two Rivers buses. The words spoken between students seemed fragmented; they were not conversations I could follow. Conversations between friends sitting together were whispered privately. In some instances, the communication seemed intended for power and position rather than for peer connection. On the Hillside bus, I heard students talk to each other in whole sentences—they included others, they said hello and good-bye to each other; on the Lakeview buses, I had an entirely different experience.

On the ride home, the driving was treacherous, and the bus was crowded. In the morning there were not many riders but at 12:30, when a snowstorm forced an early release from school, many more students had to take the bus home rather than rely on rides from parents. The bus driver, a veteran of twenty-six years, listened for instruction on a CB radio. Those of us sitting in the front seats overheard radio communications about stalled buses, windshield wipers and defrosters that weren't working, and a student who got on the wrong bus and had to be given a ride back to the school.

Students were at very high energy having been given an unexpected half-day off and the ninth grade boys in the back seat were particularly loud. One of them took out a lollipop and the bus driver, who could see him in her rear-view mirror, yelled at him to get it out of his mouth and throw it away. He threw it away and went back to his seat, and soon he and a few other boys began chanting, "Billy is gay." For this, the bus driver did not intervene, reminding me of something I heard over and over again from students: adults make corrections and give consequences for little things, but ignore the big things. School staff, especially women, who intervene in peer-group taunting, might be ignored or even made fun of, making them look and feel incompetent. For this reason, perhaps, the behavior of aggressive, older boys, in particular, might be ignored, especially when there are no other adults around. Billy, a seventh grader, was sitting near the front; he had a look on his face, half smile, and half about-to-cry. I went to the back of the bus and the students semi-defiantly asked me what I was doing. "I'm writing a book about middle schools. Stop harassing Billy," I said. Gratefully, they were willing to stop, but began to tell me that Billy "deserved it, because he harasses everyone."

The idea that some students deserve to be harassed in retaliation for other things was repeated often by many students. In the absence of effective adult intervention, students will establish their own system of social control and justice (Garbarino, 1999). In a later conversation with a seventh grade girl sitting with the boys in the back seat, I discovered that she actually fears Billy for legitimate reasons, but she does not think that adults take her sense of fear seriously. When students were allowed to explore these issues in more depth during focus-group meetings, they arrived at similar explanations: in the absence of adult guidance, fear and self-preservation often drive student interactions.

On no other occasion did I witness the intent to harm that I experienced on my first day on the Lakeview buses, but other patterns were the same: students got on and sat by themselves for as long as there were empty seats, conversations were limited, many students listened to walkmen, and some dozed off. When given the chance, Lakeview students preferred to shape their environment to be a safe distance from their peers. Securing privacy may be a survival strategy for students who perhaps fear that they could be the next targets.

Lakeview children sometimes expressed the belief that wanting or needing the sort of protective companionship Jaz had with Shaun was immature. Independence, not interdependence, is the key developmental goal for Lakeview children. Independence or interdependence, individual goals or community goals, competition or cooperation: where the emphasis is placed has far-reaching implications for the way teachers teach and the way students interact.

Tapping Student Courage and Altruism

Students not only help to shape their environments, and they not only interpret what they experience, but they also think about their roles as active participants in the expanding contexts of their lives. Many students, when given an opportunity to explore how some of their classmates are hurt in peer relationships, demonstrate profound compassion and sense of justice. Students often made efforts that exceeded institutional structures to establish mutually gratifying, supportive relationships, and demonstrated an enormous capacity for understanding, empathy, and insight. An example comes to mind. Christine and I were talking about lunchroom seating and she was telling me that some students are "outcasts" because they are so "depressed they push people away." I asked her how she thought school was for those students:

> They walk around and they look like they have absolutely no feeling . . . because all the feelings have been taken out of them by these people who are making fun of them . . . They're not upset anymore, they're just frustrated and tired of being upset . . . so they decide to make themselves not have any feelings. I think it's a lot about what people say, some of the stuff people are saying is harsh and it makes people feel like they're not worth anything . . . If people saw how lucky they were, I don't think they'd judge people so much, because if people saw what other people are going through, I think more people would want to help, maybe not, I don't know . . . That's something that

really frustrates me. There's so many things I want to do to help people, I've tried everything and I don't know what else to do.

I asked, "What do you think those students need?" Christine answered, "I think those students need some reassurance they are not alone." When I asked Ethan about the students who are called outcasts, he said, "I think if we just went over and talked to them it would make it better." Once, when Alexeia heard some of her classmates make fun of students who buy their clothes in a discount department store, she said courageously, "I don't think it is right to judge people by how they dress and where they buy their clothes." In another conversation, Micky told her peers that she doesn't like it when her classmates, "disinclude people they don't like just because of what they look like or wear."

Imagine what a resource these children could be to each other if they had opportunities to discuss these issues and voice their opinions. Imagine if their attitudes about justice and tolerance were honed into action and they had support and encouragement from adult mentors who modeled positive regard for all students. Students can be a tremendous resource to each other; however, student understanding, empathy, and insight are underutilized in peer interactions in school. Students play a huge role in how other students feel about themselves—they provide a peer context for social success or failure. They are often so willing to extend themselves toward others with empathy and generosity, but they need adult guidance and encouragement to feel empowered to take an active rather than passive role in school and in their communities.

Conclusion

Students do not necessarily lose ground when they transition to middle school, especially when their own resilient efforts are matched by a supportive, developmentally appropriate school environment (Eccles and Midgely, 1989; Carnegie Council on Early Adolescent Development, 1989; Dryfoos, 1990; Lipsitz, 1981). Most research participants thrived in middle school because they had resources on several levels working for them, including their remarkable ability to influence the tone and character of their own environments. Mountainview Regional Middle School has already integrated many of the suggestions made by the Carnegie Council on adolescent development: student and teacher teams provide smaller learning environments, each student is assigned an adult advisor, there is flexible scheduling, students are exposed to new opportunities, there is primarily heterogeneous grouping, teachers have community support, parents have access to information and ways to be involved in their child's education at home and at school. Compared to other middle grades schools, Mountainview Middle School afforded students a good deal of autonomy and opportunities to connect in meaningful ways with school adults and their peers. These are strengths that require acknowledgment, support, and resources to be sustained.

On the other hand, I came to question if students were afforded adequate opportunities for analytic thinking, social awareness, altruism, leadership, and dialogue on the issues most relevant in their lives. I did not witness facilitated discussions in which students were allowed to share their knowledge and opinions with each other. There were many missed opportunities to integrate diversity awareness in the lessons of the day. For example, students viewing the film *The Crucible* were asked questions about the clothing, lifestyle, and religious views of the people of colonial America, but not asked to probe social class, gender, religious diversity, and the ways Arthur Miller's story might have relevance today.

On a questionnaire administered at the end of seventh grade, I asked students to say whether they got too little, too much, or just right

173

amounts of intellectual challenge, homework, responsibility at school, responsibility at home, freedom at school, freedom at home, classroom worksheets, group work in school, hands-on work, teacher talking, discipline, structure/organization, time on task, and free time. Two-thirds of the students from both communities said "just right" for a majority of the fourteen areas they were asked to judge.

Most students said that intellectual challenge, responsibility at school, time on task, and structure/organization were "just right." Six students from Lakeview and two from Hillside-Two Rivers felt that there was not enough intellectual challenge. One Lakeview student commented, "I have been getting very good grades and usually the challenge is just right but sometimes it's too easy."

Students were evenly split on homework and hands-on work. Another area of agreement was in the amount of teacher talking: half of the students from Lakeview and three-quarters of the Hillside-Two Rivers students said that there was "too much" of it. The amount of free time elicited an overwhelming majority response of "too little," but three students from each community thought it was "just right."

The most discrepant answers were responding to school discipline. Lakeview students more often felt that discipline was too much; Hillside-Two Rivers students more often thought that discipline was too little or just right. Several students commented on what they perceived to be the irregular application of discipline. One student made the interesting observation that discipline was "too little for some and too much for others."

Some of the differences in student answers seemed to reflect town culture and values. For example, more students from Lakeview were unhappy with the amount of freedom they had in the seventh grade, and more students from Hillside-Two Rivers said there was too little group work. Fewer students from Lakeview found that they received the right amount of intellectual challenge, but fewer students from Hillside-Two Rivers were pleased with school structure. One girl from Two Rivers commented, "I love learning but faculty/structure are all wrong."

When asked to explain why they liked or disliked the middle school, students from both communities liked school because it was a place to see friends. "I don't like the work but I like seeing friends," was a comment several students made. Others felt positively about school for the education they were getting: "I learn what I need for the rest of my life; I love doing good and being with my friends," and "It gives me a place to vent my intellect," were two responses that were shared by others.

Attitudes toward school were generally positive: In the sixth grade, only two of the thirty students designated the answer, "I dislike school" on their questionnaires. Most students—nine out of sixteen from Lakeview and eleven out of fourteen from Hillside—said, "School is okay" in the sixth grade. A few students—six from Lakeview and two from Hillside—even said, "I love school" in the sixth grade. In the fall of seventh grade, their answers were similar, with one notable change: now, *five* students from Hillside reported that they loved school.

The thirty children in my study group entered the middle school with fears about making friends, finding their way around, keeping up academically, and getting along with many teachers instead of just one. Within a few short weeks, their fears were alleviated and most students found a place where they could experience social and academic success. The transition to middle school in Mountainview Regional School District seems remarkably smooth, so far.

However, several well-known studies (e.g., Simmons and Blyth, 1987; Eccles et al., 1993) have convincingly documented declines in self-esteem, grade point average (GPA), and after-school participation, as well as increases in victimization and anonymity in the years after the transition to the middle grades. For the most part, the resilient children in my research group seemed to meet the challenges of their new school with success—so much success that I began to wonder if I could be missing something important. I knew from my interactions with students that some of them were struggling; I could see it in their demeanor and in their grades, even when they could not find the words to explain what they were feeling. Because so many other researchers found declines in certain areas across the transition, I wondered if numerical data, such as self-esteem scores, participation rates, and academic achievement, would support the qualitative results I have reported. In the next section, I will take up these questions.

PART III

The Emotional, Participatory, and Academic Realms of Students' Lives

Introduction

When I began this study, I hypothesized that children from Hillside and Two Rivers would have a harder time during the transition. So far, my findings do not demonstrate more difficult transition for Hillside-Two Rivers children, even though they had to adjust to more dramatic changes: they got up earlier, rode the bus longer, and attended school in a new town. What would pre- and post-transition assessments of self-esteem, participation in extracurricular activities, and academic status show? Research on self-esteem across the transition to the middle grades has yielded very mixed results (Seidman et al., 1994), but research has consistently shown a decline in extracurricular participation and, in schools with ability grouping, a decline in perceived academic competence in children from lower social class backgrounds (Simmons and Blyth, 1987). Students from both Lakeview and Hillside-Two Rivers arrived at the middle school as a well-matched group in terms of grades, participation, and peer relationships. At the end of the transition year, would these two groups continue to match each other in these important areas or would one group move ahead of the other?

In Part I, I proposed that the social and economic conditions of Lakeview and Hillside have resulted in some similar and some divergent values pertaining to the role and methods of schooling and the socialization of children. In Part II, I demonstrated how children, influenced by their early socialization and community values, anticipate seventh grade, interact with peers, and evaluate their school from different standpoints.

The following three chapters will examine self-esteem, participation, and academic standing across the transition. These three chapters are combined in one section because of the theoretical and empirical connections between self-esteem, participatory belonging, and academic competence. I wondered if outcomes in these three areas would be influenced by the students' susceptibility to social comparisons and to school structures like ability grouping and selective sports teams.

179

At the age of twelve or thirteen, there may not be words to describe the especially powerful, emotional dimensions of adolescent life. In these chapters, descriptive statistics are used to further extend our understanding of how the research participants experienced the transition. There is no intent to imply generalizability—the research cohort of only thirty students is too small to make inferences—but the numerical data add to our understanding of what these particular students experienced and these results often parallel results from much larger research cohorts.

CHAPTER 9

Peer, Home, and School Self-Esteem

"I Get Gothic When I Feel Rejected"

One wintry afternoon I met with Daria, Ethan, and Jeff after school to discuss my observations of that day. I was struck by Daria's appearance: she had twenty or so braids in her auburn hair, held together with multicolored elastics and beads and silver safety pins. She wore several necklaces, bracelets, and rings, a black T-shirt, sneakers and khaki pants with loads of pockets and safety pins all the way down one leg. She seemed brooding and distant, unlike the perky, talkative sixth grader I met a year ago.

I was trying to understand the Gothic[1] look and demeanor that she and some of her Lakeview peers had adopted that is so troubling to many teachers and parents. "I get Gothic when I feel rejected," Daria explained, "I go home and put on black nail polish and wear black clothes to school." I began to slowly repeat what she just said, "So you dress like this when you feel excluded, rejected . . ." she jumped in and said, "Abandoned." Abandoned. My heart pounded with the sudden rush of understanding she just handed me. Daria, who literally wore the pain she felt, and who, in seventh grade, sometimes appeared cynical and callous, told me that she and some of her peers felt abandoned.

Later, at my computer, I began to imagine all the ways some of today's children might feel abandoned: by teachers who fail to recognize and integrate the skills, interests, and resources of some of their students; by school board members who insist that administrators should suspend students from school for dressing like Daria rather than engage them in dialogue that would lead to better self-understanding about what that dress means; by parents with busy schedules and no time; by a social culture that sees adolescence as a problem and an economic culture that sees adolescence as a commercial commodity to be exploited; by communities that have allowed materialism to veer out of control and undermine values of compassion and moderation; by clergy who fail to find

181

ways to deliver relevant spiritual messages to youth; by professionals and policymakers who have allowed "get tough" rhetoric to drown out understanding and reason. There is a wide gap in the way many of us understand the pain, passion, struggle, and alienation in adolescent lives.

In early adolescence, children begin to be more aware of life's sadness, dishonesty, and hypocrisy. The Gothic subculture's fascination with sinister rituals, piercing and cutting skin, music about horror and death, and black clothing, lipstick, and nail polish, is an expression of internal pain and loss, a statement about a spiritual and relational void. It is a bold, shocking, visual expression of what life feels like to some adolescents: artificial, empty, and disconnected. Communities, schools, and parents that fail to listen and understand this sense of abandonment will witness the tragic results as more children vent their shame, grief, and rage on themselves and others.

In the sixth grade, Daria spoke passionately about her tight circle of best friends that had been together for years. She referred to her group as the "blood sister Mafia," and told me that they held séances and secret rituals, reminding me of Brown and Gilligan's (1992) claim that girls take their relational understanding and desire underground so that they might continue to have authentic relationships in the face of increased pressure to sacrifice authenticity and honesty for overly accommodating niceness. Although she never said so, I sensed that Daria was disappointed in her group of best friends in the seventh grade. She struggled to maintain a sense of connection with her peers and with her family and her sense of identity became fragile. This struggle was reflected in very low self-esteem scores. By the end of seventh grade, this girl who had approached the transition with so much hope and enthusiasm, decided not to return to the middle school and applied to a small independent school, instead. Another Lakeview girl—a single child from a family of substantial means—experienced tremendous anxiety about fitting in with her peers. This child suffered so much in the two years she was part of the study that she became suicidal. Fearing for her well-being, her alarmed parents decided to home-school her in the eighth grade.

Understanding the Emotional Life of the Self

Over the transition, most students became more articulate and sure of themselves, barely skipping a beat. Some of them made tremendous advances in their cognitive ability—evident in their increased self-understanding, analytic skill, and capacity to coordinate and integrate perspectives from a variety of sources. But a small group of students became more silent and seemed to slide precipitously, academically and socially, during this transitional year. When I asked, these students told me, "everything is fine," but I noted that these few had become unsure, made eye contact less often, spoke with a bit of cynicism, and seemed sad and detached. By the end of seventh grade caution, rather than enthusiasm, marked my interactions with a few of the research participants. The parents of four students, all from Lakeview, were so concerned by the decline they noticed in their children that they made plans to take them out of the middle school.

There were remarkable changes in some of the members of this research group between grades six and seven. They grew several inches, I no longer recognized the voices of some of the boys when they answered the phone, their sense of humor and timing became more refined, and peers became much more central to their daily lives. It's a lot to keep up with, socially and academically, and there is an emotional price to pay for not keeping up. As I probed further, looking for evidence of how students felt about themselves, I noticed something else: there was something going on in the interaction between gender and social class and success at school, much more complex than I had previously imagined, placing girls from higher income families and boys from lower income families at risk.

I remember in particular two Hillside boys, both of whom had experienced their parents' divorce and lived with their mothers. When I asked Jake where he would place himself on a ten-point scale compared to his peers in terms of affluence, he wrote 0. Jake was as nice as can be and he often took care of his three younger siblings while his mother worked hard on her baccalaureate degree and at her job as a waitress. Academically, Jake had done real well and his standardized test scores placed him in the 99th percentile nationally in all subjects, but in seventh grade, his grades began to go down. He had a quiet nature and small build—he was one of the shortest boys in the seventh grade—and these things, along with unspoken other issues that I suspect derived from his parents separation, took a toll on his self-esteem. Matt, on the other hand, was outgoing, popular, and came from a more affluent family than any of the other Hillside students. His grades were better than average. Matt often sat at the "popular" table—the only Hillside student to do so—but he was the boy who slid down in his seat and covered his head when I asked, "Is anyone from Hillside sitting at this table?" These boys and two Lakeview girls ended the seventh grade year with the lowest self-esteem scores in the entire research group.

Considering self-esteem, argued Harter (1990), is essential for understanding the "emotional life of the self." Early in adolescence, children begin to become aware of how peer groups are arranged and where they are located in this arrangement. Social comparison as the basis for assessing one's worth has long been an explanation for the formation of self-esteem (Rosenberg and Pearlin, 1978). I hypothesized that the transition to a more economically diverse middle school would intensify student's self-assessment based on social comparison. A central question in this research, then, is the extent to which children perceived and attempted to adapt to a "normative reference group," as suggested by Merton (1957), and how their perceptions and actions impacted social adjustment in the seventh grade.

Hare (1977) argued that individuals evaluate their self-worth by comparing themselves with significant others in a reference group of their own choosing (p. 142). Class and race are powerful factors in the developing child's sense of self, Hare argued, but he challenged the belief that lower-status children would base their sense of worth on successful entry to a monolithic, middle-class reference group. Rather, the formation of self-esteem involves the physical, temperamental, and social characteristics of the developing adolescent, and his or her understanding of what parents, peers, and teachers value. Good grades, going home after school to look after younger siblings, respectful behavior, athletic ability, material wealth, employment status, community involvement, being funny, dress and looks: these are things valued differently by different families and communities. Self-esteem reflects a person's self-assessment of how they are doing compared to others that matter, on the things most valued by the people that matter (Rosenberg, 1973).

Self-Esteem and Gender

School transition researchers have emphasized four areas of assessment: self-esteem, attitudes toward school, extracurricular participation, and intrinsic motivation. The first large project to assess these areas in this age group was a cross-sectional study in Baltimore where all 1,918 students transitioned to a junior high school in grade seven. The researchers found lower self-esteem in grade seven, particularly among girls (Simmons, Rosenberg, and Rosenberg, 1973).

Simmons and Blyth (1987) followed the Baltimore study with a longitudinal study to see if outcomes were stable across time. They compared outcomes for students who transitioned to a junior high school in grade seven with students who stayed in the same K–8 school to see if results could be attributed more to the effects of school transition than to the effects of age. They found that girls cared more about how they looked, were more dissatisfied about their looks, and were less pleased with their gender than boys (pp. 64–68). These results were consistent at all four waves—in grades six, seven, nine and ten. Using a modified version of the Rosenberg Self-Esteem Scale, they found that girls who transitioned to junior high schools showed a significant negative change in self-esteem, while boys' self-esteem went up slightly from grade six to grade seven. Notably, they found that girls who were perceived to be good looking reported that they were victimized less (p. 318) and girls who stayed after school for activities reported that they were victimized more (p. 323). Furthermore, the effects of transition affected girls over a long period of time; by tenth grade, self-esteem in girls who experienced a transition in the middle grades was still below self-esteem in girls who had not experienced a transition.

Simmons and Blyth argued that gender roles might be a factor in self-esteem:

> The findings just presented indicate considerable traditional gender role differentiation among adolescents in a large Midwestern city in the mid- to late-1970s: Girls rate themselves and their sex less highly than do boys; girls value appearance and same-sex popularity more; boys are allowed earlier independence and are expected by parents to act in older ways; girls view a job as a temporary activity to be halted when they have children; boys conform less to adult prescriptions related to school (p. 89).

When Simmons and Blyth studied the effects of social-economic status and gender on self-esteem during the school transition, they found mixed results that have recurred in other studies since then, including my own:

> For boys, high social class has a solely positive effect through an interesting causal route. Boys from a higher social class background are more likely to be well regarded by peers in grade seven and therefore to show higher self-esteem. For girls, findings are more complex. On the one hand there is a small, indirect linkage favoring higher-class girls. Girls from a higher social class are less likely to be involved in problem behavior in grade seven, and thereby, they improve their self-esteem. However, for some inexplicable reason, the direct relationship between social class and girls' grade seven self-esteem is negative, with girls of lower social class favored with high self-esteem. High social class is thus not a clear resource for girls (p. 318).

The authors failed to go further with this important finding, to posit that, although *high* social class status does not appear to benefit self-esteem in girls, *low social class across race does,* and although girls from lower social class backgrounds do not appear to be at risk of declining self-esteem, *white girls from higher social class backgrounds do appear to be at greater risk.* For a long time, researchers have been incredulous with findings like these and reluctant to attribute the losses in self-esteem for girls in high socioeconomic groups, and the gains in self-esteem for girls in low socioeconomic groups, to corresponding risks and protections of social class conditions. However, the ethnographic portraits of Lakeview and Hillside provide some evidence that community cultures provide a range of opportunities and barriers to developing adolescents. Growing up in Hillside appears to be protective of girls' self-esteem but not so for boys; growing up in Lakeview appears to support boys' self-esteem but not so for girls.

The work of Carol Gilligan and colleagues from Harvard University's Project on Women's Psychology and Girls' Development begins to explain what Simmons and Blyth found "inexplicable." A team of researchers conducted a longitudinal study involving nearly one hundred girls, most of whom were white and from middle-class and upper-middle-class families. Interviews with young girls, seven to eleven years old, were striking to the researchers for their bold, clear, communication, and drive toward meaningful and honest connection, even in the midst of conflict with peers and adults. Annie Rogers (1993) characterized this resilience in young girls as evidence of strength, courage, and healthy resistance to prescribed societal gender roles. However, as girls entered early adolescence, around age eleven and twelve, researchers found a remarkable shift in the way these previously articulate girls communicated: they became more unsure, off-balance, seeming to weigh their words and their actions carefully (Brown and Gilligan, 1992). Girls read cultural and relational cues perceptively and accurately, these authors argued. As girls become more aware of societal expectations for how they should speak and behave, they begin to understand that speaking freely, boldly, and honestly could mean losing friends and approval. They become more reticent and learn to communicate in more indirect and coded ways. It is at this critical juncture in early adolescence, that girls reach a "relational impasse or crisis of connection": they risk losing authentic connection in their effort to maintain connection (p. 7).

However, some girls seem more resistant to gendered societal messages. Beverly Smith (1991) showed that some African American girls and girls from low-income families are "raised as resisters" and enter adolescence with strong self-concepts. These girls, and the home and community cultures that surround them, place value on bold, up-front communication. They are encouraged to resist the stereotypes, material-ism, and competition that are part of a status-driven culture. These girls, argued Smith, are more likely to maintain meaningful relational con-nections, even in the midst of conflict, throughout adolescence.

Boys are also at great risk of losing their sense of self. In *Lost Boys: Why Our Sons Turn Violent and How We Can Save Them,* James Garbarino (1999) described boys as especially vulnerable to depression and shame because of damaging cultural messages about masculinity. He argued, ". . . boys experiences of abandonment combine with the cultural mes-sages he receives about masculinity, messages that devalue the direct ex-pression of feelings and emphasize the necessity of burying feelings, particularly feelings of emotional connection, vulnerability, and softness" (p. 43). These cultural messages have a pervasive but less-acknowledged influence on self-esteem in boys.

Research on Self-Esteem Produces Mixed Results

Several teams of researchers failed to find a decline in self-esteem after the seventh grade transition. Thornburg and Jones (1982) found a decline in self-esteem when students made the transition in sixth grade, but not when they made the transition in grade seven, and they found no difference in self-esteem between seventh graders in K–12 schools and seventh graders in junior high schools. Nottelmann (1987) found that students who experienced a school transition felt a *higher* level of general competence than students who did not change schools in the middle grades. Petersen and Crockett (1985) found that perceptions of peer relationships improved even as body image and perceptions of family relations declined. Greene (1985) found no difference in self-esteem in transition and non-transition students. Larson (1983) studied children who transition in grade six and found that even though sixth graders in K–8 schools showed more of an increase in self-esteem than sixth graders in middle schools, the scores evened out by the end of eighth grade. The sixth graders in Larson's study, like the seventh graders in my study, said that they preferred their middle school to re-maining in their elementary school.

One of the few rural studies was conducted by Youngman (1978) in England, who noted that the wide difference in findings was due to the type of school, the geographic location of the school (urban, rural, sub-urban), and the initial characteristics of the children in the study. Like Simmons and Blyth (op. cit.), Youngman found that children with poor self-concept and children who are disenchanted with school before transition, are at much higher risk of continuing a downward spiral after the transition.

Measuring Self-Esteem

Using a self-esteem measure along with interviews and observations would indicate if students with low or high self-esteem shared common characteristics. The thirty research participants were a well-matched group: all had a C or better average, their families had been in the area for at least two years, they were generally accepted by their peers, and none of them had discipline referrals in the sixth grade. Sixteen students were from Lakeview, fourteen were from Hillside; there were fifteen boys and fifteen girls. Although I had not initially intended to ask the students about divorce, so many of them brought it up as an important experience that I decided to include it in the analysis. Fifty percent of the students from each community had experienced family disruption due to divorce.

Rosenberg and Pearlin (1978) insisted on a contextualized examination of self-esteem in their own groundbreaking self-esteem work:

> If social science is to go beyond the level of description, it is imperative to understand how a demographic variable enters the individual's life, is converted into interpersonal experiences, is processed by a particular cognitive structure, and reflects the individual's relationship to his environment (p. 72).

Heeding this advice, the remaining pages of this chapter report on how demographic variables (social class, gender, town of residence, and divorce experience) influenced self-esteem when students transitioned from grade six to grade seven and the results are understood within the multiple contexts of students' lives. The Hare General and Area Specific Self-Esteem Scale was administered to the thirty research participants who met in small groups in the spring of sixth grade (April), and in the fall (October) and spring (April) of seventh grade; therefore, each data collection point was five to six months apart.[2] The measure has thirty questions, ten in each of the self-esteem areas (peer, home, and school). Students read statements such as these: "People my age often pick on me," "Other people wish they were like me," "No one pays much attention to me at home," "I am an important person to my family," "I am usually proud of my report card," "My teachers are usually happy with the kind of work I do." Then they circled the way they felt about the statement on a four-point scale, from strongly disagree to strongly agree. Each self-esteem area can earn a total of 40 points for an overall total of 120 points.

Large research studies using the Hare measure show average total scores of 90 in the general population of adolescents and average scores of 28–32 in each of the subscales (Hare, 1984). When I have used this same measure to assess self-esteem in high-risk groups, I find general scores to be in the 70 to 80 range, with much wider variation in scores in each of the subscales.

The findings reported in the following sections are based on average scores, at three points in time, seldom exceeding the standard of error of measurement. (See Appendix 5 for a chart of all self-esteem means and standard errors of measurement reported in this chapter.) Since a number of studies have shown a significant decline in self-esteem after the transition to middle school, reporting no change in the group as a whole is worth reporting. However, it is important to remember that the research participants were selected using criteria that excluded sixth grade students who were already struggling academically, socially, or behaviorally. In the research group, we would expect to see self-esteem scores higher than in the general population.

The results reported in the following sections are based on such small numbers that they have meaning only when interpreted in the context of this work as a whole. If these findings are compelling, it is because they illuminate the story of Daria told at the beginning of this chapter, the story of the painful rivalry between Arianna and Alexeia told in chapter 10, and the story of Allen, a talented student and athlete, who became more and more unsure of himself in an accelerated math class, told in chapter 11. The self-esteem scores by themselves do not and should not stand as evidence apart from the qualitative findings.

Self-esteem is a fluctuating phenomena and a controversial and ill-defined concept. Exploring the emotional world of research participants is treacherous and tricky business—even more so when the research participants are twelve- and thirteen-year-old children. Students were reticent about emotional issues for many good reasons: they did not have the words yet to describe their inner-experience, they were self-protective in disclosing psychological information, or they did not want me to see that perhaps everything was not okay. Likewise, I was cautious. When students signaled me that they did not want to explore emotional issues, I most often did not challenge this self-protective and developmentally necessary stance. Hurtful disclosures, elicited for research in the context of a trusting relationship that could sometimes feel like counseling, could become an emotional crisis.

Stable High General Self-Esteem

When self-esteem was compared in the whole group from Lakeview with the whole group from Hillside, there were only slight differences, indicating that social class, by itself, did not play an important role in determining self-esteem in this group. It was when I looked at self-esteem by town and by gender together that I began to discern distinctions in the results: boys from Hillside and girls from Lakeview ended the year with self-esteem scores that were below the group average and, conversely, girls from Hillside and boys from Lakeview ended the year with scores that were above the group average. When these results were examined with the added factor of divorce experience, the possible reason for lower scores for Hillside boys became clearer. Boys from lower income families who had experienced their parents divorce had low and declining self-esteem scores. In the following paragraphs, I discuss each of these findings in more detail.

In the group as a whole, general self-esteem was stable across time, gaining a little at time 2 (fall of grade 7) and losing a little at time 3 (spring of grade 7). As we see in Figure 9.1, for Lakeview students, the increase in general self-esteem in the fall was minimal, from an average score of 95 to an average score of 95.91 on a 120-point scale. Hillside stu-

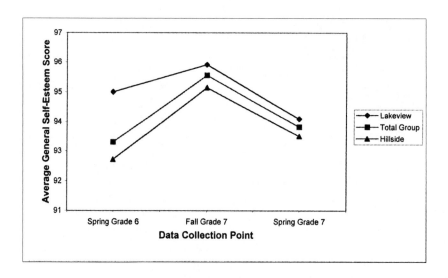

Figure 9.1. General Self-Esteem for Lakeview and Hillside Groups

dents scored a bit lower than Lakeview students in general self-esteem at the end of grade six (92.71) but gained more in the fall of grade seven (95.14), virtually matching their Lakeview peers. At the end of seventh grade, scores went down for both Lakeview and Hillside students; Lakeview students ended the school year with general self-esteem scores slightly below the sixth grade level (94.09) and Hillside students ended the school year with general self-esteem slightly above the sixth grade level (93.50).

Home, School, and Peer Self-Esteem

Looking at self-esteem in the peer, home, and school domains, there are interesting and distinct trends. Throughout the transition year, Lakeview and Hillside students had high, stable home self-esteem, with scores for Hillside edging slightly above scores for Lakeview. School self-esteem started out the same in both towns. There was a rise in school self-esteem in the fall of grade seven, especially for Hillside students. However, by the end of grade seven, school self-esteem in each town was just slightly *below* the pre-transition score. The rise in school self-esteem in the fall of grade seven might be attributed to the fact that there was a good deal of effort on the part of teachers, parents, and students to facilitate the transition process right through the first couple of months at school. For example, at the beginning of the school year, all seventh graders went on an overnight trip with their team (an annual tradition). This small boost in school self-esteem was reflected in the feelings of relief and competence expressed by many students, especially those from Hillside.

Peer self-esteem was lower than home and school self-esteem and it is here that we see the biggest difference between the towns. Hillside students have scores below those of Lakeview at all three data collection points, but in Hillside, peer self-esteem increased, and in Lakeview it stayed the same. These changes are illustrated in Figure 9.2.

Lakeview scores in each domain showed only small changes from time to time; however, there were two notable changes in the Hillside scores. First, school self-esteem at time 2 increased from 31 (on a 40-point-scale) to 32.46. By time 3, however, school self-esteem showed a sharper decrease in Hillside than in Lakeview, going from 32.46 in the fall of grade seven to 30.64 in the spring of grade seven. Even with this decrease, at the end of the year, Hillside school self-esteem was a little above school self-esteem in Lakeview.

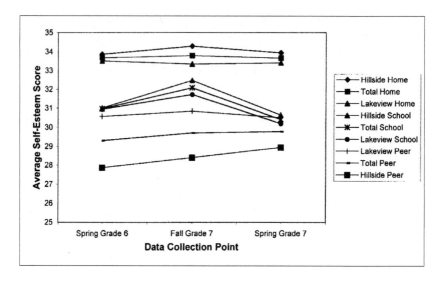

Figure 9.2. Peer, Home, and School Self-Esteem by Town

Counter to my expectations, Hillside students showed overall positive changes in self-esteem across the transition, finishing out the seventh grade with general self-esteem scores higher than at the end of grade six. In the fall of seventh grade, school self-esteem increased for both groups, but nearly twice as much for Hillside students, and general self-esteem increased for both groups, but nearly three times as much for Hillside students.

Individual Losses and Gains

It is important to know if average scores were a result of similar individual scores spread across a whole group of children or if a small number of children had big losses or gains. So, I looked at self-esteem in high, middle, and low social status groups and at the scores of each individual in those groups. Most individual scores were stable, fluctuating less than 10 points on the 120-point scale across time. In all three social class groups, home self-esteem was consistently the highest and most stable score; school and peer scores were more varied. This finding is consistent with my observations from thirty years of work with families across the social class spectrum: social class background does not determine how children feel about themselves at home. This finding also indicates that what happens at school and in the peer group really matters. The biggest individual losses across the transition were in the middle and high social status groups and the biggest individual gains were seen in the low social status group.

In general, the nine children in the highest socioeconomic group, all from Lakeview, had the most stable general self-esteem across time, but one boy and one girl lost 15 and 17 points in, respectively, peer and school self-esteem, between time 1 and time 3. A higher percentage of students from this high social class group had peer and school scores equal to or above 30, at all three waves.

The middle socioeconomic group had thirteen students—five from Lakeview and eight from Hillside. Interestingly, this middle group had lower peer scores than the other two groups. Peer self-esteem is connected to perceptions of popularity (Simmons and Blyth, op. cit.), and I learned from my research participants that popularity is connected, in part, to looking good and having nice things. The children in the middle group may value some of the same things their more affluent peers value, such as clothing from popular, expensive stores, but may be less capable of having those things. The experience of not being able to attain something that has high value may negatively influence self-esteem. One boy from Lakeview gained 11 points and a boy from Hillside lost 21 points—most of it reflected in a decline in home self-esteem.

In the low socioeconomic group there were six from Hillside and two from Lakeview. This group had the highest percentage of students with school self-esteem equal to or above 30, in the fall of seventh grade, but by the spring of seventh grade, this group had the lowest percentage of students with school self-esteem equal to or above 30. A Hillside girl and a Hillside boy each went up 14 points in school and peer self-esteem combined; another Hillside girl lost 12 points and this loss was mostly reflected in school self-esteem.

Gender Differences by Town in General Self-Esteem

Simmons and Blyth (op. cit.) demonstrated that social class background, by itself, does not appear to account for the losses and gains in self-esteem, but social class and gender together do. When we turn our attention to gender and view Figure 9.3, we see that, overall, Lakeview boys had stable, high general self-esteem across time (94.88, 95.44, 95.25). The three other groups, however, show surprising trends. Hillside boys had lower general scores at all three waves (91.43, 93.64, 91.71) and

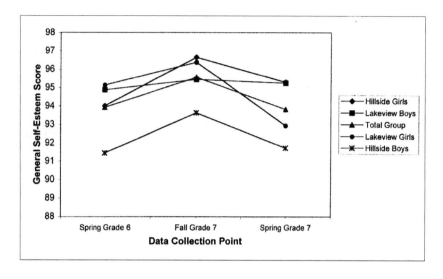

Figure 9.3. General Self-Esteem by Town and Gender

in all three domains. Lakeview girls had the highest general self-esteem in the spring of sixth grade (95.13), and their scores increased in the fall of seventh grade (96.38). However, by the spring of seventh grade, Lakeview girls showed a sharper decline than any other group (92.94), and ended the year below Hillside girls and Lakeview boys, and just above Hillside boys. On the other hand, Hillside girls started the sixth grade with total self-esteem scores lower than Lakeview girls and boys but finished the year with an average score equivalent to that of Lakeview boys—more than 2 points higher than Lakeview girls and more than 3 points higher than Hillside boys (94.00, 96.64, 95.29). Lakeview boys varied the least from time to time, while Lakeview girls varied the most.

On a 120-point scale and in such a small study group, a 2 or 3-point difference should be interpreted cautiously. However, observations and interviews with students and their parents alerted me that these changes were real and should not go unnoticed. They were possible warnings of a negative trajectory, particularly for Lakeview girls and Hillside boys. Recall that Simmons and Blyth (op. cit.) also documented a decline for girls from middle and high social class backgrounds, but no decline for girls from low social class backgrounds. They also documented stable, high self-esteem in boys from middle and high social class backgrounds. But what about the pattern of lower self-esteem in Hillside boys?

Divorce Experience and Boys' General Self-Esteem

As I met with students over the course of nearly two years, I became more familiar with their lives in and out of school. The salience of family disruption began to emerge as a key theme, especially for boys. Fifty percent of the students in both communities had experienced major family disruption due to divorce at some point in their lives; for two of them, the divorce of their parents had been recent. Some of the students had good relationships with their non-custodial parent—fathers in every case but one—but the divorce of their parents seemed to weigh heavily, nonetheless. Some had little or no contact with their non-custodial parent.

The effects of family disruption and divorce were evident in written answers to the question, "What experiences in your life make you who you are today?" Eight students referred to the impact of family disruption, sometimes using vivid language: "Watching my family hurt/torn apart," was one response.

Self-esteem was dramatically affected by divorce experience for boys, but not for girls, in both communities. In fact, it is this experience that seemed to close the gap in general self-esteem for boys from Hillside and boys from Lakeview (four from Hillside, three from Lakeview). Figure 9.4 shows an astonishing difference in general self-esteem at time 1 and at time 3 in boys who had experienced divorce and the effect is even greater for Hillside students.

Hillside and Lakeview boys who had experienced divorce had similar, below-average self-esteem scores at the end of sixth grade. By the end of seventh grade, however, these scores declined, and even more so for Hillside students. In both towns, a total of seven boys out of fifteen had experienced divorce. *None* of them had general self-esteem scores at any point in time that matched or exceeded the average scores of all boys from their town. Significantly, Hillside boys, who had not experienced divorce, ended their seventh grade year with *higher* self-esteem than Lakeview boys who had not experienced divorce. It is the experience of divorce, therefore, that seems to make the most difference to self-esteem in boys. Boys who had experienced divorce had lower self-esteem scores in all three domains, but interestingly, scores were lower in the peer and school domains than in the home domain. Comparing general self-esteem for boys with and without divorce experience: a 13-point gap at the end of sixth grade became a 25-point gap by the end of seventh grade for Hillside boys. Lakeview boys maintained a 15-point gap at both data collection points.

Divorce often means greater financial struggle for the custodial parent and their children. Boys may be less protected from feeling undue responsibility for their families than girls, particularly with regard to

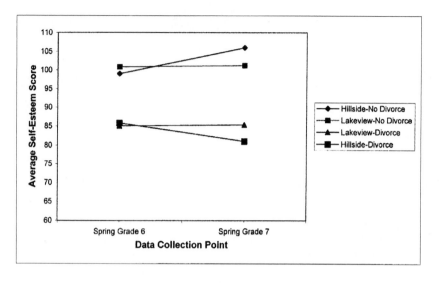

Figure 9.4. Boys' General Self-Esteem by Town and Divorce Experience

financial and practical matters and this may be particularly true for boys who are living in families with less means. It is plausible to suggest that boys' sense of responsibility along with the reality that they have limited resources and abilities to "fill a man's shoes" is a harsh set-up leading to frustration and lower self-esteem. It may be particularly at this time of life that boys feel sadder about the absence of their fathers. Add this to the reality that adolescent boys are less inclined (and often less encouraged) to talk about their sadness and feelings of loss, and the distressing results are seen in plummeting self-esteem.

Pathways to Self-Esteem

Although there are only thirty students in this study, other researchers with much larger samples documented similar findings, especially with regard to self-esteem and gender and social class. Several points are particularly relevant to this study in light of what we know about the cultural contexts of the lives of the research participants.

First, looking at average scores, home self-esteem is the highest and most stable of all three domains, at all three waves, in both communities. Home and school self-esteem are virtually the same for children from both communities. Peer self-esteem is slightly higher in Lakeview but peer self-esteem improved over the transition to seventh grade for Hillside students and stayed the same for Lakeview students. School self-esteem improved in the fall of grade seven, and then declined by the end of grade seven in both communities, to just below the sixth grade mean. I found what Simmons and Blyth (op. cit.) found: one of the most significant predictors of seventh grade self-esteem was sixth grade self-esteem.

Second, by the end of grade seven, girls from Hillside and boys from Lakeview had the highest general self-esteem, while Hillside boys and Lakeview girls had the lowest self-esteem. Boys who had experienced the divorce of their parents obtained the lowest self-esteem scores. Although the sample from which this information was obtained is very small—only seven boys—the difference in self-esteem between boys who had experienced divorce and those who had not is so large that it warrants a closer look by researchers and by practitioners.

School self-esteem showed the greatest overall change, especially in Hillside. Researchers working with much larger study samples of students from low-income communities have also found that school plays a critical role in how students feel about themselves (Seidman et. al., 1994; Willie, 1994). The good news here is that findings like these give support to the idea that schools can have a consequential impact on the lives of low-income children. Good schools can and do have a positive effect in the lives of students, *especially* in the lives of students from low social class backgrounds.

A pathway for high self-esteem in boys from all social class backgrounds appears to be family stability and a sense of congruity across the home and school domains. A pathway for high self-esteem in girls appears to be entering adolescence in the community environment that emphasizes connection and belonging through altruism and de-emphasizes physical appearances and social status. Hillside girls continued to be involved by volunteering in their communities and by playing helpful roles in their families. These contributions made by girls from working class families were encouraged and recognized. Altruism and being yourself without pretense are values that are encouraged in the way many children grow up in Hillside and these values were protective of girls' self-esteem.

The Ascendancy of Peer Relationships

Understanding community values with regard to education, social interactions, political power, and future goals provides a structure for understanding adolescent self-esteem. In the seventh grade, children are not only adjusting to a new school, they are adjusting to many other role changes and physical changes associated with puberty, as Simmons and Blyth (op. cit.) point out. Some of these changes set the emerging identity of the young adolescent and home values at odds with each other. It is, at the very least, a time of questioning and internal tension as children make the enormous shift of focus away from home toward peers and the public world. It is an accomplishment worth noting when self-esteem remains stable at this time.

Anyone who knows twelve- and thirteen-year-old children understands Mr. Jordan's counsel the night of the middle school open house for parents: "I hope you have a sense of humor, 'cause you're going to need it. Things are going to get very interesting." It is just at this time of life that children begin to differentiate their parents' values from the values of their friends' parents, and their own values from their peers' values. Many adolescents begin to get a gnawing feeling that no one in their family is like them or understands them. Rules, family customs, what gets put on the supper table, and everyday ways of doing things, suddenly seem strange, even ridiculous. *Peers* are the ones who understand what is important: music, fashion, communication styles, and that hallmark early adolescent sense of humor.

It is at this age when children begin to talk about a small army of other students as friends whom parents have never met or even heard of before. And, from these friends, they learn about new fashions, new privileges and responsibilities that they want to try out, and new ways of looking at the world. It is likely that the early adolescent pleas, "But, Mary can wear . . ." or "But, John's mother lets him . . ." are refrains heard in virtually every household that has occupants between the ages of ten and fifteen.

The Relationship Between Home and School Values and Goals

The process of identity development during adolescence requires that children extend themselves beyond the family system toward their peer and school communities. However, what goes on at home matters tremendously during this time of life. Seeley, Sim, and Loosley (1956) found in Crestwood Heights that high-status families actively monitored their child's experience at school and in the community because they felt much was at stake, namely, their child's future education and career options. In my conversations with Lakeview parents, I frequently heard the perception that the future will not take care of itself. Rather, future outcomes depend on careful planning, an appropriately cooperative and capable child, and intervening when necessary. Early adolescents are very savvy to the goals, values, and expectations held by their parents. In fact, they pick up from their parents and teachers, with amazing accuracy, subtle signs of hope, expectation, disappointment, or pleasure.

And some of the signs were not so subtle. By the seventh grade, most children from Lakeview and a few children from Hillside were very much aware of the selection process for competitive sports teams and eighth grade algebra. The consensus of values between home and school appeared to be directly related to self-esteem in children—positive self-esteem for children who succeeded in attaining what their families viewed as important and negative self-esteem for children who failed to attain what their families viewed as important.

Parents from both communities were unanimous in their desire for their child's future happiness and success, a college education, good grades, peer acceptance, and a secure job, but there were differences in how parents were able to be involved in helping their children secure these things. Some parents were active on school committees, or they coached a team, or volunteered on school trips. Other parents had work schedules that prevented them from attending meetings and school events. Some parents had educational backgrounds that allowed them to help their children with homework; others didn't have that privilege. Parents with college degrees had some knowledge about how to navigate the maze toward higher education; for others, this pathway remained a mystery.

As Seeley et al. (1956) argued, there is likely to be a convergence of values, goals, and knowledge between schools and middle class families. The focus on future life goals and the emphasis on academic, athletic, and social success through a competitive process are aims that middle-class and upper-middle-class families are likely to value, that schools are likely to accommodate, and upon which children are likely to base their self-evaluation.

When there was high home value and high parental action to influence an outcome at school, such as being selected for a sports team, getting a part in a play, or being chosen for a leadership position, I found that students and their parents endured devastating disappointment when the outcome was not in their favor. Although, intuitively, it seems a good thing when parents, schools, and students value the same things, parents and educators must be aware of the possibility that too much of a good thing could mean colluding with rigid goals that could be counterproductive to a child's sense of competence, motivation, and self-esteem.

Hillside students and their parents did not place as much importance on being selected for special positions. This appears protective to students' self-esteem, giving them a little more flexibility in responding to unfavorable circumstances. For example, I heard Hillside students respond to disappointment like this: "I really wanted to get on the basketball team, but didn't get picked, so I'll play on the town team instead," "I didn't get the class I wanted with all my friends, but this way I'll make new friends," "I didn't get into eighth grade algebra, but maybe I didn't need the extra stress anyway."

This resilient manner in dealing with disappointment was an adaptive strategy that worked well for the students that exercised it. Still, educators and parents must consider if missed opportunities might have harmful long-term results. It *does* matter whether or not someone gets into eighth grade algebra, or plays on a sports team, or is chosen for a special position. There is danger if it matters so much as to become a source of anxiety about one's competence and worth, and there is danger if it does not matter enough. Clearly, children who feel they are incapable of achieving what is valued by people that matter—whether that means getting honor roll grades, being selected for a sports team, or playing an important role at home—may show declines in self-esteem. Rosenberg (1973) explained:

> In the long run, then, we would expect most people to value those things at which they are good, and try to become good at those things they value. They may still consider themselves poor at those things which to them are unimportant, but this is likely to have little effect on their global self-esteem" (pp. 250–251).

Students evaluate themselves and their options differently, and community culture, family values, opportunities at school, and individual temperament combine to pose both risks and protections to self-esteem in developing adolescents.

Conclusion

The transition to middle school is a formidable task. For the students in this research group, the process was well supported by parents, teachers, and administrators. Hillside students approached the transition with more uncertainty than did their Lakeview peers. Some of them were aware that Hillside Elementary School was among the schools in the state with the lowest standardized test scores and they wondered if they would be prepared for seventh grade work. Many of them were unfamiliar with the Lakeview community and, although they enthusiastically anticipated making new friends, they worried that they might fail at this important task. They arrived at the middle school and many of them found themselves to be up to the challenge and thriving, giving them a sense of competence reflected in higher self-esteem scores. Lakeview students, whose elementary school is a few hundred yards from the middle school, were not faced with quite as much change and, perhaps, did not perceive the transition to be as challenging as did their Hillside peers. The risk of failure did not loom as large and, therefore, mastering their new environment was, perhaps, not as affirming.

Lakeview girls who struggle with their self-image and boys who had experienced divorce need support during this time to prevent potential long-term losses. School and community programs to help children maintain their sense of self during the transition are warranted.

Good self-esteem, though desirable and influential, will not promote favorable lifelong outcomes by itself. That takes equitable access to future educational opportunities and a secure sense of belonging to school and town communities. Participation in after school activities is one way that children and their families feel more a part of their school community. The next two chapters will look at equity and access with regard to extracurricular activities and higher-level academic groups.

CHAPTER 10

Extracurricular Participation

Benefits of Extracurricular Participation

Students named a variety of reasons for valuing participation in activities and no one summed it up better than Will. In his answer to the question, "If you are active in sports or clubs, what is it about these activities that you enjoy?" he wrote, "The exercise, the fun, the thinking, the friend activities, the excitement, the challenge, the wins, the losses (both teach you many things), the feeling you are good at it!" With philosophical flair, Will covers a lot of the benefits to participation cited by researchers. Participation in school activities requires, as Will points out, thought, social interaction, and an ability to accept both success and failure. In my interviews, I also learned that when good cross-town friendships were formed they were almost always initiated in after-school activities.

Researchers have examined the connections between extracurricular participation and self-esteem, student identification with the school, and academic performance. School and community activities potentially provide students with different ways of interacting with their peers, opportunities to excel in diverse arenas, avenues for contributing to the life of the school, and relationships with a coach or faculty advisor. Simmons and Blyth (1987) argued that participation in sports and other activities helped students feel recognized and integrated into peer and community networks: "Extracurricular participation can be regarded not only as an index of the students' integration into peer society, but also as an index of integration into activities approved of by adults in the larger culture" (p. 239).

Using the large national data set, High School and Beyond, Marsh (1992) found that extracurricular participation was,

... favorably associated with (in order of the size of effect) social self-concept, academic self-concept, taking advanced courses, time spent on homework, post-secondary educational aspirations, GPA, parental involvement, absenteeism, senior year educational aspirations, being in the academic track, college attendance, parental aspirations, and senior occupational aspirations (p. 557).

Coladarci and Cobb (1996) were not able to reproduce the positive effects reported by Marsh, and found instead that, "higher achieving students tended to participate in more extracurricular activities than did lower achieving students" (p. 97). Yet they did find a correlation between participation and social self-esteem, and concluded that, "the enhanced self-esteem that students appear to derive from extracurricular participation, while small, is a psychologically important effect and should not be taken lightly by educators or policy-makers" (p. 100).

By high school, students have been selected out of certain activities, or they select themselves out to make room in their lives for jobs, friends, more down time, and other interests. The relationship between extracurricular participation and social self-esteem suggests that school policies that deny some students opportunities to participate in after-school activities because of grades or in-school behavior may be denying those students a way toward a better connection with their peers and a sense of belonging to the school community.

Participation in extracurricular activities started out evenly among all sixth grade research participants, but after the transition to grade seven, participation went down in both communities, more so in Hillside-Two Rivers. Simmons and Blyth and their colleagues (1978, 1979, 1987) found that middle school students had higher levels of anonymity and lower levels of participation in school activities in grade seven; participation dropped more for girls than for boys. By comparison, extracurricular participation went *up* in grade seven in the K–8 schools they studied. Furthermore, K–8 students had a higher participation rate when they transitioned to high school than their classmates who went to junior high schools.

The potential increase in feelings of anonymity is a real threat to some students who must transition to middle school. Participation in extracurricular activities can offset this sense of disconnection. Future educational and career opportunities may be enhanced by active participation, and school activities are an avenue for greater parental involvement. These possible benefits, alongside the potential negative outcomes of alienation from school, suggest that it is wise to maintain an accessible extracurricular program, especially in regional, rural districts.

The Participation-Identification Model

In his research on dropping out of school, Finn (1989) suggested the "participation-identification" model as a way to understand how children bond with the school, and the developmental process that leads to successful or unsuccessful completion of secondary school (p. 118). Finn argued that alienation from school is a process that starts in the early grades triggered by a lack of opportunity for the child to become integrated and invested in the school community. "The failure of a youngster to participate in school and class activities, or to develop a sense of identification with school, may have significant deleterious consequences," he asserted (p. 117). Finn links school participation with positive self-image, success at school, and a sense of wholeness across domains. Participation leads to an emotional connection with the school that serves as an asset when problems arise, suggested Finn:

> . . . without a consistent pattern of participation in school activities, and possibly without the reinforcement provided by academic success experiences, it is unlikely that the youngster will come to identify with school. The emotional ingredient needed to . . . overcome the occasional adversity, is then lacking (p. 131).

Finn (ibid.) proposed four levels of participation: level 1 participation refers to the student's ability to be attentive and prepared in class, level 2 refers to engagement and participation in class beyond what is required, level 3 has to do with involvement in the broader school context by participating in extracurricular activities and by taking more responsibility in school (i.e., running errands, reading announcements during break), and level 4 refers to having a say in the governance of the school through committee membership (pp. 128–129). Engagement at some level is a necessary prerequisite to dropout prevention (p. 132), and each level of engagement fortifies the possibility of engagement at the next level. All but one student in this study participated at level 3 in the sixth grade, and a few of them, at level 4.

Dropout prevention is an important issue for schools in this state where a recent study reported cumulative dropout rates averaging 25% with a range of 0 to 50%[1]. This should be of particular interest at the middle school level, where Finn says the decision to drop out is made. Mountainview Regional School District does not keep dropout records by town, but researchers have found that low socioeconomic status is highly correlated with dropping out of school (Rumberger, 1987; Wehlage and Rutter, 1986). Over and over again, school transition research has found low-income boys to be particularly at risk of feeling alienated from their new school. The self-esteem scores reported for Hillside boys in the previous chapter are consistent with this concern.

Finn's analysis presents school identification-participation as an internal state—a sense of belonging and valuing—and he does not address the structural, social, economic, and historical external forces influencing a child's sense of attachment to school. I believe that the child's involvement and attachment to school is a function of the child's predisposition and interests *and* of the school's ability to welcome and integrate children of diverse abilities and resources. So, the central questions of this chapter are: Who participates in extracurricular activities and who does not? Does the middle school provide a culture of participation and an environment where student involvement and leadership are sustained and strengthened? Are some students more likely than others to benefit from school identification-participation?

"A Set-Up Like This Makes It Prone to Division"

A feeling of disconnection or lack of positive identification with school and peers is a concern that recent research on school violence has made all the more urgent (Garbarino and deLara, 2002). Despite broad consensus among researchers, parents, students, and educators concerning the social benefits of participation, there is disagreement about whether it is the school's responsibility to provide equity in after-school activities. An article in the local newspaper published January 26, 2000 argued that while participating in activities helped to integrate students from different communities, it might be especially hard for students from outlying communities to participate:

> Students from outlying towns probably often do decide that participation in extracurricular activities will be too tiring or pose too many difficulties from sheer distance. But taking part in what the school has to offer and thereby mixing in with other kids is one way to combat the bane of adolescence—cliques. Every school has cliques, not just regional ones, but a set up like [regional school district] makes it prone to division. The delineations are there in black and white—"I get off a bus and you don't." (Allyn, 2000)

Allyn claimed that busing, in itself, divides students, and that students from outlying towns may choose not to be in activities because of the added toll it would take. Allyn's contention with busing has not been fully examined through research; however, Howley (2000) argued that busing rural students to regional schools has a social cost to families and students, and some pay a higher price than others, ". . . in the form of increased private transportation costs, lost sleep, lost family time, and so forth" (p. 57). He recommends a research agenda that evaluates the benefits and losses of rural busing to students and families.

For many years, people in outlying towns have questioned whether the gains of long-distance busing outweigh the losses in a regional school district. Gains such as a wider range of academic opportunities, better facilities, more after-school activities, and exposure to greater diversity in the student body provide substantial benefits to students from *all* communities. However, increased transportation costs, loss of sleep, less family time, tensions between towns, and, perhaps, an increased sense of alienation and anonymity for students and parents unable to be involved in school activities, exact a price that some feel may offset the benefits. In 1976, as the number of regional school districts began to increase at a steady pace, a U.S. Department of Health, Education, and Welfare report authored by Sher and Tompkins stated that arguments in favor of regional schools based on economy, efficiency, and equality are mostly wrong. But by the middle of seventh grade, most of the Hillside participants in this study and their parents believed that the diversity and expanded opportunities at the middle school were worth the price. Only one of the students wished she had stayed at Hillside Elementary School for seventh grade. However, there may be other children from outlying towns, with fewer social, familial, or economic resources, who may not be able to access these benefits and may be disadvantaged by the multitown arrangement.

Students Value Extracurricular Activities

The students involved in this study from both communities were active in town and school activities and they valued their participation for a variety of reasons. When the active students in this study were asked, "What is it about these activities that you enjoy?" answers reflected a wide range of benefits to students. Some students appreciated sports as an avenue for health and vitality. For example, Isabelle said, "I enjoy getting the exercise after school." Dez liked to "stay healthy" and Matt felt good about "the strength it takes" to be in sports. Many other students reported that they liked after-school activities because of the "excitement," the "fun," and the opportunity to do something they loved to do. The social aspects of participation—friendship, teamwork, and connection with others—were very important to students. Nearly half of the students noted that they participated in activities because they liked, "working with people," "being with friends," "bonding with teammates," and "being in groups." Frank from Hillside said that football gave him a chance to, "hang around with my friends from my home town." Three other students, all from Hillside-Two Rivers, remarked that opportunities to meet new people and be with students from *other* towns was something they enjoyed about after-school activities.

Students also articulated the gratification of feeling competent at something that takes hard work to accomplish. A number of students said they liked to do activities that they were good at, and others went a step further to describe the internal satisfaction of feeling competent:

> I like to feel I've accomplished something when I come home from practice or a game and sports give me that feeling (Zoe);

> In field hockey, I love the sport, it makes me feel on top of the world, especially when I help my team (Becka);

> In cheerleading, I get to show off my flexibility (Alexeia).

After-school activities can be a way for students to discover talents, indulge passions, and explore possible future options. Students from both communities made a connection between extracurricular activities and vocational and academic goals. Christine said, "I want to become a singer, that's why I do chorus." Analysa took the baby-sitting course because she likes children. And Amber joined the International Languages Club to learn more about Spanish and French culture.

For some students, activities seemed to be a valuable emotional outlet. Zoe said that being in drama, "gives me a chance to not act like myself." Dez, a very accomplished cross-country skier, reported that the sport gave him a chance to ". . . let off steam if I'm mad," and the very reasonable and kind Ethan said that he likes dodgeball because, "I like to make people who annoy me my targets."

Many answers were similar across town and gender, but a few variations may reflect the differences in town cultures. For example, four Lakeview students and none of the Hillside-Two Rivers students named competition and winning as important. Three students from Hillside valued their connection to a church activity for its spiritual benefit to them. More Lakeview students linked extracurricular activities to future goals but more Hillside-Two Rivers students appreciated outlets for altruistic feelings. Five students from Hillside-Two Rivers and only one from Lakeview mentioned the importance of community service and mentoring opportunities. Hillside-Two Rivers students explained the gratification they felt in helping others in these ways:

> I have been the ultimate role model for most of the little kids (Ethan—but watch out for him in a dodgeball game!);

> I get to help second, third, and fourth graders learn math concepts (Oceana);

> . . . helping first graders learn more about God in crafts, stories, plays and other things (Amber);

> I like teaching littler kids about the Bible (Jaz).

The Hillside-Two Rivers community places a high value on helping out others, and this was reflected in students' answers and the activities they chose to do. However, I unfortunately found that students had fewer opportunities to contribute in this way when they got to the middle school because the middle school did not provide service opportunities. It is clear that extracurricular activities can benefit students; however, for a variety of reasons, many students do not, or cannot, participate.

The parents of research participants valued active involvement in social, athletic, civic, and service organizations, and they encouraged their children to participate in activities. Table 2 shows that students were engaged in a variety of sports and clubs in the sixth and seventh grades and many of them joined more than one activity.

Communities and schools afforded these students ample opportunities to become involved and overall participation among research participants from both towns was almost even. But a few students were less active. The middle school intramural program provided a popular alternative for students who could not do other activities.

School-wide Extracurricular Participation

Participation was high among the thirty students in this study but I had been hearing in the community that students who do not live in Lakeview could not participate as much. Take, for example, the headline of the article in the local newspaper mentioned earlier, proclaiming: "Bused kids exhausted, excluded." Since participation in extracurricular activities has many benefits to students, it is important to know if some

Table 2. Enrollment in Extracurricular Activities in Grades 6 and 7

Extracurricular Activities from High to Low Enrollment

Numbers Participating	Lakeview Grade 6 N=16	Hillside Grade 6 N=16	Lakeview Grade 7 N=14	Hillside Grade 7 N=14
7–10 participants	Basketball Drama	Basketball	Band Basketball	Band
4–6 participants	Chorus Band Baseball Soccer Church Group	Baseball Football Chorus Peer Helper	Soccer Volleyball	Football Track
1–3 participants	Lacrosse Hockey Student Council Babysitting Club Skiing Field Hockey Football Computer Camp	Gymnastics Babysitting Club Church Group Hockey Soccer Skiing Softball Band Lacrosse Volleyball Student Council Youth Counselor	Skiing Lacrosse Baseball Tennis Floor Hockey Drama Hockey Field Hockey Track World Language Math Team	Basketball Church Group Baseball Volleyball Drama World Language Math Team Coach's Helper Hockey Lacrosse Skiing Youth Counselor
Not Available and/or No Participants	Volleyball Track Gymnastics Softball Floor Hockey World Language Math Team Peer Helper Youth Counselor Coach's Helper	Field Hockey Track Tennis Drama Computer Camp World Language Math Team Coach's Helper	Football Gymnastics Softball Computer Camp Babysitting Club Peer Helper Youth Counselor Coach's Helper Church Group	Soccer Field Hockey Gymnastics Floor Hockey Softball Chorus Youth Counselor Student Council Babysitting Club Peer Helper

students are indeed excluded. At the end of the 1999–2000 school year, I surveyed all middle school students about their involvement in after-school activities. Teachers administered the five-minute survey in their classrooms. Mountainview Middle School offered twenty activities plus intramurals that year and students were asked to circle all the school activities and sports they participated in. Students who were not involved in school activities were asked to explain why they did not participate. (The Student Participation Survey is Appendix 6.) On this survey, I asked only for participation in *school* activities and did not ask students to report on community activities.

Three hundred and twenty-six seventh and eighth grade students completed the survey, 72% of the total student body of 453 students. Students from all six towns completed the survey; however, since this is a comparative study of two communities, Lakeview and Hillside-Two Rivers, I have limited the focus of this chapter to the data collected from students residing in those towns (75% of the sample). Intensity of commitment varied in different activities; for example, interscholastic sports teams and drama club met at least every weekday for the entire season but intramurals and other activities met only a couple of times a week. I weighed all activities the same regardless of intensity.

Interesting participation patterns emerged in this larger sample when participation was examined by town and by gender as shown in Figure 10.1. Hillside-Two Rivers girls said they participated the most in school activities, followed by Lakeview girls, Lakeview boys and, well below anyone else, Hillside-Two Rivers boys. For girls, participation *increased* from grade seven to grade eight and, for boys, it decreased slightly. I learned from this survey that active students were inclined to be involved in more than one activity and girls were active in a higher average number of activities than boys. This finding is counter to Simmons and Blyth's (op. cit.) finding that girls do not participate as much as boys after the transition to middle school.

I was initially surprised to find that a third of the students from Lakeview, both boys and girls, said they did not participate in school activities. However, when I probed the reasons for not participating I learned that many of them participated in well-funded popular community activities instead.

A quarter of the girls and nearly two-thirds of the boys from Hillside-Two Rivers did not participate. Not only were 64% of the boys from Hillside-Two Rivers not involved in school activities, but the boys who were involved were involved in fewer activities than other students. These students, in contrast to Lakeview students, were not likely to be involved in

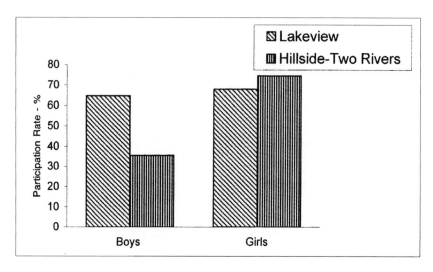

Figure 10.1. Boys' and Girls' Participation in After-School Activities by Town

activities sponsored by the community, so actual participation in clubs and sports is even lower in Hillside-Two Rivers than this chart indicates.

Some activities had a disproportionate number of students from one town. Girls from both communities were well integrated in drama, intramurals, and softball; boys from both communities came together in football, baseball, and intramural sports. However, despite the earlier active experience of Hillside-Two Rivers students in basketball, there were three times as many boys and girls from Lakeview in basketball than from Hillside-Two Rivers. Field hockey and girl's soccer were almost exclusively populated by girls from Lakeview, and boy's soccer was Lakeview's domain. Track was the one sport that had a disproportionately high number of boys and girls from Hillside-Two Rivers. An important benefit of extracurricular participation is the development of friendships among students from different towns but some activities were not integrated enough to enhance the development of cross-town friendships.

Perhaps most striking was the absence of Hillside-Two Rivers students on the student council, especially in light of the fact that these students had active leadership and service roles in their elementary school. Ten Lakeview students, six girls and four boys, and *none* of the Hillside-Two Rivers students, served on the student council during the 1999–2000 school year.

Reasons for Not Participating

There were many factors influencing student involvement in the middle school. Middle school sports teams are interscholastic and, therefore, they are competitive, selective, time-consuming, and expensive. In a regional economically diverse school district, participation is more accessible to students who have transportation, come from families that can afford the fees, have had prior opportunities to play the sport, have been coached well, have attended sports camps where they can improve their skills, do not have after-school responsibilities at home, and so on. While there may not be *intentional* exclusion of students from outlying towns in extracurricular activities, including these students takes intentional, committed, systematic efforts on the part of school staff and parents.

It will be important for teachers, administrators, coaches, and school board members to assess the impact of these findings on future opportunities, sense of belonging, and power distribution among middle school students. It is also important to explore the reasons why some activities are integrated by town and others are not.

Although 49 out of 144 Lakeview students (21 girls, 28 boys) reported that they were not involved in school activities, 34 of them reported that they were involved in community activities instead. Ice hockey, for example, is a well-supported town sport played by a large number of boys from Lakeview where there is an indoor rink that is in constant use. When asked why they did not participate in school activities, Lakeview students wrote:

> I had conflicting schedules with . . . school sports. I enjoyed the out-of-school sports more;
>
> My reason is that the school does not offer the sports I like, such as lacrosse and hockey;
>
> They also don't offer the highest level, which I compete at;
>
> I am really into hockey and it takes up most of my time.

On the other hand, of the 11 girls and 38 boys (out of 102) from Hillside-Two Rivers who reported that they did not participate, only three participated in activities outside school. If Hillside-Two Rivers students were not involved in school activities, they were not likely to be involved at all.

One in four Hillside-Two Rivers girls did not participate in extracurricular activities, and these girls, more than any other group, reported that they had other responsibilities. Again, the differences in town lifestyle and culture are evident in the answers these girls gave for why they were not involved in after school activities:

> . . . would never be home early enough to do chores;

> I have to go home take care of my little brother, house, and my dog. My parents get home between 5:30 and 10:00 p.m.;

> I need to be home after school for my little sister. I also have responsibilities at my house;

> I didn't have time and have too much to do;

> I had too much work and chores to do anything else.

Students who are needed at home may benefit from knowing that they serve an important role in their family. There may be gratification that comes from having this kind of responsibility, or there may be stress and resentment, depending on how students interpret their lives and what their families and communities value and recognize. Hillside-Two Rivers girls in my study seemed to take pride in the way they contributed at home. Well-meaning programs that seek to involve more students in after-school activities need to be aware of the vital role some young adolescents play in their families, and the way the students understand this responsibility.

Two-thirds of the boys from Hillside-Two Rivers did not participate in extracurricular activities. Boys frequently said they did not participate because they were not interested in the activities offered or because they didn't want to. Boys from all towns, but especially from Hillside-Two Rivers, gave answers like these:

> . . . after 6 years of school sports I got sick of it and I have better things to do after school;

> Skool sux did not want to (sic);

> I don't like most of those sports;

> Waste of my time;

> I don't like to do anything with the school;

> I do not like organized sports and it's too committing;

> All the activities are things I <u>hate</u>.

In these answers there is a tone of irritation, disconnection, even anger, reminding me of school transition research that has found a higher level of alienation from school in seventh and eighth grade boys. The resentment expressed by some boys toward "jocks" perhaps also surfaces in these answers.

Clearly, not all students want to take part in extracurricular activities. Students find other meaningful ways to spend the hours after school. One girl said for example, "I don't really like all those activities because I like going home with my family." But it is unfortunate that some students who want to be involved are excluded because of not having the insurance, the money, the transportation, or the experience needed. The following answers demonstrate that some students face barriers to participation:

[I] feel like I have to be playing forever before I'm on a team, like I can't come without experience (Two Rivers girl);

I haven't participated in the activities because all the sports I wanted to do I needed insurance and my family did not have it (Lakeview girl);

Money problems (3 students, different towns);

I wouldn't have a ride back and forth (8 students, different towns);

I didn't really know what the activities were (2 Hillside girls).

Important questions concerning student involvement in activities may remain obscure because individual taste and talent, the complexity of cross-town relationships, and structural constraints are entangled and deeply embedded in how and why students are engaged or not engaged in extracurricular activities. Transportation, financial resources, parental support, and experience are obvious constraints for some children but are there tacit conditions that favor privileged students? One student, for example, explained to me that since coaches are mostly from Lakeview, they know the students and families from Lakeview, and therefore, they might feel some pressure to pick Lakeview students for positions on selective teams. Given the differences that exist between towns, this is an entirely understandable interpretation, whether Lakeview students are actually favored or not.

When I explored questions about how and why some students participated in activities and some did not, I found the issues to be more complex than the information I gleaned from the survey. The following story about Arianna and Alexeia demonstrates the interconnected influences that determine student participation: the student's hopes and desires, the student's attempt to protect himself or herself from disappointment, cross-town tensions, the values of parents regarding how and when to intervene in their child's school domain, school and community resources and commitment to extracurricular activities, and the sole explicit factor: school policies and criteria for participation.

Arianna and Alexeia: The Risk of Hoping for Working Class Kids

When I met eleven-year-old Arianna as a Hillside sixth grader, she was already taller than most of her classmates, played a mean game of basketball, and was involved in town and school activities. An honor roll student, Arianna told me she loved school and especially liked writing and science and dreamt of being a veterinarian some day. But she expressed feeling nervous about going to the middle school because, she said:

> My sister, I was asking her about seventh grade and she goes, "Well I don't think nobody gets along with the people from [Lakeview] because they're stuck up and they don't like anybody." . . . They don't like us. I don't know. They feel like it's their town that they're boss of.

Arianna was not sure whether to believe her sister or not. In the next few minutes of our interview, Arianna also told me important things about how she interprets what her sister said. First, she guessed that it would be different for her than for her sister: "I think I might have friends from [Lakeview] because I do field hockey and track and stuff, so I think I might be friends with those people." Second, she told me that, to her, the town someone is from doesn't matter, "I don't care where they're from. I'll be their friend." But she wondered if the kids from Lakeview would be friendly toward her: "The people in [Hillside] are friendly, they just don't care, they're friends. Other people from other towns . . . they just don't act like they want to be our friends." Much later in the interview, after a long discussion about popularity and acceptance, Arianna considered this possibility: "I think it might just be my sister, who she is . . . the people she hangs out with. I don't know, but I just want to get along with the kids from [Lakeview]. I want to know what they are like. They could be exactly like us." She asked me, "Do you ask [Lakeview] kids? Do they say anything about us?" I was touched by how important these issues were to Arianna, the sincerity of her concerns, and by how common these concerns were to other Hillside-Two Rivers students.

In the sixth grade, Arianna was already considering issues of relative power ("they're the boss of"), possible obstacles to making new friends, and ways that she might get to be friends with Lakeview students (by being on sports teams). Being cautious about her judgments, she looked for information from me to further inform her perceptions. These are vital considerations for children coming to the middle school from outlying communities. Arianna's willingness to contemplate the possibility that her sister might be wrong and that she could have a different experience is a sign of resilience on her part. After all, she is active, athletic, smart, and friendly. Who wouldn't want to be her friend? Still, given her concerns, it takes a lot of courage to risk hoping that she will make friends from Lakeview and play on middle school sports teams.

Arianna and I met again in December when she was well into her seventh grade year. She was doing well, and told me she loved the middle school and most of her teachers. A few minutes after we began talking, however, she said she didn't make the basketball team. In fact, despite her experience and desire, Arianna did not play on any middle school teams, and when she tried for the team again in the eighth grade, she was again cut. "Let's talk a little bit about that, Arianna. I feel sad for you," I said. I was surprised to hear her response: "I didn't really care. It's a real commitment. Practices are almost every day . . . it's really hard, so I didn't really care. Me and my other friends are going to do the rec team, so it didn't bother me so much." In response to what was actually available to her, Arianna tried to reassess the value she placed on being a part of middle school sports teams. Instead, Arianna found satisfaction in playing intramural and town basketball, and she helped her mother coach the elementary school team.

During our seventh grade interview, I sensed reluctance on Arianna's part to pursue the discussion about basketball. When I asked her if she thought the decisions had been fair, her voice lowered to a whisper:

> One girl was the coach's daughter and she was good . . . I knew she was going to make it; there was no doubt about it [and] her friends mostly made it. I told the coach that people are saying that most of the [Lakeview] kids would make it and not from other towns. He said, "I don't think that was true." I do, I still do.

The measured way Arianna murmured these last words made me feel that she would very much like to not believe what she was telling me; her disappointment was palpable even though she found other ways to be active. It hurts children when they begin to understand that they might be excluded because of where they come from, or the color of their skin, or their family's religious beliefs. Ironically, the coach was a Lakeview father and parent of two girls in this study. Conversations with these girls revealed that they knew about the way some students wondered if their father had played favorites and they were distressed and offended by this speculation.

It is likely that Arianna will not play basketball in high school, since the bar will be set even higher, and she will not have had the experience. Arianna has faced many disappointments in life and she rebounds from disappointment in a flexible and resilient manner. Like many of the Hillside-Two Rivers students in this study, she has learned to adjust her desire to what is actually available to her. This strategy ("I didn't really care . . . it's really hard.") is both adaptive and dangerous. At what point might the scale be weighted by indifference rather than by hope, by frustration rather than by flexibility, by disappointment rather than drive, perhaps even threatening future aspirations like college and a lucrative career?

Twenty-one of the girls who played middle school basketball in the 1999–2000 school year were from Lakeview; seven were from Hillside-Two Rivers. Both towns had equally active elementary school teams. It is unfortunate for Arianna, and others like her, that she did not have the opportunity to be a part of this interscholastic team—to work real hard and do real well, to make good friends from other towns, to be exposed to students from other school districts, to contribute something she values to the school she loves, to gain the sense of competence and school identification this opportunity might have afforded her. In general, fewer opportunities are afforded to Hillside students to develop their athletic ability. School districts have the responsibility to nurture the interests, talents, and dreams of low-income children and to enable them to be a central part of the life of their schools and communities. Given the benefits of interscholastic sports participation, it is reasonable to suggest that some of the positions on teams should go to Hillside students who show talent and drive even if they have less experience or play less well at the time of try-outs than their Lakeview peers.

Although Arianna seemed to move beyond this disappointment quickly and to find other ways to be involved in the sport, something happened later in the school year that made me wonder how Arianna was really feeling about herself and the middle school. Arianna seemed to place her frustration and her anger squarely on the shoulders of a girl from the same town whom she had been to school with all her life. The tension between the two girls became a major issue for them and for many of their classmates, and it went on for months, causing a lot of concern to parents and teachers. Through the second half of seventh grade and well into eighth grade, these former friends wrestled with deep misunderstanding and animosity toward each other.

Alexeia, who became the target of Arianna's rage, *was* chosen for the basketball team and, to make matters worse, she was taken out of the classes she shared with Arianna and placed in accelerated classes halfway through the seventh grade year. I was stunned by the power of Arianna's feelings and the poignancy of this drama between two old friends, parting ways because of the sudden status differences that existed between them. Arianna said she was mad because, "[Alexeia] changed and I don't like the way she is now. She ignores me. The people she started hanging around with are not my type of people . . . they're snobby. She acts like she's too good for us."

Alexeia had been able to do what Arianna hoped to do in the seventh grade: make good friends with students from Lakeview and become an important player on the middle school basketball team. Alexeia was moving away from her old friends, Arianna felt betrayed, and the change was tense and painful to them both. Alexeia sought help from others to try to figure out what to do. She tried many times to talk with Arianna, but these efforts seemed to make Arianna even angrier. When I talked with Alexeia, she was distraught; this awful tension—not speaking to each other or saying mean things—had been going on for months. She said she wanted to be friends with her old friends and be able to have new friends too.

This is a dilemma played out over and over again in the lives of successful students from working-class towns and neighborhoods. For them, doing well may mean facing misunderstanding, losing friends, being accused of hanging out with snobs, and being accused of thinking they are "being better than everyone else." Crossing borders, making new friends, excelling in school, being in what students called the "smart class," moving on in life, may result in resentment from old friends who are left behind. This is one of the costs of successful integration. It is understandable how some students would resist making choices that might move them away from what is familiar, thereby avoiding this painful dilemma.

Alexeia, like other kids who move toward what is new and different, felt like she was on thin ice. This is a risk—a big one. How Alexeia handles these issues and whether she continues to move ahead or retreat back to what is familiar, depends on what kind of support and understanding she gets from trusted people at home and at school. And it depends on something else much more unpredictable: her new Lakeview friends. The cruelest experience of all is to come up against the possibility that her new friends may not see her as one of their own. If the lines get re-drawn, leaving her out of her new peer group in the next year or two, then what? Working class children often face this dilemma whenever they are perceived by their peers (or by their parents or teachers) to be reaching higher than they should.

Arianna's sense of betrayal, Alexia's sense of rejection and confu-sion, and Daria's sense of abandonment described in the previous chap-ter, and the experiences that triggered these powerful emotions, were a central part of what happened in the seventh grade for these three girls. But despite the salience of these experiences, and the powerful impact on their lives, these stories were played out in the emotionally isolated dimension of early adolescent lives, not fully explored, or understood, or discussed. Daily, students make choices, formulate their dreams and identity, and make decisions in this lonely context. There are whole worlds of early-adolescent emotion and stuggle, resilience and courage, right under our noses, but hardly seen.

Three Mothers, Three Perspectives

While I was in the middle of this study, I had dinner with a friend of mine from Lakeview who said that although she doesn't feel it is ab-solutely defensible, she will "do anything to manipulate [her] kid's envi-ronment." We were discussing her son's desire to be on the seventh grade basketball team. She said that she tried to let the coach know how impor-tant it was for her boy to be on the team, and wondered if I would call the coach and "put in a good word" for him. My friend, a gifted fifth grade teacher, is well aware of the inequities of students' lives; she taught in Two Rivers and saw for herself the differences in what children have—differ-ences in clothes, health care, housing, preparedness for school, and so on. But she is not hesitant about advocating for her seventh grader, and expects that other parents would do the same. Her son eventually made it on the team.

Ironically, the next day, I ran into Arianna's mother, Cathy, who also had a seventh grade son trying to get on the basketball team. Arianna, now an eighth grader, had just learned that she was again not chosen for the team. Cathy was much more forthcoming about her opinions than she had been in the past. She told me that she feels the middle school is a place where kids have to face prejudices about being from Hillside. She thought her son, like her daughter, would not get on the team, and maybe it would be because his grades were not good enough or maybe it would be something else more undefined. I asked her if she would talk to the coach about getting her son on the team. "No, I wouldn't do that, I've never done that," she said, surprised I would even ask. While Cathy worries that her children may not get the chances other kids get, she does not try to advocate for her child over someone else's child; she has never intervened in that way. In another conversation, I asked a Two Rivers parent if she would try to get her son into an eighth grade algebra class and she responded in a similar way—the decision would mostly be up to him and what the teachers recommend. Another Hillside parent said that he does not intervene in these decisions and that he wants his son to "be able to accept that things don't always work out the way you want them to."

After many conversations like these, I began to understand that this response is not indifference, not even a *laissez-faire* attitude on the part of Hillside and Two Rivers parents, but rather, based on an intentional, personal value system about the role parents should take in their child's school life, and the need for their children to learn how to manage disappointment on their own. Cathy feels that school is mostly the domain of her children and that they must learn to face disappointment, though at the same time she questions the inequities she has seen as a lifelong resident of this area. Perhaps Hillside-Two Rivers parents are reluctant to "manipulate their child's environment" out of deference to the decisions of the school or because they do not perceive themselves to have influential power in the school realm. However, these answers indicate another purpose that reflects the experience and values of Hillside-Two Rivers families: these parents feel their children can benefit from learning to face and overcome disappointment. Cautious enthusiasm characterizes the way many Hillside-Two Rivers people think about an unpredictable future. This feeling is evident in comments like these: "Ethan has a lot of hopes and dreams, and I want him to understand that they may not work out; he needs to learn to accept disappointment."

A few days later, I telephoned the boys basketball coach, an athletically talented Hillside mother whose son was also in my study (he played baseball, not basketball). She told me thirty-eight seventh graders tried out for the team and she could only take thirteen. She spoke with the physical education teachers about the attitudes and athletic talents of the students who tried out, and she spoke to the principal about their academic performance and effort. "I never looked at where they came from," she said, "It has to do with grades, ability, and attitude. When I went to school there if you were from Hillside you were looked upon as dirt, but I don't see that now." I asked about whether she received any pressure from parents lobbying for their kids, and she said she did not. But she went on to speculate that some Lakeview coaches may feel pressure to include the children of their friends, even if the influence is not spoken.

Some Lakeview children may benefit from what I have come to think of as a system of affirmative action for people who have social class privilege. Unlike their Hillside-Two Rivers classmates, Lakeview students are more likely to have been well-coached on competitive town teams, they are more likely to go to sports camps in the summer, to be known by the coaches, to have proper clothing and equipment, and they are more aware of the rules of the game when it comes to try-outs.

Although there are vast discrepancies in opportunities for children, I do not believe that there is a conspiratorial effort to exclude certain children. These stories demonstrate that participation and inclusion is the function of a much more complex and enmeshed set of factors than that. However, I believe, as Bruce Hare argued, that while it may not be a school conspiracy to maintain structured inequality in our society, "such a process requires a conspiracy to stop it" (1984: p. 195). It takes the highest kind of integrity, on many levels, from coaches, parents, teachers, administrators, and school board members, to avoid the subtle, and not so subtle, pressure to favor certain children. It takes honest and bold community dialogue focusing on these issues to improve our understanding of how and why parents intervene or not in their child's school life and what is behind students' decisions to participate in extracurricular activities. And it takes a real commitment on the part of parents and educators to put these issues on the table and to acknowledge and change what needs to be changed.

Conclusion

The active students in my study spoke convincingly about the many benefits of participating in school activities: a sense of connection, healthy and fun recreation, an emotional outlet, a way to reduce stress, a way to express leadership and altruism, an opportunity to explore interests and future goals, a sense of exhilaration and competence—these are all good reasons for vibrant community and school activities for children of all ages. Extracurricular participation is an essential asset for future college applicants; institutions of higher education seek students who are well rounded and involved. Furthermore, after-school activities afford students an important opportunity to establish a mentoring relationship with another adult—the coach or advisor—who can get to know them in a different venue within a smaller group of peers. Importantly, some extracurricular activities provide a chance to make friends with students from other communities.

Considering the volume of research evidence that shows lower participation in middle grades schools, and lower participation in large schools, student participation at Mountainview Middle School was impressive. However, for a variety of reasons, ranging from structural and resource constraints to deeply rooted economic and cultural forces that limit inclusion, participation in extracurricular activities varied from town to town. Lakeview students were likely to become involved in well-organized town sports if they were not in school sports, but these options were not available to most Hillside-Two Rivers students. In light of the self-esteem data that showed Hillside-Two Rivers boys to have lower self-esteem scores, it is very concerning that so many boys from that community do not participate in extracurricular activities.

These findings raise important issues concerning the goals of middle school inter-scholastic sports teams. At the middle school level, should the priority be to have highly competitive, winning teams? Should the priority be to select out the best students and get them ready for high school teams and state and regional competition? Or should middle schools promote extracurricular involvement as a way to be involved in the school community, a way to interact in a diverse group of students, learn new skills and develop new interests? I would argue that there would be much more gained than lost in making middle school activities less competitive and more accessible to a wider range of students.

In no other context are issues of equity and access more critical than when it comes to academic opportunities for students. Academic status, like participation status, had a dramatic influence on the social adjustment experiences of the thirty students in this study. In the next chapter, I will explore ability grouping at the middle school, where students from different communities were placed, and how they understood the way they were grouped.

CHAPTER 11

Ability Grouping

Perhaps no other school policy influences student experience more than how students are evaluated and grouped academically. Middle schools have typically embraced heterogeneous grouping but, in economically diverse school districts, heterogeneous grouping is criticized by some parents who worry that their children may be held back by their less motivated classmates. The year I conducted this study, Mountainview Middle School experimented with grouping by ability—some students were selected to be in an advanced group. To understand the social arrangements among students at the middle school, I had to understand how their social interactions were structured institutionally. In this chapter, I examine student and parent attitudes toward education, how students performed on standardized tests, the nature of ability grouping at Mountainview Middle School, and how this grouping influenced social interactions and the way students perceived their own and their peer's intellectual competence.

"My Main Thing Is a Good Education"

In the spring of their seventh grade year, research participants were asked to indicate whether getting good grades was very, a little, or not important. More than 75% of the students from both communities indicated that good grades were very important to them, and none of the students indicated that grades were not important. As sixth and seventh graders, most of the students achieved solid A and/or B grades. When students were asked in the sixth grade about the importance of going to college, fifteen from Lakeview and thirteen from Hillside-Two Rivers responded that going to college was very important.

Positive attitudes toward education were also reflected in good school attendance. Despite the greater distance Hillside-Two Rivers students had to travel to get to school, their attendance in seventh grade was even *better* than their Lakeview peers. On average, Hillside-Two Rivers students made it to school all but 6.29 days in the seventh grade; Lakeview students were absent an average of 7.69 days in seventh grade. They were also late less often—an average of 1.29 days and 5.94 days, respectively—probably because they took the school bus more consistently than Lakeview students.

However, not everyone experienced social and academic success. By the end of seventh grade, two students from Hillside-Two Rivers and *six* students from Lakeview received grades at or below a C average—lower than any previous year in school. Three students from Hillside-Two Rivers changed their answers about going to college from very important to a little important. Why might very capable students from both communities get such poor grades, and what might have caused some of the students from Hillside-Two Rivers to alter their future aspirations? Four of the six students from Lakeview with lower grades were girls, leading me to the tentative interpretation that whatever was going on for Lakeview girls that negatively influenced their self-esteem, might also explain a slide in academic self-perception and performance. Concerned parents of these girls shared this speculation.

College education was not the privilege of some of the parents of research participants but while this study was in progress, five mothers—four from Hillside-Two Rivers and one from Lakeview—were enrolled in college courses. Parents from both communities shared similar aspirations for their children: happiness, success, a job they enjoy, confidence, independence, and a college education. Hillside-Two Rivers parents *all* said they wished a college education for their children and they were willing to make great sacrifices to improve their child's options. I was moved by comments like these when I asked, "What do you hope for in the future for your son or daughter?":

That he can be anything and do anything he wants to;

[That she] doesn't have to struggle like her father and I do;

We have funds set aside for the kids to go to college, neither of us graduated with a high school diploma;

I wish for him a lot more than I had—he can go beyond that;

She's staying in school all right and then she's going to college. I've already talked to her about that and told her I'd pay for it;

My main thing is to get a good education—they can never take that away from you.

Hillside-Two Rivers parents were unequivocal about their desire for higher education for their children, but inequitable access to the information necessary to make college possible, along with limited resources, may make the road to higher education more challenging for these families. Lower expectations for working-class students can also be a barrier. I found that teachers and parents, concerned about the stress level some students had, sometimes didn't push them as hard on homework and class work. This well-meaning accommodation, if it is a consistent pattern, can limit future options.

Lakeview parents also desired a college degree for their children; however, I found that going to college was such an unquestioned expectation that parents often didn't mention it until I asked. Their comments reflected hopes that their children would develop worthy future goals and strong moral values—values that they felt might be threatened by a material-focused culture:

> [I hope he] becomes a giving and caring adult—it's important that he learns that he is not only in this world to please himself;

> I want him to be driven by something other than money;

> That she is proud of who she is and has self-worth;

> That he becomes more aware and appreciative of what he has, and of what is around him.

Students from both towns expressed similar interests in veterinary work, marine biology, and architecture. Lakeview students also aspired to careers in law, the arts (acting, singing, writing), and medicine. Hillside-Two Rivers students were also interested in teaching, communications, sports, and owning their own businesses. In the seventh grade, students had similar academic histories, ambitions for the future, and values about the importance of education. However, education and employment trajectories are influenced by long-standing, pervasive attitudes about social class and intellectual ability, and, increasingly, they are influenced by standardized testing and a meritocratic system based on factors that have long favored children from middle and high social classes.

A Meritocracy Based on Narrow Interpretations of Intelligence

Standardized tests, including cognitive and psychological assessments, have become a more and more powerful screen for future mobility and educational and career opportunities. Tests are administered every year or two and used, along with other criteria, to assess student ability, course placement, subject matter mastery, and school effectiveness. Like most other economically struggling communities nationwide, Hillside-Two Rivers students scored much lower, on average, than students from Lakeview and state-wide on standardized tests. The knowledge of lower scores made many parents and their children concerned about whether they would be adequately prepared for middle school. Information and dialogue are imperative to demystify these tests so that students, parents, and educators can understand them for what they measure and what they do not measure.

Achievement tests measure performance and acquired knowledge in a decontextualized way. They do not measure applied knowledge, nor do they measure aptitude; some students test well, and others, for a variety of reasons test poorly. Although tests are often viewed as predictive of future potential, they cannot define the sorts of things that lead to success: "They don't find wisdom, originality, or humor, or tough-mindedness, or empathy, or common sense, or independence, or determination—let alone moral worth" (Lemann, 2000: p. 345).[1]

When research participants were in the seventh grade, I examined the fifth grade test scores for all the students in their grade who attended Lakeview or Hillside Elementary School. The highest scoring students were a boy and girl from Hillside-Two Rivers who had total battery scores in the 99th national percentile. However, overall there was a 30-point difference in average national percentiles between the towns, and the biggest gap was in math, with nearly a 34-point difference. (A comparative summary of the 1997 results of the California Achievement Test is Appendix 7.) Even though the subject area scores were very discrepant, it is important to note that students in both communities had a similar range of cognitive skills (CSI) scores. This indicates that the acquired knowledge of Hillside students did not match their cognitive ability. A Hillside-Two Rivers student obtained the highest CSI score of the entire group. The technical report published by McGraw Hill (1993) demonstrates that CSI scores do not vary by social class, race, or gender but achievement test scores do, and this fact reflects the differences in schooling, resources, and opportunity for affluent and poor children.

The factors leading to gaps in achievement test scores between affluent and low-income communities are numerous and complex: class size, percentage of special needs students in each class (5–8% in Lakeview, 20–25% in Hillside), gender make-up of students, parent and teacher expectations for their children, the understanding of children as to the purpose of the test, the availability of a place to study at home, parental ability to assist with homework, access to technology, the relative

value placed on school, sports, and home commitments, the overall quality of the student's housing and health care, the availability of adult mentors, opportunities to be exposed to future career and educational
options, and the list goes on. But test scores become part of student's self-
knowledge and the basis for academic decisions nonetheless.

Using tests for grouping by ability threatens to produce a self-fulfilling prophecy in school performance. Students may evaluate their intelligence and the intelligence of others based on test results and group
placement. Once test scores are known, very high and very low testers
are at risk of virtually becoming, in the minds of teachers and peers, what
their national percentiles represent (Lemann, ibid.). Many students in
this study had strength in cooperative, associative, creative, applied, and
democratic intellectual endeavors. There is not a standardized test on
Earth that can measure what some children are good at.

Testing and ability grouping result in school and societal divisions by
social class, and also result in a polarization of attitudes toward school,
with some students becoming more confident, enthusiastic, engaged,
and identified with school as leaders, while others become increasingly
less confident, alienated, disengaged, angry, and identified as "losers"
(Oakes, 1992). In the end, tests and ability grouping may say as much
about a societal drive to maintain a hierarchy by class and race, as they
say about student achievement. Students often learn the lesson that they
deserve to be where they are solely because of their individual merit and
not because of the advantages or disadvantages of their lives.

"Kids Have Other Ways of Being Smart"

Testing threatens to over-emphasize certain subject areas and types
of knowledge, and under-emphasize others, riveting teacher and community attention and resources on a very narrow range of abilities. Mu-
sical, spatial, kinesthetic, and personal domains of intelligence described
by Gardner (1983) get very little play in many over-stressed schools with
limited resources. Many children thrive in areas considered less important in school and unfortunately miss the opportunity to shine in front of
teachers and peers. For students like Christine, analytic and artistic abilities do not find an adequate outlet in school:

> They don't have a music [chorus] program, they have a small art
> program, those are some people's really strong strengths. But
> those don't get recognized . . . people don't seem to be paying
> much attention to those things, they just pay attention to their

core classes. I think teachers and many grownups have trouble understanding that . . . kids have other ways of being smart . . . Half of the stuff we do is memorization. That has nothing to do with being smart.

I lament what Christine so eloquently describes. Unless we find ways to enable schools to be effective with diverse learning styles, we risk losing the enormous intellectual and creative contributions of students like Christine.

The Making of a Privileged Learning Atmosphere

Mr. Jordan munched on trail mix and sipped coffee from a travel mug as he prepared his class to read the article, *The Legend of King Arthur*. As papers shuffled and students began to settle, a girl stood up and drawled a few lines from a play with full flair, delighting her classmates and her teacher. As he taught, Mr. Jordan moved around the room, commanding attention with humorous and relevant descriptions of legend, chivalry, plot, and hyperbole. He and his students exchanged differences of opinion about who in the sports world could be regarded as a legend and a student spoke up about a spelling mistake on the blackboard. This is the Galaxy group; eighteen students selected for accelerated learning based on math achievement and teacher recommendations. This sort of demonstrative confidence in students, and teacher good humor, were common in this class. The atmosphere was relaxed and the exchanges between Mr. Jordan and students had a friendly, egalitarian tone.

The next day, I was again in Mr. Jordan's English class, this time with what was called a "regular" (heterogeneous) group of students. The chatting stopped quickly when Mr. Jordan quipped, "When you're ready let me know. I'll wait." This time, the students followed along as Mr. Jordan read aloud, but two students seemed to be somewhere else and, in general, these students seemed to lack the self-assurance I observed the day before. The bantering I witnessed between Galaxy students and their teacher was considerably toned down in this class.

The Striders teaching team wanted to give promising students a challenging scholastic experience without being held back by peers whose grasp of the subject matter was not as strong. One group out of four on this team was arranged by ability and designated for accelerated learning in the core classes. They made an effort to frame this experience in a way that would not be detrimental to students in regular classes. Although a different tone and atmosphere prevailed, *all* students were instructed by this experienced team of teachers with an energetic commitment to teach.

This experiment in homogeneous grouping was an unprecedented move in this otherwise heterogeneously grouped middle school. Ability grouping had arrived, despite the reluctance of the principal and guidance counselor. Teachers wanted to be fair. They used what are considered to be objective selection criteria—grades, test scores, and classroom performance—they did not know what town most of their students were from. However, I did know. Of the eighteen students originally selected, twelve of them had attended Lakeview Elementary School and two had attended Hillside Elementary School. Four others were from Deer Run, Farm Crossing, or new to the school district. Later in the year, another Hillside-Two Rivers student was selected for this group because she was doing so well in math. The imbalance is clear when we know that Lakeview students made up 41.5% and Hillside-Two Rivers students made up 34.7% of the seventh grade class.

On another seventh grade team, an algebra-prep class was taught during the seventh period of the day to a select group of students who were otherwise heterogeneously grouped. My observations of this group led me to reflect on how grouping by ability might affect the one or two Hillside-Two Rivers students who are selected for placement in accelerated classes. The following description is from field notes written in January 2000:

> The class began as it did the previous day: students came in, sat down, and busied themselves with the work that was assigned on the black board. When Ms. Streeter left the room to tend to an unpredictable classroom coverage problem, students began to chat happily and work on their assignment with the student on either side of them. The noise escalated as students transformed this tightly controlled math class into a lively social environment. Isabelle called across several students to a basketball teammate: "Do you have an extra pair of socks? I didn't bring any." A couple of students bickered, "You couldn't get a basketball scholarship if your life depended on it." A group of girls leaned heads in together looking at pictures.

> For some, this was an intimate, friendly space, but one student sat at a table separate from the others. He was not part of the peer interactions; his head was down on the desk. He should be on top of the world, being such a talented athlete, but as only one of two Hillside-Two Rivers students in this class (the other is a girl), he seemed sidelined in this lively social exchange.

How does this homey social atmosphere feel to the one or two out-of-town students in the group? Are there subtle and not so subtle ways that Hillside-Two Rivers boys get the message it is somehow okay for them to excel in mechanics and carpentry and sports, but not okay for them to excel in academics? Does this student worry that his classmates wonder what he is doing there, or worse, has he internalized the stereotypes that call to question the intellectual capabilities of Hillside people, and wonder *himself* what he is doing there?

Later, when he was asked by his teacher to give answers out loud, this very capable, articulate, high-performing student faltered nervously. This student can do the work, his high academic achievement has demonstrated that, but his lone position in class may take an emotional and social toll. In all, two Hillside-Two Rivers girls involved in this study went on to eighth-grade algebra, but all four boys from this community who took a pre-algebra course in grade seven, did not take algebra in grade eight. All of these boys had standardized math scores above the 80th percentile (two of them, above the 90th percentile), and at the beginning of the year, their math grades were As and Bs. But by the end of seventh grade, their grades, and their self-esteem, declined. By comparison, all nine of the research participants from Lakeview who were in algebra-prep in seventh grade went on to eighth grade algebra. These outcomes verify what many ability grouping researchers fear: that for students from low social class backgrounds, academic grouping is influenced by things other than ability.

When I asked students why they were not in algebra, they told me they were dedicated to football and baseball; their sports and school schedules, along with home responsibilities, were already demanding enough, they didn't need the extra stress. "The teachers told me it was my decision; I didn't think I was ready for eighth grade algebra," one of them said. The problem some students face is not an ability problem but, perhaps, one that is derived from the difficult demands many students face—long days and multiple responsibilities—along with pressure to perform in the context of subtle social and cultural messages about academic ability.

The reasons why so few children from Hillside-Two Rivers go on to eighth grade algebra are academic, political, social, cultural, and psychological, and they are poorly understood. At an age when peer-group belonging has primary power in their lives, middle school students are reluctant to be noticed as unusual. I could not help but wonder if it felt safer to be with lots of familiar faces in a heterogeneously grouped math class than to be the only boy from Hillside-Two Rivers in what was called the "smart class" by students. It seems plausible that when Hillside-Two Rivers students look around and see so few others from their town in accelerated math, they adjust their expectations to conform to implicit societal expectations.

Math literacy and equity are so important that it inspired civil rights activist, Bob Moses, to conceptualize and implement the Algebra Project to enable black, working-class children to learn algebra. The Algebra Project responds to the reality that children from disenfranchised communities are tracked-out of courses that give them access to higher-level education and jobs (Moses and Cobb, 2001). In his community organizing work, Moses began to see algebra as a "gatekeeper" course and he compared math literacy today with voting rights in the sixties. "The older generation may be able to get away with it [being illiterate in math]," he argued, "but the younger generation coming up now can't—not if they're going to function in the society, have economic viability, be in a position to meaningfully participate, and have some say-so in the decision-making that effects their lives" (p. 14).

Many people are not aware of research evidence that suggests eighth grade algebra is indeed a gatekeeper course—a very significant dividing point that determines who will go on to regular high school classes and who will go on to higher-level classes (Muller and Schiller, 2000). Course selection, quality of teaching, and academic status within schools are connected to long-term educational and occupational outcomes. I found that parents who had been able to go to college and who understood the rules of the game were much more likely to insist that their children be placed in accelerated classes. But many families lack information about the long-term implications of course selection.

Research in Ability Grouping

As I visited the classrooms described in chapter 7, I began to see a disturbing pattern: the nature of classroom pedagogy, peer relationships, student participation and freedom, and student-teacher relationships seemed to contrast sharply in homogeneously and heterogeneously grouped classes. Students in accelerated classes were predominantly from Lakeview and they seemed comfortably at home in this less diverse context. They were more assertive, they shared a more egalitarian relationship with their teacher, and they defined their classroom space more forcefully than students in regular classrooms, where the space and tone were clearly and non-arbitrarily set by the teachers. They more often stated their own opinions and interpretations, and teachers seemed more relaxed, friendly, and tolerant of behavior that might be considered out of line in heterogeneously grouped classes.

There is evidence that ability grouping reinforces societal and educational inequality and affects future options (Oakes, 1985; Oakes, 1992; Oakes, Gamoran and Page, 1992; Rosenbaum, 1976; Slavin, 1993). Jeannie Oakes studied tracking practices in twenty-five junior and senior high schools with 13,719 students, and found that students tracked in lower ability groups experienced *less teaching* and the most passive teaching strategies (such as doing worksheets). Frequently, they were exposed to a watered-down curriculum, lower expectations, more conformity to rules, and less responsibility and freedom. Many very capable children from working-class families sit in unchallenging, tightly controlled classrooms where they become increasingly disenchanted and are given little opportunity for relevant, critical analysis and discussion (Oakes, 1985). High track classrooms were structured to encourage competence, independent learning, and less conformity. In these classrooms, both students and their teachers perceived themselves to be more capable, intelligent, and likely to succeed (ibid.). Students in high-ability groups often begin to assume that they are handicapped rather than benefited by diversity.

Ability grouping is based on the controversial assumption that children learn better, and teachers teach better, when children are grouped with others who learn like them. But there is little evidence that high academic achievers do better, in the long run, when they are grouped by ability compared to high academic achievers who are not, and at the same time, there is mounting evidence that low academic achievers do more poorly when they are grouped by ability (Oakes, Gamoran, Page, 1992). Schools have begun to heed the advice of researchers and organizations from the NAACP to the Carnegie Institute and are finding ways to provide excellent education in heterogeneously grouped classrooms (e.g., George, Jenkins, and Morgan, 1997).

Students in different ability groups receive a different type of education and ultimately internalize different beliefs about their competence and potential. But I learned something else from this study. My observations and interviews led me to wonder if ability grouping can also hinder social and moral development by decreasing the student's exposure to diversity at exactly the time in life when social comparisons are heightened and students are at a critical juncture in their perspective-taking abilities.

The Classroom as a Social-Cognitive Context

Middle grades students need experiences that will help them integrate skills in intergroup understanding and in reciprocity in interpersonal relationships. Arguments that emphasize the cognitive development benefits of ability grouping grossly under-emphasize the constraints ability grouping might engender to social and moral development, specifically to reciprocal perspective-taking skills. To be able to function effectively in relationships of all types—at work, at school, with friends—it is imperative that students learn empathy and respectful awareness of others. Classroom environments that provide opportunities to develop these sensitivities are perhaps more urgently needed by middle school students whose self-judgment and self-consciousness may lead to an aversion to difference and a self-protective tendency to target other students.

Ability grouping has been studied for its effects on academic and career outcomes, but questions concerning the social development aspects of ability grouping have not been explored. As a fundamentally social context, every classroom has an implicit social curriculum; there is much more being learned than literary terms and fractions, with perhaps more powerful and long-range implications. What are students learning about themselves and their classmates in situations where there is ability grouping? What reality do students absorb about themselves and others in terms of social power, perceived ability, the value of their contributions, and how deserving they are of teacher attention and approval? Based on this knowledge, how might they adjust their dreams and aspirations?

Ability grouping is a powerful force in the way students think about themselves and their peers; it influences social acceptance and perceptions of who is smart, who has sway in shaping the atmosphere of the school, and ultimately it establishes narrow standards for leadership and success. My greatest concern about ability grouping in the seventh grade is that, at just the time students need environments that improve interpersonal competence and intergroup perspective taking, homogeneously grouped classrooms threaten to derail progress toward healthy social development, limit opportunities to make friends across town lines, and encourage stereotypes.

Selman (1980) and Selman and Schultz (1990) identified five levels (0–4) of social development and described the equally important trajectories of development toward autonomy and development toward intimacy. I introduce these concepts and describe levels 1–3 here as a framework for understanding the social development significance of student responses when they were asked to write about their ability grouping experience. These levels are not fixed; home and community environments and other conditions can affect one's level of operation (Selman, ibid.).

At level 1, the individual is able to move beyond impulsive, self-absorbed ways of interacting, toward unilateral interactions that are characterized by the individual's ability to understand that others have needs and desires. However, social connections are made based on the degree to which self-needs are met by others. Interpersonal interactions are predominantly one person giving orders and the other complying. The needs of others are seen as a potential barrier and connections quickly disintegrate when unilateral needs are not being met. Children with "first-person perspective taking ability" consider how others feel about them, but are not aware that their actions affect others who have complex feelings of their own.

Level 2 reciprocity is consolidated generally between the ages of 9 and 12, so seventh graders are just at the crux of this critical stage of development. At this level, there is a more complex understanding of one's emotions and motivations, and there is awareness that others have an inner life too. Children at level 2 have a greater ability to differentiate and coordinate perspectives and are capable of self-reflection. They are aware of multiple and potentially conflicting feelings, intentions, and desires in themselves and others. This is precisely the time when children begin to be able to imagine what it would be like to "walk in another person's shoes" and to develop a capacity for empathy, compassion, and understanding across differences.

Beyond reciprocity is mutuality—level 3. It is at this level of development that powerful, collaborative commitments to others are developed. There is potential for deep attachment, an awareness of how lives are interconnected, a capacity to coordinate and contextualize multiple perspectives, and a consciousness that competing needs and resources can be resolved through consensual decision-making and mutual accommodations. At this level, people are aware of the relativity of social and political power and their position in this social field.

As I listened to students, I began to hear something startling from very bright and articulate high-status students. While these students seemed to be operating securely at level 2 (reciprocal) in their more intimate interpersonal relationships, I heard more and more unilateral thinking over the seventh grade transition when intergroup relationships were in question.

Trent: Inspired and Engaged But Not Challenged

At the end of the year, students in the Galaxy group were asked to write a critical analysis of ability grouping. Notably, students in the regular classes were not asked to write about their experiences in a critical analysis paper. I find their reflections extraordinary in light of research in ability grouping; students report many of the same benefits, concerns, and questions raised by researchers. Listen to what they have to say in excerpts from these papers:

> Some students on the team refer to us as the "smart class." Although we may be the best math students, we are not the best, as a group, in the rest of our core classes. I have found that the group of students have a tendency to socialize a lot during class. The atmosphere is usually joyful, yet always a chance of turning unfriendly.
>
> Learning is a social experience, and I had no trouble fitting into that. As far as academics go, well, that's a different story. I need to be challenged. Although I had great teachers, with great methods of instructing their curriculum, I think I would have liked to see more of a challenge to really get me thinking.
>
> As individuals, there were kids who were exceptional students in other classes too . . . this not only improved my learning in math but enhanced my education in English, science and geography as well.
>
> Enhancing your learning falls under being challenged, inspired to learn, and engaged in activities. All three categories . . . are equally important to one another. I know I was much better off this year with a special grouping, compared to no grouping at all. I have high hopes that next year Mr. [Jordan] will once again be able to elude the powerful hand of the administration to continue his concept of homogeneous grouping.
>
> (Trent, Lakeview)

In this insightful piece of work, this student points out what social cognition theorists tell us: learning is a social experience and being with other students who were good in different subjects enhanced his learning. He and many other students in the Galaxy group were aware that they were referred to as the smart group. And he describes what I observed, that the students in this group have "a tendency to socialize a lot" and he informs us that the "atmosphere [can turn] . . . unfriendly." This insight may reflect the competitive nature of this class and may be one of the reasons why some students opt out of accelerated classes.

Students felt they had special exemption, permission to go a little further than what is usually the norm in classrooms. When I told students in an after-school focus-group that I thought I had observed a difference in teacher style and student behavior, a student explained: "With the other groups the teachers don't joke around as much. They are more strict. In Galaxy they know they can joke around but that we will still get the work done. They think with the other groups things might get out of control so they don't joke as much."

Several other students also commented on the behavior of their classmates, and wondered if being together for a whole year may have led to an inordinate amount of loud, out-of-hand behavior and classroom socializing:

> While the class was more intelligent, mathematically speaking, we were loud and out of control quite often . . . we've all grown familiar with each other. If we'd been moved around occasionally, we might have been calmer, and thus more controllable.

> Now I must face the issue that is unavoidable: our group is loud. We've been this loud for a while. But I think most of it is that we got so used to seeing the same people every day . . . But maybe that isn't a result of the grouping at all. Maybe we are just loud people by nature.

> The grouping got a little out of hand though in the fourth quarter . . . all during class we would be talking and laughing because we knew each other so well . . . we would always have to stop and wait for people to be quiet and it wasted time.

Trent also points out that students need to be "inspired, engaged, and challenged" and he says that while he *was* inspired and engaged, he was not adequately challenged. His experience affirms what I thought I saw during classroom observations: teachers were more inclined to present their interpretations and opinions rather than facilitate analytic thinking and problem deconstruction on the part of their students. Students appreciated when they were challenged. One student wrote, "We would discuss and debate many issues in today's world . . . our excelled minds took all the information like a sponge."

Trent concludes that the experience was an overall success but his critical analysis, insightful as it may be, is unilateral in its approach—a lack of perspective taking that I believe might be *encouraged* by ability grouping. This unilateral stance was predominant in almost all of the eighteen papers that I read. Trent enjoys the idea that this arrangement is an unauthorized and innovative move on the part of his teacher and he hopes his teacher will "again be able to elude the powerful hand of the administration to continue his concept of homogeneous grouping."

What he does not know is that his teacher is actually playing a much more politically powerful hand in this school district than the principal. School board members and many Lakeview parents would like to see more, not less, ability grouping.

Dez: "Other Kids Don't Have the Advantage That I Do"

Dez states even more clearly the advantage of being placed with higher achieving students and he understands that this advantage is something that not all students have.

> Seeing the same faces everyday can sometimes be unpleasant . . . but in its own way it is a gift. The group has changed my learning abilities in many ways . . . has given me something to strive for. I am not as smart as the other kids, but I try to follow along and stay with the group. There are not as many troublemakers in our class to disturb the other students.

> Since I have been with this group for a long time it would be weird going with other students that weren't as advanced as I was. I don't see myself as better than anyone else but the other kids don't have the advantage that I do being with these students. I had my friends and was challenged and engaged.

> (Dez, Lakeview)

Recalling the social aspects of learning, that children construct reality through interactions with others, (Piaget, 1948; Vygotsky, 1962), this student says what proponents of *heterogeneous* grouping argue: "the group has changed my learning abilities in many ways . . . has given me something to strive for. I am not as smart as the other kids, but I try to follow along and stay with the group."

Dez also makes the comment, "There are not as many troublemakers in our class to disturb other students." Even though students in this class recognized that they were "loud and out of control quite often," they did not see themselves as troublemakers. These students have teacher approval and consent; the troublemakers do not. Implicit here is that the real troublemakers are in the lower level classes. Although this student is careful to say that he does not feel "better than anyone else," and he recognizes that others simply do not have the advantage he has, he concludes that he would feel "weird going with other students that weren't as advanced."

Students felt positive about ability grouping because they saw their classmates as assets and because ability grouping excluded students who they thought might threaten their academic experience:

> I felt I belonged there and I didn't have to wait on anybody who didn't get it. Being with students who scrambled made me excel at a faster rate.

> You can be sure your partner will get the job done right the first time. There were many different people with the same goals as you . . . we could really count on each other.

> The people in my class made me want to do better, bring myself up to their standards even though I didn't and still don't know exactly what they are.

> Being in the "smart group" I think my grades rose because I was with smarter people and I tried to impress them . . . they would give me extra help if I needed it.

> Having other students around you that were engaged into their work helped pressure and challenge me to succeed and try harder on my school work . . . the other students helped to create an atmosphere that was both social and academic . . . It felt good to sort of stand out.

> We weren't held back from moving forward. We finally had the group we wanted. [I was] inspired to do more because everyone was as smart or smarter than me.

> It kept most of the trouble students away from the people who really go to school to learn.

What comes across most clearly in these comments are perceptions that their classmates were assets to their learning and that some of their peers in regular classes would hold them back and prevent them from learning.

Jeremy: "It Is Hard When There Are No Good Examples"

Some students were not able to benefit from this academic grouping, and chose not to be in eighth grade algebra, as comments from the following two students, both from Two Rivers, demonstrate:

Students should have a choice about being in it or not. I wanted to be in it at the beginning but then I did not want to be in it. Teachers in all classes expected more from you. I really like the classes, they were packed with information; but there was a lot of silliness.

I will admit that I need to work on my homework skills and study skills but it is hard when I never really see my parents and there are no good examples in my family. It is hard to come in to school after waking up and not seeing my parents at all. My dad does not get home till 8:00 p.m.

(Jeremy, Two Rivers)

This student again reminds us of the remarkable range of experiences and contexts in which students live their lives. Here is a student well aware that he needs to work on study skills and the social and practical reasons why this is hard for him. I know from conversations with this student that he is serious about going to college and that he believes one way to get there is to excel in football. As he continues through school, I wonder if his teachers will encourage his tremendous intellectual potential, and find ways to help him overcome the substantial barriers he faces. Jeremy's sole classmate from Hillside Elementary School faced similar barriers:

I felt it was going to be a challenge and I was ready. As time went on though I felt good about all my classes except oddly enough, math. I had a chance to get out of the group . . . but for some reason I told Ms. Lyons I could bring my grade up and wanted to stay in the group . . . it all seemed a little more laid back. Even though sometimes we did have more work than other classes, the atmosphere was nicer, not so much class pressure . . . so that was really the only reason I wanted to stay in the group . . . with a laid back atmosphere I didn't get as much done in class as I had hoped.

I was not able to get my math work done at home because I didn't understand most of it and I had no one to ask for help . . . I should've gotten out of the group but . . . I felt it was too late. But if a kid comes around like me you should have a fifteen minute talk with him/her and ask them what they seriously think. And then make a decision to keep them in or take them out.

(Fred, Two Rivers)

Again, this student points out something I perceived during my observations: the atmosphere was more laid-back. However, the laid-back and more independent learning environment may have resulted in making it harder for this student to get his work done and perform at his capacity. Many students need a structured environment in which to work. This is especially true, this student tells us, if there is no one at home to help them out. With declining grades, he felt he should get out of the group, but couldn't bring himself to tell his math teacher that. He advises his teachers that "if a kid comes around like me" they should talk to him and find out what he "seriously thinks" and then make a decision. Jeremy and Fred are both capable students with tremendous potential and challenging life circumstances. To succeed in this environment they needed more structure and teacher guidance than this opportunity afforded them.

Lisa: "Everyone Was Competing for the Role of 'Smartest Person'"

Lisa is direct and certain in her critique of this practice. Even though her placement in this class benefited her academically, the social price for her and other students not in the class, is too high a price to pay:

> The atmosphere was competitive. Everyone was competing for the role of the "smartest person." If being the "smartest" was out of reach, they would try to be the funniest or something else.

> It met my academic needs [but] . . . It did not meet my social needs. In the first quarter, I was making lots of new friends . . . when I was moved to the "smart group" in Q2, I lost the friends I made and did not make any new friends. This made me spend more time after school socializing.

> In math, I do not feel any different because it is not just the "smart group" (us) and the "dumb group." I was extremely challenged knowing that we were the "leaders" of the group. I was not inspired and not engaged. For my socialization's sake, I would never want this kind of grouping again.

This critique is riveting for its cutting interpretations. The class was competitive and students were engaged in a drive to be the smartest, or if they failed at that, they tried to be the best at something else. She lost friends when she was placed in this class and did not make new friends in this competitive group. Here is a student who says out loud what is often not said about student perceptions: if there is a "smart group" there is also a "dumb group"—a notion she rejects, along with the idea that the students in this group were the "leaders" of the team (quotation marks are hers). She concludes that she was not inspired, not engaged, and does not ever want this kind of grouping again.

Other students also made it clear that they were aware of being the "smart group." Some students, especially girls, were bothered by these perceptions. The following comments illustrate how grouping influenced self-perceptions and how students reacted to the "smart group" designation:

> I'm glad that being smart is cool. Special assignments made us feel as though we were leaders of the team.

> I have been in the "smart group," well that's what others would call it. I call it "the people who set higher standards for themselves."

> The 1 thing I disliked about the group was what the other classes thought of us. I always hated being called "the Smart group." I would try to explain that all we were was a bunch of kids taking a pre-algebra course, but everyone still thought we were smarter than them.

> I think the thing I disliked most was being referred to as the "smart group." I doubt that there is anyway around this. I think this would bother me because people would be like, "oh you're in the smart group," and they sort of didn't act the same . . . I don't even like it when people in the class referred to us as the smart group because it seemed like they were mocking the others.

These comments reveal that some students were self-consciously aware of how others might think about them, however, the reciprocal skill of being able to imagine the feelings and perspectives of students who were not in the accelerated class is not demonstrated. Some students even called for more rigid restrictions in selecting students for homogeneous grouping. "Put only the people in there who are really smart" and "kick out the slackers" were examples of this sentiment.

Students had mixed feelings about how the group worked for them socially. Some felt the group gave them a chance to have better and stronger friendships, an opportunity that many adolescent social development experts would advocate. Others said that they "got a little tired of each other," and the "jokes just aren't funny anymore." Overall, the biggest criticism was that the grouping prevented them from making other friends. Several students wanted more diversity in their peer group and missed having opportunities to meet other students:

> In the beginning of the year, I was really looking forward to getting to know a lot of different people by the mixing up of the groups. And it got a little tiring seeing the same faces day after day . . . So I hope that for next year, I might get more chances to meet people I don't know very well.

> [Another problem is] seeing the same people every single day. Sure it built friendship within the group, but it's only a fourth of the team. [He recommends incorporating other kids into the group.]

> When you are with different people the classes don't get as boring because it is a change of atmosphere.

> [I am] a little disappointed about not being able to get to know as many kids as I would have if it had been a regular placement.

Several students were able to imagine what their classmates thought about them, and how other students influenced their education, but the following student goes a step further in his analysis demonstrating empathy in a way that no other student did:

> Academic needs were met. [But] this year's grouping would have been better without the [separate groups]. The group was formed by taking all the brightest kids and putting them together. This left all others in the dark with no other student to learn from. I myself learn a lot from other students, and I don't think it's fair not giving the other kids a chance to do the same. In conclusion, I don't think a group like this should be put together next year.

Here is a student who, reflecting on how other students enhance his own education, is able to consider how homogeneous grouping might negatively affect other students. He suggests that other students are disadvantaged if they do not have the opportunity to learn from their peers, and for this reason, he does not agree with ability grouping.

The Yurt Concept of Mutually Reinforcing Accommodations

There is a cooperative game that I enjoy playing with school groups: Everyone stands holding hands in a circle and they count out 1, 2, 3 . . . and so on. On cue, all the children with odd numbers in the circle lean as far forward as they can; all the children with even numbers lean backward. If the group moves forward and backward at the same time, the result is a very secure zigzag circle where no one is off-balance. As long as the children keep their feet planted firmly on the ground, and hang on to their partners hands, the pull in opposing directions makes the circle strong and stable—like a yurt.[2] But the circle becomes unstable when one person lets go.

Over time, I began to notice that the opportunities that students had, the decisions that were made, the way they felt about themselves and others, were influenced by individual temperament, desire, and motivation, combined with complex social, political, and cultural forces. The pushes and pulls of everyday life—responsibility at home, family finances, the example set by older family members, community values, the level of athletic ability and drive, and a multitude of other factors—created a strong and stable system of reinforcements that accommodated the choices available to students. This understanding of behavior-in-context is explained by adolescent psychologist Cynthia Lightfoot in this way, ". . . the actions of persons, and the contexts in which those actions are meaningful, are understood not as independent realities, but as interdependent, internally related, and recursive elucidations of each other" (1997: p. 136).

Four very capable and motivated students from Hillside-Two Rivers—all boys—chose not to be in eighth grade algebra. Based on what I know about the stresses in their lives, I have sometimes supported students in making decisions like that when they seemed overwhelmed by their academic work. But Fred's own hopes are revealed in something he told me one afternoon: "If I wanted to spend my whole life in Two Rivers, I wouldn't be doing my work," he said. There is a mismatch in Fred's life between hope and ability—Fred had plenty of those things—and the actual opportunities Fred and other students from working-class families have available to them.

To their credit, the teachers of Mountainview Middle School did not let students like Fred off the hook too easily. As educators, and in light of the potential consequences of academic decisions made at this time, it is our responsibility to make educational equity the complex and socially based issue it is, and to search for ways, through dialogue and collaboration with teachers and parents, to better prepare students for academic decisions, and to support and guide students of all backgrounds.

As I tried to make sense of the inequities I observed in extracurricular participation and academic opportunities, I found over and over that I could not attribute these discrepancies solely to the exclusion of students based on town and social class biases. There was something much more intricate going on, and students and their parents were part of the transaction. It seems we are caught in an invisible web—a system of "mutually reinforcing accommodations" that works mostly behind our backs in subtle unacknowledged ways. This web entangles students, peers, parents, teachers, administrators, and many others, visible and not visible.

I have struggled to find a way to articulate this concept. The phrase, "mutually reinforcing accommodations," was inspired by Bronfenbrenner's (1979) context-conscious, dynamic theory of human development: "The ecology of human development involves the scientific study of the progressive, mutual accommodation between an active, growing human being and the changing properties of the immediate settings in which the developing person lives, as this process is affected by relations between these settings, and by the larger contexts in which the settings are embedded" (p. 21).

The following example from my research demonstrates the multiple-level interacting and recursive forces that result in inequitable outcomes in students' lives: A boy from Hillside approaches middle school with confidence in his athletic ability and dreams of being an important player on his middle and high school teams. He wants to excel in sports more than anything. He has good grades in math so he is enrolled in pre-algebra but finds himself in a group of Lakeview students who all know each other; he is isolated from other kids from his town. When it's his turn to answer in class, his voice is uncertain. He seems self-consciously aware of his minority status. He sits apart from the other students at a table by himself. When it is time for the test to see who is going to eighth grade algebra, it's baseball season. He is playing hard and he is tired. His grades go down and he doesn't do so well on the test. His teacher wonders if he can really keep up next year, and the student begins to wonder himself if he is capable of rigorous academic courses. There is also a seductive and powerful message that sparks the imagination and desire of many ambitious working-class children: "If you keep playing well, college scholarships, money, and fame will be available to you." A college degree was not the privilege of either of his parents. Eighth grade algebra seems like an unnecessary added stress in an already stressful life. His parents, like others from Hillside-Two Rivers, are inclined to take into account their child's stress level, academic interest, family responsibilities, sports schedules, teacher recommendations, and so on. This student, his mom, and his teacher decide that he should skip eighth grade algebra.

It is unlikely that a similarly capable Lakeview student did not make it to algebra in eighth grade because there is a parallel system of reinforcing accommodations for high social status students. If a Lakeview student is in an accelerated class, he or she will be in the company of mostly Lakeview peers. Academic, sports, and social goals are set early and carefully monitored by parents and other adult mentors. Future career and higher education opportunities, and the means to access them, are much more clear to students from families with resources and information. Many Lakeview parents are vigilant in their efforts to move their children toward the things they value and they are willing to manipulate their child's environment whenever necessary, so much so that Lakeview students may be placed at risk because they face more rigid academic and occupational expectations. Even when high standards are implicit rather than explicit, students unable or unwilling to meet expectations experience a high level of stress.

And they may absorb competitive and exclusionary values and unilateral ways of thinking. A Lakeview student, also an athlete and with similar grades as his classmate from Hillside, did not wonder if *he* belonged in accelerated math or highly selective sports teams, but he did wonder if *other* students belonged there. He wished that the teachers would make the group more exclusive and "kick the slackers out." He sees some of his classmates as a threat to his advancement. When he looks for verification for this point of view, he finds ample agreement in many implicit and explicit societal messages. How will this student become educated about his own privilege and the system of mutually reinforcing accommodations that support this privilege? The lack of social perspective-taking in otherwise bright students is alarming, especially in light of the probability that students in accelerated classes are more likely to be in positions of leadership, authority, and power in the future.

The important point here is that the structure I refer to as a system of mutually reinforcing accommodations is not just about reproducing privilege for some and inequality for others. We have enough evidence here to also suggest that a wider interpretation of success and less emphasis on individualistic goals may be beneficial to healthy development, while narrow interpretations of success and less emphasis on communitarian goals may threaten healthy development.

Conclusion

My concern is that ability grouping may actually derail a child's development toward reciprocal thinking and acting particularly as it applies to intergroup social awareness and competence. Both Lakeview and Hillside students experience gaps in their schooling and both potentially face negative results. If the Hillside-Two Rivers students do not go to college, they may not have the opportunities for the scholarly work and lucrative careers that they are eminently capable of. If Lakeview students don't learn empathy and appreciation for diverse skills and ideas (their own as well as others), they may face life-long frustration in their interpersonal relationships, at work, in future educational settings, and in making close friends. In today's world, no one can claim to be well educated without an ability to form mutually respectful relationships across diverse boundaries.

As educators, we make efforts to accommodate what we think we hear from children and their parents; we try to respond to political and social pressures. However, we sometimes risk giving students what they want and not what they need, with potentially harmful results. Students who are most vulnerable to the stratifying mechanisms in schools (testing, ability grouping, course placement, disciplinary actions leading to suspension) are students from low social class backgrounds, students in isolated family situations, and students with cognitive, emotional, or neurological problems. We are poor predictors of the future especially when it comes to human potential and we should *never* feel comfortable about forecasting failure for our students. What students need are high expectations and the parallel support to meet them.

Eighth-grade algebra is here to stay and everyone should have access to it. Schools, families and community-based agencies must do everything in their power to understand the complex process of selection and self-selection, to inform parents and students of the long-term implications of their choices, and to provide support to students so they can choose wisely, and if they choose algebra, they can succeed.

CHAPTER 12

Success and Struggle in the Transition to Middle School

Successful or unsuccessful adjustment over the transition from elementary to middle school was a result of interconnected dynamics in several arenas: community and family cultures and educational and social values; the environments and resources of sending and receiving schools; the social, cognitive, emotional, and physical needs and resources of students; and the economic conditions of their lives. The thirty students in this study faced the transition with cautious enthusiasm. As elementary school students they had experienced a secure connection to their schools, homes, and communities. They had reason to be hopeful about continued success but worried that things beyond their control might compromise this success.

The challenge of transitioning to a new school, combined with the biological, emotional, and social stresses of early adolescence, produce significant strain in early adolescent lives, even when they face new tasks in the context of responsive schools and supportive families. At this critical developmental juncture, new academic and social roles and responsibilities require complex organizational and interpersonal skills. Most adolescents have the capacity and the drive to have deeper, more meaningful relationships with their peers and with the significant adults in their lives. Academic and social accomplishments or perceived failures are all the more significant to adolescents in the context of increased autonomy and self-determination. How well they do, and how well others treat them over the transition year, become benchmarks in self-evaluation that may boost or bruise their sense of efficacy, self-esteem, and future possibilities.

Several factors contributed to successful transition for most research participants in this study. Their communities and families valued and encouraged active involvement, academic achievement, and a positive sense of self. Hillside and Lakeview Elementary Schools and Mountainview Middle School joined families to intentionally prepare students for the transition, and offered classroom and after-school activities that provided opportunities for competition and cooperation, autonomy and intimacy, social and cognitive development, individual development and a sense of community. Some teachers held *all* their students to high standards and provided sufficient support to help them meet high expectations.

A very significant factor was the hopeful adaptive strategies of the students themselves, such as the resilient way some students recovered from disappointing outcomes and their ability to shape their microenvironments to be familiar and friendly. Students in this study sought out and benefited from adult role models at school and in their communities and, importantly, school staff and community adults were willing to be enlisted in this way. Finally, most of the students in this study had good health, enough rest, physical safety, a place and time to study, and technical resources like a calculator, a computer at home, pencils and notebooks—things that not all children have.

The work of this project has been to understand as Lewin (1951) suggested, that any event is a result of a "multitude of factors," (p. 44) and to find ways to integrate realities that, at first glance, seem contradictory. Along with stories of successful adjustment to middle school, there was also evidence of struggle that placed some children at greater risk during the transition year. For example, I found distinct town cultures that were each rich with historic and social resources, but the Hillside-Two Rivers community is unknown to most outsiders. Superficial characterizations of poverty in Hillside-Two Rivers and wealth in Lakeview continue to result in a polarization of these communities, mask the deeper structure of everyday life in each community, and threaten clear analysis of problems and strengths by the citizenry of each town.

During this vital period of identity development, students may be especially subject to damaging societal messages. Commercialism exploits the vulnerabilities of early adolescents—there are material, status, and appearance expectations that are confusing, unrealistic, and often damaging to evolving self-concepts. Rigid gender roles are problematic for both girls *and* boys and cultural stereotypes place low *and* high-income children at risk. These issues pose serious challenges to children in the formation of positive self-identity.

Successful school adjustment is also threatened by structures that limit opportunities to middle school students, such as competitive and exclusive inter-scholastic sports teams, homogenous grouping, and lack of access to school leadership roles. The harmful results of these factors are perhaps represented in a decline in self-esteem in boys from Hillside-

Two Rivers and in girls from Lakeview over the transition year, the disproportionately small numbers of Hillside-Two Rivers students in accelerated classes, and the low participation rates of Hillside-Two Rivers boys in school and community activities.

For many students nationwide, the transition to middle school represents an adjustment to a bigger and more diverse environment. A longer bus ride, an earlier start to the day, a variety of teachers and classes, and more choices and responsibilities pose new challenges and opportunities. In supportive and inclusive environments, students can enjoy deeper and more meaningful connections with peers and non-familial adults, a sense of gratification in being able to handle new situations well, and a greater sense of competence.

In the next few pages, I will summarize the key findings, connecting them to the research questions. Chapter 13 will summarize the implications of these findings for policy and practice.

Students' Funds of Knowledge Were Irregularly Integrated

My observations at Mountainview Regional Middle School, my individual and group conversations with students, and the answers on student questionnaires, suggest that most, but not all, of the thirty research participants felt a sense of congruity across home, school, and community domains. Children brought to school interests, social interaction styles, values, skills, and desires that were shaped by their families and communities and influenced the way they participated in class and interacted with adults and peers. They were received by a functional middle school that offered a range of teaching styles, varied extracurricular opportunities, and more than adequate resources. Children actively defined the tone, pace, and means of communication in the school environment and used endlessly creative strategies to adapt to and change their surroundings. Perhaps the most pronounced example of this is the way children shaped their environment during less controlled times of the day—the school bus, halls during break, and unsupervised classroom situations.

Comparing Hillside-Two Rivers and Lakeview, we see neighboring towns that share a strong sense of citizenship, healthy self-sufficiency, active social and political involvement, and rich natural resources. We also see two communities with contrasting and complementary lifestyles. In Hillside-Two Rivers, I found that many students had close family and neighborhood ties, a strong sense of communal goals, a here-and-now orientation, an appreciation for the traditional past, and a faith in the goodness of the local community. The cultural environment of Lakeview emphasizes independence, active involvement, upward mobility, future-oriented goals, optimism, and individuality. Families from both communities hoped the schools would reflect these values. As students approached middle school, some Lakeview parents criticized structures, such as heterogeneous grouping and cooperative learning, that they believed would interfere with individual goals and educational attainment, and some Hillside-Two Rivers parents worried that their children may not have as many options for meaningful involvement at the middle school. Hillside-Two Rivers parents also wondered if the people responsible for their child's education knew enough about their community to foster positive self-image in their children. *There are stereotypes of both towns, but Hillside-Two Rivers students came to know and appreciate Lakeview during the seventh grade, while their own community remained unknown to their Lakeview peers, and therefore, still subject to misinterpretation and distortion.*

My research results indicate that most of the thirty students, regardless of social class background, found ways to integrate their personal styles, values, interests, resources, and skills during the school day. However, there is evidence that Lakeview students may have enjoyed more explicit institutional validation for these "funds of knowledge" (Moll et al., 1992) and may have been able to integrate them more fully during core academic classes and structured times of the day. Hillside-Two Rivers students were able to integrate their funds of knowledge more successfully during unstructured times of the day and in ancillary courses such as Spanish and physical education. Furthermore, while Lakeview children utilized and contributed personal and familial assets that were recognized and acknowledged, the assets brought by many Hillside-Two Rivers students remained invisible. For example, Hillside-Two Rivers students contributed a cooperative, tolerant attitude that made it more okay to "just be yourself," but even though Lakeview students told me they were relieved to find less emphasis on clothing styles and a more relaxed attitude about popularity in the middle school, they did not attribute this improvement in atmosphere to the presence of a more diverse group of peers. *While Hillside-Two Rivers students seemed aware of the new opportunities Lakeview offered them—new friends, a nice down town to explore, new styles and tastes—Lakeview students did not seem conscious of how they benefited from their Hillside-Two Rivers classmates.*

A healthy, diverse school environment enables full and active reciprocity between the students' background and the school. When the contributions of Hillside-Two Rivers students go unnoticed, they are left feeling ambivalent toward their own community. Cross-town and own-town attitudes reflected in interviews and answers on question-naires, demonstrated that over the transition year students from *both* towns developed a more positive attitude about Lakeview and a more negative or neutral attitude about Hillside-Two Rivers. There is a two-way loss when diverse resources are not noticed and utilized: Lakeview children may continue to judge themselves based on narrow criteria such as clothing and material belongings and Hillside-Two Rivers children may not fully grasp the options they have when peers and adult mentors do not validate their strengths and resources.

The middle school experience might be improved for *all* students if the complementary assets of both communities were more fully recognized and integrated. With vision, imagination, and adult leadership community service could have as much prestige as competitive sports. Cooperative and connected patterns of communication could have as much currency as fast-paced, TV-influenced, hierarchy-driven interactions. All teachers and students could be familiar with the historic and social richness of all the towns in the school district. Accelerated classes in all subject areas could have social class diversity. Creative and associative learning styles could be utilized as much as logical and linear styles.

Positive Self-Identity Requires New Ways of Thinking

Contrary to my expectations, I found that good outcomes for Hillside-Two Rivers children *and* for Lakeview children could be at risk but in different ways. Remember sixth grade promotion night—Lakeview children on the stage, Hillside children seated in the gym with their teachers on the stage? For better or for worse, the socialization of many Lakeview children leads them to look outward at their world and audience. They want to know, "What do you think of me? Am I good? Better than the next kid?" Hillside children on the other hand may be cued in many subtle ways that they are not the actors, but the audience. Some Lakeview children may thrive with the challenge of meeting these expectations, but for others, the experience of social comparison and pressure to perform may be excruciating, perhaps even leading toward lower performance and self-esteem. Hillside children, on the other hand, may be elated to have higher academic expectations and extracurricular opportunities but may face frustration when they yearn to have a place on the stage and find that no one was expecting them and there's not enough room.

More than any other group, white, middle class boys experience a sense of congruity in their identity development—a consistency between their desires and the cultural and institutional frameworks that nurture these desires. Lakeview boys led the pack in self-esteem, participation, and ability grouping. They find ample reinforcement for their view of the world and for their place in it. However, over the 18-month period of talking with students and observing them in a variety of settings, I noticed something amazing happen: As I continued talking with Hillside students, listening carefully for their meaning, and what they were communicating to me about their experiences in seventh grade, their interactions with me became more fluid, more sure, more deep and analytical. The more we talked and explored the situations of their lives, the more skilled and confident they became at communicating their perceptions to me. At the same time, when I probed the perceptions of Lakeview students for their personal meaning, they became more tongue-tied, and unsure. It appeared that when asked to consider new and different information about themselves and others, these extraordinarily articulate students became more and more uncertain about what they were saying. Lakeview students, more than Hillside-Two Rivers students, experience school in ways that confirm and reinforce their structure of reality. But shouldn't good schooling be more than that? Seldom, if ever, do we ask some students to confront the hard social and ethical questions they are so capable of confronting. As a result, their understanding of themselves and others may be handicapped by myth.

Students with Secure Relationships Maintained High Self-Esteem

Students were universally concerned with making new friends and keeping old friends as they approached middle school. Positive, consistent, and meaningful peer relationships are so vital in the lives of adolescents that when this essential ingredient is missing, successful adjustment to middle school is threatened. Students from both communities were not sure they would be accepted in their new and more diverse school, but by the end of the seventh grade, most students reflected positively on their seventh grade year and felt they were successful at making friends.

However, several students from both communities felt they did not fit in with their peers and many students did not make good, lasting friendships with classmates from other communities. In fact, some students commented that the efforts made at the beginning of seventh grade to make friends from other communities were all but lost by the end of seventh grade. Students were more likely to make friends in other communities when they belonged to extracurricular activities that were integrated by town. Despite early promise of a more integrated school experience, town of residence remained a salient dividing line for students. Indeed, town of residence became *more* salient as the year went on and selections for accelerated math and sports teams were being made.

I found that the needs of students for secure friendships transcended their need for status. Students told me repeatedly that it didn't matter where they sat in the lunchroom or how popular they were as long as they were with friends. Students with good, lasting friendships seemed more at ease about their place in the middle school. In the end, the fulfillment of this preeminent desire to feel a sense of belonging to one's peer group became a leading factor in how students reported their seventh grade experience. At the same time, students emphasized the value of their relationships with parents, teachers, coaches, neighbors, and other significant adults.

Self-esteem scores were one indication of how students fared in the social and emotional realm across the transition. The results produced these key findings: 1) Home self-esteem was higher and remained more stable for children from both communities across the transition; 2) school self-esteem went up in the fall of grade seven but, by the end of grade seven, went down to just below the sixth grade average; 3) peer self-esteem was slightly higher in Lakeview than in Hillside-Two Rivers, but peer self-esteem improved over the transition to seventh grade for Hillside-Two Rivers students and stayed the same for Lakeview students.

High socioeconomic status did not result in high total self-esteem as expected. By the end of grade seven, girls from Hillside-Two Rivers and boys from Lakeview had the highest total self-esteem, while boys from Hillside-Two Rivers and girls from Lakeview had the lowest self-esteem. These results indicate the importance of considering gender as a factor in school adaptation and, even more importantly, they indicate that socioeconomic status influences the experiences of boys and girls differently.

There is evidence to further suggest an interaction between gender, low social class, and family disruption. Boys who had experienced the divorce of their parents, from low and low-middle social class backgrounds, obtained the lowest total self-esteem scores at the end of seventh grade. Perhaps this is because boys may feel more cultural pressure to fill in as the "man of the house" and provide economic and emotional support to their mothers and siblings without the resources to do so, at a time of heightened academic responsibility and social pressure.

Girls from middle and high social class backgrounds may be especially vulnerable to messages that insist that nice clothes, popularity, and good looks are essential. Some Lakeview girls became unsure of their self-worth over time regardless of their security at home and their successful involvement in extracurricular activities. Hillside-Two Rivers girls seemed to care less about looking and acting in fashionably designated ways and their home and community cultures allowed them this freedom. They were more relaxed and more able to develop a sense of their self-worth based on other factors, like the quality of their relationships and the ways they contributed in school, at home, and in the community.

A pathway to high self-esteem for boys in this study was economic and family stability, good grades, and moderate home responsibility. A pathway for high self-esteem in girls was entering adolescence with strong community and family messages that allowed them to just be themselves, and opportunities to contribute in meaningful ways at home and at school.

The transition to middle school is a formidable task in itself requiring efforts in a variety of domains. Even when the process is well supported by parents, teachers, and administrators, as it was in this case, this transition represents an enormous developmental challenge. Hillside-Two Rivers students approached the transition with more uncertainty than their Lakeview peers did. Although they valiantly protected themselves from negative outside appraisal of their community, they were aware of demeaning stereotypes and they quietly wondered how their classmates from other towns might view them. Most of them arrived at the middle school and found themselves to be up to the challenge, boosting their sense of competence.

Lakeview students were not faced with as much change and did not perceive the transition to be an academic challenge. The threat of failure did not loom as large for Lakeview children and, therefore, mastering their new environment was, perhaps, not as affirming. However, when Lakeview children struggled in their new environment, they did so with full knowledge that they were the ones thought to be most likely to excel. There is an expectation of success for Lakeview students, making difficult adjustment all the more hurtful. The communities that children come from provide both protections and risks in the social and emotional domains during the transition to seventh grade.

The Benefits and Hazards of Social Class Background

Some students faced more challenges than others and I observed and heard many examples of sharply contrasting realities from the lives of students. For example, some students got rides to and from school from their parents, had a good computer and Internet access at home, always had what they needed (notebooks, binders, a calculator, pens, etc.), were able to buy trendy clothes, went special places during school vacations, and knew their parents were familiar with the school and with their teachers and coaches. Other students had to get themselves up and ready in the morning, took the school bus because that was their only option, knew their parents would not get to games because they had to work late, took care of siblings on school vacations, were aware that money was often an issue in their household, and doubted that their teachers and coaches knew their parents. Participation and interaction patterns are at least somewhat influenced by factors that are often unknown to school staff. Insuring a good fit and educational equity requires a broad view of students' lives.

Most students were active in school and community activities in grade six, but overall, participation declined in the seventh grade. Extracurricular activities are important because participating students have opportunities to make good friends among a more diverse group of peers, have a mentoring relationship with an adult coach or advisor, are afforded numerous health and enrichment benefits, and gain experience that is valued on college applications. When I examined participation rates for all middle school students, I found that participation in extracurricular activities varied from town to town, for a variety of reasons. The competitive, selective nature of some sports, unequal opportunities for children to develop adequate skills before seventh grade teams are selected, responsibilities at home, and problems connected to rural transportation posed barriers to participation. Lakeview students were likely to be involved in well-organized, and well-resourced town sports if they were not in school sports, but these options were not available to most Hillside-Two Rivers students, who had lower rates of participation in grade seven. It is concerning that so many boys from Hillside-Two Rivers do not, or cannot, participate in extracurricular activities.

The selection process for sports teams was one way students were grouped by institutional criteria; academic grouping was another. Following national patterns of homogenous grouping, only two or three students out of eighteen or nineteen were from Hillside-Two Rivers in each of the seventh grade accelerated academic groups. All four boys who were research participants from Hillside-Two Rivers with high standardized math scores were not in eighth grade algebra. School performance and educational attainment are the result of a complex combination of opportunities and resources: The presence of adults who have succeeded in school and who encourage educational goals; access to accurate information about the future implications of course selection; the student's sense of competence and motivation; peer relationships; and teacher, parent, and community expectations. Cognitive ability certainly matters, but I have begun to wonder if it may indeed be one of the least important factors when it comes to academic achievement in the middle grades.

Parents from Hillside-Two Rivers were less likely to intervene in their child's educational placement and sports opportunities, and they were less likely to convey to their children that it is important to be chosen for high-status positions. But while Hillside-Two Rivers students may be at risk of not having as many opportunities as Lakeview students, Lakeview students may be placed at risk by explicit or implicit expectations for high performance positions when the expectations are not realistic or not desired by the student. Lakeview children who do not meet their own or others' expectations may feel they have no one to blame but themselves; Hillside children may not be expected to perform at the high level many of them are so eminently capable of. Either way, children from both communities were harmed or privileged by what I have referred to as a system of "mutually reinforcing accommodations"—a network of interactions between community values, parent and teacher expectations, student temperaments, and broader cultural messages. In none of the cases was harm or privilege absolute.

Student responses to ability grouping at the end of the year seemed to indicate that ability grouping might deter social awareness and reinforce stereotypes. My greatest concern about ability grouping in the seventh grade is that, at just the time students need environments that improve interpersonal competence and intergroup perspective-taking, homogeneous classroom situations threaten to derail progress toward these goals and encourage intergroup biases.

Parents and policymakers who believe that children must have homogeneous grouping to get ahead, may not be aware that top-level institutions of higher education are now considering expanded indicators of academic potential; high SAT scores and As in honors classes are no longer enough. They are also looking at whether or not the student is well developed in areas previously not considered, for example, service to the community and evidence of cross-cultural understanding. Talented students deserve to know that if getting into a top-level school is important to them, they will be judged on a variety of indicators including their awareness of and sensitivity to diversity. It is "human breadth, not narrow brilliance" that institutions of higher education are looking for, and "the personal qualities of students have never mattered more" such as "teamwork and the ability to educate others," a recent article in Harvard Magazine claimed (March-April 2001, p. 70).

An important insight from this study is that, in the end, *Lakeview children have more opportunity but less liberty to make their own academic, career, and social choices; Hillside-Two Rivers students may have more degrees of freedom in defining social and academic success but fewer opportunities.* Narrow and restrictive definitions of success harm some Lakeview children who need room to grow in areas that may not be as well regarded by their parents, teachers, and peers. For Hillside-Two Rivers children, a more flexible range in determining success may give some of them the "freedom" to fall short of their academic capabilities and may handicap future options.

Sounding the Alarm

Even though most research participants adjusted to middle school successfully, I was constantly made aware of the anxiety many of them continued to feel about their peer relationships. And I was increasingly cognizant of how painful school can be for students of all social class backgrounds when they feel they do not fit in.

On May 31, 2000, the week I finished data collection for this project, a fifteen-year-old boy from Hillside went home after school one afternoon, made a video for his parents, took his father's gun and went into the woods in his backyard and took his own life. He was buried with a burn mark on his cheek—a classmate seared his face with a hot glue stick a couple of days before he pulled the trigger. As the tragedy of his too-short life was told to me by his friends and his grandmother, I heard echoes of stories from other adolescents who considered suicide or who vented their rage on other students: He had endured years of targeting by his peers, he pretended he didn't care, he made others laugh at him by doing silly things, when he told others what he was going to do they didn't take him seriously, he was a risk-taker sometimes pushing his own safety perilously near the edge to get a response from his peers, he was small for his age, he struggled in school, and he sometimes seemed withdrawn. Many people did not fully grasp the immeasurable pain he carried. Like many boys whose emotional pain is a source of shame, he did everything he could to mask his feelings. Peer rejection began to be unbearable to him when he transitioned to the middle school from Hillside Elementary School.

My research participants were seventh graders when this happened. I spent a lot of time wondering if any of the Hillside-Two Rivers students who rode the bus with this boy every day thought to themselves, "That could be me."

At the memorial service, one of his friends remembered something that speaks volumes: "I moved here a few years ago from Lakeview. He was the first person I got to know," his friend said. "I had gone to school in Lakeview and I was surprised by how silly he acted. He used to tell me, 'Relax. This is Hillside. You're supposed to just act how you act.'" The room full of Hillside people smiled through their tears, appreciating this gentle, true characterization of life here: You just "act how you act." There are no pretenses; it's okay in Hillside to just be yourself and act silly. But it wasn't okay at school—a school that must have seemed very far away from home for this boy.

In the weeks that followed, I learned that he loved the out of doors, liked to fish and ride his four-wheeler, and played hacky-sack at lunch with a homemade ball. A couple of days after the service his two grandmothers and grandfather came to my office looking for answers about how this could have happened, and to ask me and my coworkers to do everything we could to prevent this from happening to other families. His grandmother said, "I just thank God he didn't do harm to another student." But she grieved how he was treated at school and relayed this story: "One teacher called him 'Hillside' instead of his real name. Why would a teacher do something like that?"

For weeks I kept asking myself, who is responsible for the death of this child? Was it other kids whose cruelty finally drove him over the edge? Teachers who did not recognize and intervene in targeting and stereotypes? A family who failed to get him help through a long period of depression? The culture that shames and silences boys who struggle with self-image? Community programs like my own that fail to extend their reach far enough to involve troubled adolescents before hopelessness becomes intolerable? The gun lobby that enables people to have guns without safety locks?

In the summer months that followed, two other teens, with family connections in both Hillside and Lakeview, died in car accidents. Worried teens and parents from both communities came together to discuss the circumstances that may lead to teen depression. How children live and die is never the result of any one factor in any one domain; it is a shared responsibility. Preventing tragedy and supporting success takes efforts on multiple levels.

CHAPTER 13

Implications for Research, Policy, and Practice

A Research Agenda

Giroux (1988) argued that schools are "cultural and political spheres actively engaged in the production and struggle for voice . . . Schools do not allow students from subordinate groups to authenticate their problems and lived experiences through their own individual and collective voices" (p. 206). Four research recommendations arise from this project and from the very real "struggle for voice" I encountered.

Consult Students and Teachers About Policy and Practice Decisions

The students in this study were reliable, articulate, and authentic sources of knowledge and enthusiastic research participants. Researchers need to consult young people more often in order to gain better understanding of the conditions of their lives and to inform educational policy and practice. The insights of these students regarding social and academic grouping, for example, provided valuable information that could not have been derived from any other source. Teachers also possess untapped knowledge about classroom interactions. School districts would do well to enable teachers to undertake more systematic exploration of teaching through school-based action research projects. School districts must provide resources for data collection, personal reflection, team analysis, and effective links to policy and curriculum development.

Study These Issues in Larger, More Differentiated Populations

This study examined the adjustment to middle school in a relatively low-risk but economically diverse group of students. A handful of students in my study struggled during the transition year, leading me to wonder about these questions: Would I find Mountainview Middle School to be as strong in meeting the needs of a broader group of students? Would some students benefit from a K-8 model where they would not have to undergo a disruptive transition at the age of twelve and then again two years later? Would the patterns of high and low self-esteem be the same in a larger population? A similar comparative study with a broader range of students would provide valuable information about how students who face academic and social challenges fare during the transition.

Document Resilience and Strength Using Creative Methodologies

Some researchers have critiqued the standardization of middle-class values in school programs (e.g., Bourdieu & Passeron, 1977; Bowles & Gintis, 1976; Freire, 1970; Giroux, 1983) but very few researchers have explored, in-depth, the beneficial values and lifestyles of low-income communities (for an example, see Willie, 1985). More research about how people thrive needs to come out of the experience of people from less known communities. Many questions about children's experiences in school are phenomenological in nature and therefore require phenomenological approaches. Ethnographic community and classroom comparisons provide multidimensional, contextualized information that have relevance to teachers, administrators and policymakers.

Collect and Analyze Population Specific Data on Educational Outcomes

When I tried to access information concerning drop-out rates, college enrollment and completion, standardized test results, and course selection, I found that school districts seldom collect information or examine results by gender, town of residence, or socioeconomic status. Careful collection and analysis of this sort of data would provide communities and schools with important and valuable information. While general information is sufficient for some purposes, corrective efforts require population-specific information in order to appropriate resources and implement useful programs to overcome deficits. Finally, there is a need for much more understanding of schooling in rural areas, the lives of rural youth, and the issues families and communities face.

An Agenda for Policy and Practice

Review Policy and Practice Decisions and Promote Equity

When making educational policy decisions, such as dress codes, expulsion rules, tracking structures, standards for sports team selections, student evaluation methods, graduation requirements, or how academic credit is awarded, it is important to investigate and fully understand the way the policy would affect diverse students. To limit risk to vulnerable students, questions like these need to be addressed: Whom does this policy (or practice) protect? Who might benefit and who might be hurt? Are there students who would be placed at greater risk if this policy/practice were implemented? Does the outcome justify the potential risks of this policy/practice? What or who is the impetus for this change? Whose values or desires are affirmed by this policy/practice and whose values or desires are not considered? If this is not a reasonable risk, are there other ways to attain similar results? Policy development in schools must be better informed by actual data, and less influenced by the political pressures exerted by a small, vocal group of people who wield more than their fair share of power.

Initiate District-Wide Diversity Committees

School districts, perhaps *especially* those in rural predominantly white areas, do well to initiate diversity committees with broad community membership whose job it is to work for educational equity for all students. These committees might, for example, research ability grouping practices, review curricula, suggest professional development programs, make recommendations for changes in structures that are found to be inequitable and unsound educationally, and design and implement mechanisms for better access, participation, and involvement from families in outlying areas.

Recognize and Promote Resilience in Youth

In my research participants, I found many of the traits listed in Emmy Werner's (1990) summary of research on resilience in children. Children who were more stress-resistant at school shared a number of common traits, according to Werner: They were well-liked by peers and adults; they were reflective rather than impulsive; they believed they were capable of influencing their environment positively; they employed creative coping strategies to overcome adversity.

Werner also cited researchers who found that resilient children "possessed well-developed problem solving and communication skills . . . were not only sociable but also remarkably independent . . . able to concentrate on their school work . . . [and] displayed a healthy androgyny" (p. 103). When teachers and parents are aware of the adaptive efforts of children and when they acknowledge and support these strategies, they create environments that promote resilience.

Most students experienced the transition successfully and when they ran into trouble, they had family and school resources in place to help them out. Many students were able to bridge highly disparate environments by creatively implementing the tools and resources from home. Take, for example, the way Jaz found ways to replicate a "family feeling" in her new school environment by enlisting the support of an older boy on the school bus to be like an older brother. Other students similarly established connections with peers and adults to be "like family." We need to find ways to recognize and support this natural resilience in children so that they can keep doing what makes them strong.

Prevent Negative Outcomes for Vulnerable Children

All children need to feel a sense of security and connection. Depression and anxiety among adolescents is higher than ever; today, one in five children need extra help to cope with psychological and emotional distress (Garbarino & Bedard, 2001; Kazdin, 1993). Preventing bad things from happening takes community-wide awareness and effort. Children thrive or fail in the context of peer, home, and school environments. It is not accurate or helpful to place blame in one place or another, nor is it effective to focus intervention efforts only on children who are perceived to be at risk. Social interaction problems require social interaction solutions in broader classroom, school, and community contexts.

When it becomes clear that some groups of children may be placed at higher risk due to certain conditions, it is important to intervene. What we know from this study is that girls from Lakeview and boys from Hillside-Two Rivers, especially those who have experienced family disruption, had lower self-esteem scores at the end of seventh grade. Programs that enhance self-esteem in girls, such as small-group activities, creative writing, and discussions after school are an appropriate response. Counseling, mentoring, and small group programs that provide support and understanding to boys who have experienced the divorce of their parents are essential. Children from low-income communities need opportunities to participate more in school and community activities as a way to expand their options. Boys and girls both need opportunities for sustained, authentic relationships with peers and adults who do not reinforce gender stereotypes but who offer healthy role modeling in being comfortable with oneself—physically and emotionally. In addition, parent education on the effects of divorce and other specific issues in boys and girls development in early adolescence is needed. To accomplish these things, much more collaboration among organizations, schools, churches, and families is needed to more effectively address the issues of today's adolescents.

If adolescents do not find what is familiar to them to help them survive in school, they will recreate something they can understand— whether we like it or not. Cliques and gangs are an effort to secure a sense of belonging and safety when the environment threatens physical or emotional harm. Students, perhaps particularly at this age, need guidance in dealing respectfully with diversity, they need assistance with friendship-building skills, and they need support when they are having friendship problems.

Build and Sustain Alliances with Parents

Healthy development and positive educational outcomes are enhanced when children sense cooperation and respect between home, school, and community domains. In rural, regional school districts, the connection between home and school changes dramatically when children leave their own-town elementary schools to transition to multi-town middle schools. For out-of-town families the middle school is farther away in miles, as well as in things less tangible. The curriculum and structures are more complex, there are many more students per grade, parents must learn a whole new vocabulary along with their children, the work is harder, and so on. It takes a very committed administrative and teaching staff to build alliances with parents to involve them in their child's learning in a way that is meaningful. Finding ways for all parents to be positively involved in their child's education is essential and requires thought, respect, and resources from school administrators and teachers.

Continue Heterogeneous Grouping

It is an irony that a country that so prides itself on the fluidity of its class structure sets up systems to fix class in place and at every turn. I am opposed to rigid ability grouping in middle schools because it restricts opportunity for the next five years and beyond. At this particularly important time of social development there is potential for increased interpersonal and intergroup understanding. Ability grouping threatens to encourage unilateral thinking and acting and harms respect for diversity.

I know of one middle school where eighth grade algebra is the standard curriculum for everyone. Teachers at this heterogeneously grouped school, cognizant of college admissions standards and the way eighth grade algebra determines the math trajectory through high school, decided that if algebra was advantageous for some students it should be an advantage accessible to *all* students. Most middle school students, if prepared properly, are developmentally ready for algebra and can learn a lot of math in one year. Sixth and seventh grade teachers need the resources to make this a possibility.

Show How We All Benefit From Diversity

Children from different towns need more accurate information about each other. Rural education needs more attention. Communities and neighborhoods need to insist on values of compassion, altruism, respect, and honesty. Adolescents need guidance so they can discern damaging marketing messages and consumer standards that honor greed and self-centeredness. We all need to recognize how much we benefit and how much stronger we are, individually and collectively, because of diversity.

These are some suggestions I have heard: One mother suggested that starting in grade school, all the children in the school district could come together for a day or two of cooperative games and discussions. These days would take place in the six towns of the school district, hosted by the different elementary schools. A teacher suggested that when the seventh grade teams do their September overnight they could visit each of the towns outside Lakeview and conduct programs that highlight local history and geography. Students could, for example, conduct oral history interviews with residents, visit the landmarks of each town with the local historian, make dinner together in the community church, and learn about the natural history of the area. Another parent called for community discussions with participation from parents, students, teachers, and administrators. My most cherished hope is that this work will generate ideas like these and encourage people to talk with each other about how these issues play out in their own schools and communities.

Promote Justice, Compassion, and Understanding

In the end, I learned that social class presents assets and barriers to children, regardless of their background. Lakeview students are more vulnerable to social comparisons and pressure, but have more opportunities; Hillside students are more flexible in the face of disappointment, but have fewer options available to them. If we want our children to be smart but not arrogant; flexible but not easily pushed away from their hopes and dreams; compassionate toward others but not self-denying; confident but not preoccupied with themselves; proud but not exclusive, then we would do well to provide them with diverse environments and the means of functioning well in them. That way, Hillside-Two Rivers students might someday be on the field hockey or soccer teams, or might in the future be fully represented in eighth grade algebra, student council, and honors courses, or may someday hear from their classmates, "I've been to Hillside, it's a great town!" And Lakeview students might someday know it's okay to "just be yourself," and have the freedom to interact without fear on the school bus, or the choice to sit any place at all in the lunchroom without concern about losing status.

Children need adults to reaffirm strong community values, including compassion and generosity, so that they will know that material and occupational status can never be the basis for judging the worth of people. Communities can improve outcomes for all children, if they heed the lessons from students on these pages: support good teaching and good schools, nurture other ways of being smart, encourage student's natural resilience, make our communities and schools strong through diversity, and encourage the empathic and generous tendencies of students toward others.

This account of how thirty students made the transition to middle school raises issues of equity and fairness, issues of self-concept and stress, but when we look at the whole context of adolescent lives, we see much more than missed opportunities. We see tender lives, filled with promise and hope.

Comparisons of Educational and Economic Factors*

		Hillside	Lakeview	State
1.	Less than 9th grade education	7.7%	5.2%	6%
2.	9th to 12th grade, no diploma	24%	10.8%	12%
3.	Four year college degree	9.3%	19.2%	15.2%
4.	Advanced degree	3%	8.6%	6.9%
5.	Poverty below age 18	16.3%	4%	7.4%
6.	Poverty ages 18–64	8.6%	4.6%	5.4%
7.	Median Family Income	$26,932	$34,640	$41,628
8.	Unemployment	15%	2%	6.2%
9.	Families receiving Medicaid	40.8%	21.1%	NA
10.	Mothers under age 20	17%	6%	6.9%
11.	Language testing	4% advanced 12% proficient 51% basic 29% novice	5% advanced 30% proficient 50% basic 10% novice	NA
12.	Math testing	6% advanced 14% proficient 39% basic 39% novice	13% advanced 29% proficient 44% basic 12% novice	NA

* Items 1-10 from 1990 Census Data, reported by the Department of Employment Security; Items 11–12 from 1995 State testing data from Kids Count, [State] Children's Alliance, 1996.

Rubric for Defining Socioeconomic Status Categories

Education:

1   Less than high school
2   High school diploma or GED
3   Some college
4   College graduate
5   Graduate study

Occupation:

1   Disabled, unemployed
2   Service worker, waitress, custodian, home day care
3   Skilled workers, carpenter, dispatcher, electrician, bookkeeper, shop supervisor, assistant teacher
4   Administrative assistants, teachers, respiratory/occupational therapist, case technician, recreation director, forester
5   Managers, executives, business owners

Property Value:

1   < $50,000 or renting
2   $51,000–$100,000
3   $101,000–$150,000
4   $151,000–$200,00
5   > $200,000 (or primary home > $150,000 plus summer home)

Number of Caretakers in Household

0   One adult caretaker present
1   Two adult caretakers present

Scores of

5 through 7 = low SES
8 through 11 = middle SES
12 through 15 = high SES

Recommendations of the Carnegie Council on Adolescent Development

Interestingly, rather than suggesting a reversion to K–8 schools, Simmons and Blyth (1987) made suggestions for ways middle schools could reduce negative outcomes and enhance development over the transition. The Carnegie Council on Adolescent Development (1989) took the conclusions of these authors and others to come up with the following list of recommendations for middle schools:

1. Large middle schools should be divided into smaller communities for learning, student and teacher teams, and an adult advisor for every student.

2. Middle-grades schools should transmit a core of knowledge to all students; schools must teach young adolescents how to think critically, about healthy lifestyles, and skills for active citizenship.

3. Middle-grades schools should maximize opportunities for success, through cooperative learning, flexible scheduling, and new opportunities.

4. Teachers in middle grades should be specifically prepared to teach young adolescents, and must understand the developmental, cultural, and educational needs they bring.

5. Teachers should be able to influence curriculum decisions, should have roles on school governance and policy-making committees, and roles as instructional leaders for their peers.

6. Schools should be environments for health promotion, including access to health services specific to the needs of adolescents. They should encourage a healthy atmosphere through nutritional food, no smoking rules, alcohol and drug education, physical fitness programs, and school safety measures.

7. Families should be allied with school staff through mutually respectful and trusting relationships; parents should have roles in school governance and policy making, ways to be involved in their child's education at home and at school, and access to all the information they need to help guide their child's educational decisions.

8. Schools and communities should be linked in educating young adolescents. School-community partnerships should offer meaningful opportunities for community service, ensure access to mental and physical health and social services, encourage ways to supplement the education and support of middle school students, connect teachers and students to community resources, and expand career guidance for students.

Sample Student Questionnaire

> Home, School, and Friends
> A Youth Questionnaire About Belonging, Hoping, and Caring
> Seventh Grade ~ Fall 1999

Dear_____,

   Now that you have gone from grade 6 to grade 7, I would like to hear your first impressions of the Middle School. So, this is a questionnaire about you as a seventh grader. Your answers to these questions will help me to know how seventh grade meets (or doesn't meet) your expectations, what activities you like to do, who you like to be with, what responsibilities you have, what you think about certain things, and who you go to when you need help. Some of the questions are the same as last time, but your answers may have changed. Some questions are different.

   Please take all the time you need and answer the questions carefully and honestly. Don't worry about spelling but do your best. If you have any questions, please ask me. These are *your* answers; there are no right or wrong answers to these questions. If there is something more you want to tell me about your answer, or if these questions make you think of other things that I did not ask, we will have a chance to talk after.

   Thank you!
   Donna

Name:_____Age:_____Date:_____

Team:_____Advisory:_____

Please list other schools you have been to since kindergarten and
the grades you were there:

If your address or phone number has changed
since last time we met, please give your new....

Address:_____

Phone:_____

Part I ~ Sentence Completion

1. When I thought about seventh grade, I expected to *be...*
   and now that I am in seventh grade, I *am...*
2. When I thought about seventh grade, I expected to *feel...*
   and now that I am in seventh grade, I *feel...*
3. When I thought about seventh grade, I expected to *have...*
   and now that I am in seventh grade, I *have...*
4. This year, I hope...
5. At home I feel...
   and at school I feel...
6. At home I act...
   and at school I act...
7. One thing I wish people at school could know about me is...
8. Now, I go to school with students from six towns and I have discovered . . .
9. Hillside...
10. Lakeview...

Part II ~ Belonging and Participating

1. Please write down all the organized *school* activities, sports, and clubs you are or have been active in this year so far. Tell how many times a week you do this activity. Do not count the activities that you did in the sixth grade.
    School Activity: How many times per week?

2. Please write down all the organized *community* activities, sports, and clubs you are or have been active in this year. Tell how often you do them and tell what organization sponsors this activity (e.g., town rec. program, church, business). Include organized activities you did this past summer.
    Community Activity: Times/wk.   Sponsor:

3. If you *are* active in sports or clubs, what is it about these activities in general that you enjoy?

4. If you *are not* active in sports or clubs, please tell the reasons why you do not participate.

5. If you do not like sports and clubs, please explain what you do not like.

6. Have you ever been a leader in school or in the community? ___Yes ___No
    If yes, in what way have you been a leader?
    For how long?

7. What time do you get up on school mornings?
    Do you: Take the bus?_____Get a ride?_____Walk to school?_____

8. *Please answer all the questions that apply to you:*
    What time does the school bus pick you up?
    How far do you walk to get the bus?
    If you get a ride, who takes you?
    If you walk to school, how far do you walk?
    What time do you get to school?
    If you take late bus, what time do you get all the way home?
    Where does late bus drop you off?

9. In which class (subject) at school do you participate the most?

10. What or who encourages you to participate a lot?

11. In which class (subject) do you participate the least?

12. What or who discourages you from participating?

Part III ~ Interacting with Friends, Classmates, Teachers, and Communities

1. Please think of all the people you count as your *close* friends. Next to the towns listed below, tell how many close friends you have from that town. Are they new or old friends? Then tell how often you see them:

    0 Never   1 Rarely   2 Sometimes   3 Often   4 Every Day

	Number of Friends:					
Name of Town:	New or Old?	How often:				
Hillside		0	1	2	3	4
Two Rivers		0	1	2	3	4
Lakeview		0	1	2	3	4
Farm Crossing		0	1	2	3	4
Deer Run		0	1	2	3	4
Meadow		0	1	2	3	4
Other (please specify)		0	1	2	3	4
Other (please specify)		0	1	2	3	4

2. Do you have a nickname you like?
    What is it?
    How did you get it?
    What do you like about it?

3. Are you called anything you don't like?
    What?
    What do you dislike about it?

4. What do you like *most* about your classmates?

5. What do you like *least* about your classmates?

6. What do you like about your *most favorite* seventh grade teacher?

7. What do you dislike about your *least favorite* seventh grade teacher?

8. On a scale of 1–10, where 1 means that your family *always* worries about money and faces difficulty making ends meet, and 10 means your family *never* worries about money, and has everything they want, where would you place your family compared to other students at your school?

    1   2   3   4   5   6   7   8   9   10

9. If you live in Lakeview or Meadow, for what reasons and how often do you go to Hillside? If you live in Hillside or Two Rivers, for what reasons and how often do you go to Lakeview? Please circle the town you are answering about.

    0 Never   1 Rarely   2 Sometimes   3 Often   4 Every Day

Town:	Reasons for going:	How often?				
Hillside		0	1	2	3	4
Lakeview						

Part IV ~ Hoping and Planning

1. Please check the response that is most right for you most of the time:
    ___I love school   ___School is okay   ___I dislike school

Please explain your answer:

2. Please check one:
    ___ I pretty much got what I expected at the middle school
    ___ I expected some things and did not expect others
    ___ The middle school is very different from what I was expecting

Please explain your answer:

3. Please rate how important these are to you.

    1 Not Important   2 A Little Important   3 Very Important

Hope/Plan	How important to you?		
a. Getting good grades at school	1	2	3
b. Participating in activities	1	2	3
c. Being athletic	1	2	3
d. Being popular	1	2	3
e. Graduating from high school	1	2	3
f. Graduating from college	1	2	3
g. Having a well-paying job	1	2	3
h. Having a job I enjoy	1	2	3

4. If you plan to go to college or technical school, what are you interested in studying?

5. What kind of work would you like to do?

6. Do you know what kind of training and education you must have for this work?

Part V ~ Working at Home and in the Community

1. Please list all the chores and responsibilities you have at home and tell how often you do them:

    0 Never   1 Rarely   2 Sometimes   3 Often   4 Every Day

    Chores/Responsibilities: How often:

2. Did you work this summer or do you work now *for pay*? Please list the type of job (i.e., babysitting, farm-work), the location (i.e., restaurant, store, office), and how many hours per week you work(ed).

    Job: Location: Hours per wk.:

3. Have you served as a volunteer at school or in your community since we last met? Please list the volunteer positions you have had, the location, and how many hours per week you volunteered.

    Volunteer Job: Location: Hrs. per wk.?

Part VI ~ Caring

1.   How often do you get help from the people listed below? Use the numbers to say how often each person helps you with your schoolwork, athletics, personal problems, spirituality, your future, and other things. Some people listed may not apply to you, for example, you may not have a coach or a stepparent. If this is the case, leave it blank. Otherwise, fill in all the spaces with a number. If you mark "other," please write what kind of help you mean.

0 Never   1 Rarely   2 Sometimes   3 Often   4 Every Day

	Type of Help:					
Helper:	School work	Athletics	Personal	Spiritual	Future	Other
Friends						
Other Students						
Mom						
Dad						
Step-parent						
Grand-parent						
Other Family						
Teacher						
School Counselor						
Other School Staff						
Coach						
Counselor (out of school)						
Neighbor						
Someone at Church						
Other						

Table of Self-Esteem Means

Table A5. General and Area Specific Self-Esteem by Town, Gender, and Boys Divorce Experience*

Time and Variable**	Total Group N = 30	Lakeview Total N = 16	Hillside Total N = 14	Boys Lakeview N = 8	Boys Hillside N = 7	Girls Lakeview N = 8	Girls Hillside N = 7	Lakeview Boys (No Divorce) N = 5	Lakeview Boys (Divorce) N = 3	Hillside Boys (No Divorce) N = 3	Hillside Boys (Divorce) N = 4
T1General	93.93	95.00	92.71	94.88	91.43	95.13	94.00	100.80	85.00	99.00	85.75
	(1.96)	(2.84)	(2.73)	(4.34)	(4.16)	(3.98)	(3.82)	(5.03)	(3.61)	(6.11)	(4.09)
T1Peers	29.30	30.56	27.86	30.75	28.86	30.38	26.86	32.40	28.00	31.33	27.00
	(0.70)	(0.85)	(1.05)	(1.50)	(1.14)	(0.91)	(1.78)	(1.94)	(1.53)	(1.20)	(1.08)
T1Home	33.67	33.50	33.86	33.75	33.00	33.25	34.71	36.40	29.33	35.00	31.50
	(0.82)	(1.14)	(1.23)	(1.47)	(2.02)	(1.84)	(1.49)	(0.68)	(1.76)	(2.52)	(3.07)
T1School	30.97	30.94	31.00	30.38	29.57	31.50	32.43	32.00	27.67	32.67	27.25
	(0.85)	(1.34)	(1.05)	(1.96)	(1.51)	(1.95)	(1.36)	(2.92)	(1.33)	(2.67)	(0.48)
T2General	95.55	95.91	95.14	95.44	93.64	96.38	96.64	101.30	85.67	105.67	84.63
	(2.36)	(3.12)	(2.52)	(4.08)	(4.41)	(5.01)	(2.70)	(4.65)	(2.60)	(2.33)	(1.43)
T2Peers	29.70	30.84	28.39	29.69	28.29	32.00	28.50	31.10	27.33	32.00	25.50
	(0.79)	(0.94)	(1.26)	(1.39)	(1.77)	(1.22)	(1.94)	(1.95)	(0.88)	(1.00)	(2.10)
T2Home	33.78	33.34	34.29	33.81	33.14	32.88	35.43	35.90	30.33	36.67	30.50
	(0.80)	(1.26)	(0.96)	(1.35)	(1.37)	(2.22)	(1.31)	(1.25)	(1.45)	(0.67)	(0.96)
T2School	32.07	31.72	32.46	31.94	32.21	31.50	32.71	34.30	28.00	37.00	28.63
	(0.86)	(1.36)	(1.02)	(1.85)	(1.91)	(2.12)	(0.89)	(2.40)	(0.58)	(2.08)	(0.80)

T3General	**93.82**	**94.09**	**93.50**	**95.25**	**91.71**	**92.94**	**95.29**	**101.20**	**85.33**	**106.00**	**81.00**
	(2.36)	(3.60)	(3.08)	(4.02)	(5.66)	(6.26)	(2.86)	(4.18)	(3.71)	(4.93)	(3.24)
T3Peers	**29.77**	**30.50**	**28.93**	**28.88**	**29.00**	**32.13**	**28.86**	**30.00**	**27.00**	**34.00**	**25.25**
	(0.84)	(1.03)	(1.38)	(1.42)	(2.12)	(1.33)	(1.94)	(2.12)	(1.00)	(1.00)	(2.06)
T3Home	**33.65**	**33.41**	**33.93**	**34.63**	**33.14**	**32.19**	**34.71**	**36.80**	**31.00**	**37.67**	**29.75**
	(0.89)	(1.41)	(1.07)	(1.28)	(1.81)	(2.55)	(1.23)	(1.16)	(0.58)	(1.86)	(0.85)
T3School	**30.40**	**30.19**	**30.64**	**31.75**	**29.57**	**28.63**	**31.71**	**34.40**	**27.33**	**34.33**	**26.00**
	(1.12)	(1.81)	(1.30)	(2.06)	(2.21)	(3.01)	(1.44)	(2.25)	(2.67)	(3.18)	(1.47)

*The standard error of measurement is reported in parentheses below each mean score.

**Time 1 (T1) is spring of grade 6, time 2 (T2) is fall of grade 7, and time 3 (T3) is spring of grade 7.

APPENDIX **6**

———————

Student Participation Survey

Dear Students,
I need your help with a research project I am doing about students and the middle school. I would like to know if you participate in activities and sports. Your answers will help me understand if certain students are more able and likely to participate in activities and sports than others. I am very grateful for your help.
Thank you!   *Donna San Antonio*

---

1. Please circle the town you live in:
Meadow	Two Rivers	Deer Run
Hillside	Farm Crossing	Lakeview

2. What grade are you in?   ___ Grade 7   ___ Grade 8
3. Are you a   ___ Boy   ___ Girl

---

4. Please circle all the activities and sports you participated in this year, but do not circle activities that you started and then dropped:

Art Club	Drama	Jazz Band
Math Team	Mock Trial	Student Council
Yearbook	Football	Soccer
Field Hockey	Basketball	Skiing
Baseball	Softball	Track

   Cross Country   Intramurals (name sport)_____
   Family & Consumer Sciences Club   Kids in the World of Science
   Technology Club/Photography   Other_____

5. If you did not participate much in sports or activities, please explain what prevented you from participating. Please use the back of this form and take as much space as you need to explain. Your reasons for not participating are VERY important. For example, these are some answers I have heard: after-school responsibilities at home; transportation problems; getting home too late; too much homework; after school job; activities cost too much money; they do not offer the activity I am interested in; I wasn't chosen for the team; don't feel I fit in with the other students; I didn't want to participate. WHAT ARE *YOUR* REASONS?

APPENDIX **7**

Town and Gender Comparisons of California Achievement Test Scores

Test Scores of the Thirty Students in the Study Group

My study group of thirty students took the California Achievement Test in May, 1997. The Lakeview national percentile (NP) scores were higher, on average, than Hillside-Two Rivers scores by nearly 21 percentile points (total battery). The biggest gap was in reading with a mean difference of 22.20 percentile points. Girls from Lakeview had *higher* scores than boys, except for in math; girls from Hillside-Two Rivers had *lower* scores than boys on every count, the biggest gap being language, which was lower by 17 percentile points.

Seven Lakeview students had total scores above the 90th percentile. Three Hillside-Two Rivers students had total scores above the Lakeview average, and these three students scored above the 90th percentile. There was a much wider range of total scores in Hillside-Two Rivers (5–99) than in Lakeview (45–99). Table A7.1 lists

Table A7.1. California Achievement Test Results (Grade 5) for Hillside and Lakeview Research Participants (Means for Reading, Language, Math, and Total Battery and Range for Total and Cognitive Skills)

	Hillside-Two Rivers	Lakeview	Hillside-Two Rivers	Hillside-Two Rivers	Lakeview	Lakeview
	All (n=14)	All (n=16)	Boys (n=7)	Girls (n=7)	Boys (n=8)	Girls (n=8)
Reading	62.36	84.56	66.71	58.0	81.25	87.88
Language	60.71	78.06	69.29	52.14	71.63	84.5
Math	60.57	77.63	61.43	59.71	80.13	75.13
Total Battery	60.86	81.75	66.0	55.71	79.0	84.5
Total Range	5–99	45–99	5–99	27–99	45–94	58–99
CSI Range	88–141	94–133	88–134	88–141	101–133	94–124

average scores for each test section, total battery, and the results of the Test of Cognitive Skills (CSI).

It is important to note that students in both communities had a similar mean and range of cognitive skills (CSI) scores, even though the subject area scores are very discrepant. In Lakeview the CSI mean was 113.5 and in Hillside-Two-Rivers it was 108.5. This indicates that Hillside students' acquired knowledge did not match their cognitive ability. A Hillside-Two Rivers student obtained the highest CSI score of the entire group. The technical report published by McGraw Hill (1993) demonstrates that CSI scores do not vary by social class, race, or gender; however, achievement test scores do vary.

Test Scores of All Hillside and Lakeview Students

When I examined scores for all Lakeview and Hillside students who took the CAT5: In Lakeview, 2.5 % of the students scored at or below the 10th percentile (total battery), and 32.5% of the students scored at or above the 90th percentile. In Hillside-Two Rivers, 16.67% of the students scored at or below the 10th percentile, and 8.33% of the students scored at or above the 90th percentile.

When all students were taken into account (not just the students in my study group), the between town difference in mean scores was even larger. When the mean total national percentiles of research students were compared to all students, there was a ten-point positive difference for Lakeview students, and a twenty-point difference for Hillside students. This again demonstrates that the research participants were not necessarily representative of their classmates and this is even truer in Hillside. Rather, they represented a group of students who had experienced schooling more successfully.

When towns are compared, there was a 30-point difference between the mean total national percentiles, and the biggest gap was in math, with nearly a 34-point difference. Math is the subject on which so many future decisions and options are based. Table A7.2 shows these results.

In Lakeview, mean national percentile scores were just about the same for boys and girls in reading and language, but boys scored 10.5 points higher, on average, than girls in math. When scores for all students were taken into account, Hillside boys did not maintain their edge over Hillside girls. In reading, the average scores of boys and girls were about the same, but Hillside girls had an average 8-point lead in language and 7-point lead in math.

One interesting finding points to the possibility that the gender make-up of the classroom may have influenced achievement, especially for boys: In one Hillside classroom there were 18 boys and 6 girls. In this class, the boys had mean math scores that were twice as high as their peers in more gender-balanced classrooms (50.83 vs. 26.68)! We have had a good deal of discussion about how girls might benefit in classrooms that are all-girls. The finding that boys scored much higher when there were mostly boys in the classroom may indicate that there may be advantages to boys in same-gender classrooms too.

Table A7.2. California Achievement Test Results (Grade 5) for *All* Hillside and Lakeview Students (Means for Reading, Language, Math, and Total Battery and Range for Cognitive Skills)

	Hillside-Two Rivers	Lakeview	Hillside-Two Rivers	Hillside-Two Rivers	Lakeview	Lakeview
	All (n=72)	All (n=76)	Boys (n=45)	Girls (n=27)	Boys (n=36)	Girls (n=40)
Reading	42.85	71.41	42.74	42.96	72.82	70.0
Language	44.82	67.46	40.64	48.99	65.92	69.0
Math	38.45	72.32	34.73	42.16	77.54	67.1
Total Battery	40.11	72.29	36.76	43.45	73.34	71.23
CSI Range	68–141	71–138	68–134	70–141	80–133	71–138

There are other factors that have an effect on average test scores. One such factor is attendance on test day. There was a higher absentee rate in Lakeview on test day, which may have resulted in higher mean scores for that community. In Lakeview, 80 out of 91(88%), and in Hillside-Two Rivers, 73 out of 76 students (96%) took the test. More Lakeview students than usual stayed home on test day and it is reasonable to posit that the students who didn't come to school on test day were students who were more likely to perform poorly on the test.

Another factor may be class size. During the school year that these tests were taken, Hillside Elementary fifth-graders were in classrooms that averaged 25 students, and Lakeview fifth graders were in classrooms that averaged 21 students.

This small difference in numbers is more significant when we also realize that Hillside teachers work with many more students with special needs. Lakeview teachers had 7 students who were identified to have a learning disability (7.7% of the total number of students), while Hillside teachers had 17 special education students in three classrooms—22.4% of the total! These are the sorts of hidden factors that often go unexamined when test results are analyzed and when comparisons by towns and schools are made.

When factors like these are accounted for, and when we consider the fact that the results of the cognitive skills test are similar across social class backgrounds, and the powerful influence good teaching and school resources can have on students, we then begin to understand the significance of environmental, structural, political, and societal factors in determining actual performance.

Notes

Introduction

1. To maintain confidentiality, all the names of people and places have been changed throughout the book. In order to keep the location of this study confidential, I have not disclosed the name of the state, including at times when the name of the state would be used in a citation. For example, URLs, full names of state offices, names of local history books and newspapers are not disclosed in the notes and references.

2. Free and reduced lunch figures for the 1997–2000 school years are from the State Department of Education.

3. Number and race of students was provided by the school district's central office for fall 2000 enrollment.

4. From the Kids Count Annual Report of the [State] Children's Alliance, based on 1990 census data.

5. The 2000 census data were being released by the Office of State Planning as this book went to press. Income, population, race, and poverty data were available but employment and education data were not yet available.

6. From the Kids Count Annual Report of the [State] Children's Alliance, 2000.

7. National Center for Education Statistics (NCES), U.S. Department of Education.

Part 1-Introduction

1. The small community of Two Rivers (population, 1,273 in 2000) is included in the description of Hillside. Two Rivers has its own town government and K–3 elementary school. Students from Two Rivers attend Hillside School for grades 4–6. Many Two Rivers families have a Center Hillside mailing address and they share the same social services. Often outsiders refer to students from Two Rivers as though they are from Hillside. Families participate in many of the

same town activities, and they are part of many of the same social and economic networks and faith-based communities.

2. Population and race data are from Office of State Planning Web site.

Chapter 2: Hillside

1. Written by Rena McLauthlin Merrow (1867–1947), this poem appeared in the 1999 "Old Home Week" flyer printed by the local newspaper, the County Independent. It is sung to the tune, "Christmas Tree, Oh Christmas Tree." The town name has been changed to Hillside from its actual name to maintain confidentiality.

2. Town statistics are from records kept at Hillside Town Hall, year 1999.

3. Historic information in this chapter is taken from a history of Hillside, written by Edward M. Cook, a summer resident of Hillside and assistant professor of history at the University of Chicago. The history book was published in 1989 by Peter E. Randall.

4. From 1990 census data compiled by the Office of State Planning (OSP); 2000 educational data were not yet available.

5. Income and poverty information from 2000 census statistics summarized on the Office of State Planning Web site.

6. Free and reduced lunch data are from the State Department of Education.

7. The figures cited in this paragraph are from 1999 Hillside and Lakeview town records.

Chapter 3: Lakeview

1. Office of State Planning; most recent figures are for 1997.

2. From the Town of Lakeview Web site.

3. From Lakeview and Hillside tax collectors for the first half of 2000.

4. From a school district publication reporting on various indicators of academic achievement.

5. Q. David Bowers: *The History of [Lakeview] 1170–1994: A Chronological History of the Town and its People.* [Lakeview] Historical Society. Vol. 1 (1996) p. 219.

6. 2000 census data from the Office of State Planning Web site.

7. Q. David Bowers: *The History of [Lakeview] 1170–1994: Places and People.* [Lakeview] Historical Society. Vol. 2 (1996) p. 36.

8. Cited in Q. David Bowers: *The History of [Lakeview] 1170–1994: A Chronological History of the Town and its People.* [Lakeview] Historical Society. Vol. 1 (1996) p. 63.

9. In 1999 the base tax rate in Hillside was $22.36 per $1,000 and in Lakeview it was $15.72 per $1,000. These figures are from the tax assessors of each town.

10. Cited in David Bowers: *The History of [Lakeview], 1770–1994.* [Lakeview] Historical Society. Vol. 1 (1996) p. 61.

Part 2-Introduction

1. The researchers actually began the study with 924 students in two types of schools: K–6 and K–8. Their 1987 publication reports, ". . . the small number of black students in comparable types of schools made it necessary to limit analyses to only white students. Earlier publications have dealt with black-white differences in key areas (Simmons, 1978; Simmons, Brown, Bush, and Blyth, 1978)" (Simmons and Blyth, 1987: p. 27).

2. The authors do not indicate if the schools were regional or local, large or small, and they do not clearly distinguish middle schools and junior high schools.

Chapter 4: Mountainview Middle School

1. From the 1999–2000 District Report Card. The nearest metropolitan area, two hours away, had an average per pupil expenditure of $9,025 in the 1999–2000 school year.

2. Free and reduced lunch percentages for Mountainview Regional School District are from the State Department of Education; per pupil expenditure and free and reduced lunch percentage for Metropolitan Public Schools from the MPS budget office.

3. From the handout, "Major Distinctions Between Middle Schools and Junior High Schools," adapted from *The Definitive Middle School: A Handbook for Success*, by Imogene Forte and Sandra Schurr, 1993.

4. Mountainview Middle School Student Handbook, 1999–2000 school year.

5. From the 1999–2000 District Report Card, averaging 1993–1998 school years.

6. Teacher's educational backgrounds, residence, and salaries are from the annual school district report.

Chapter 6: Transition for Parents and Teachers Too

1. From the parent information and surveys packet prepared by the middle school guidance counselor and sent home in March 2000.

Chapter 8: Less-Structured Environments

1. From "School Takes Tough Stand on Dress Code Enforcement" in the local weekly newspaper, 10/5/2000.

2. Vito Perrone (personal communication, spring 2000) gave me the concept of "school friends." He has found this trend in other rural, economically diverse regional school districts.

3. Personal communication with the Director of Transportation of Mountainview Regional School District.

4. These earlier and later times also apply to students who live in Deer Run, fifteen miles south of Lakeview.

Chapter 9: Self-Esteem

1. *The Oxford Concise Dictionary,* ninth edition (1995), gives this definition of Gothic/Goth: A style of rock music derived from punk often with apocalyptic or mystical lyrics; a member of a subculture favoring black clothing, white and black make-up, metal jewelry, and Goth music.

2. In this and the following chapter on participation, I have sometimes replaced the more awkward designation of Hillside-Two Rivers with simply, Hillside. In these chapters, I intend Hillside to include Two Rivers.

3. Overall self-esteem measured by the Hare Scale is correlated .83 with the Rosenberg measure of general self-esteem used widely in the transition research cited in these chapters. Test-retest reliabilities of the Hare Self-Esteem Scale, administered at three-month intervals, are reported to be .65, 56, .61, .74 for peer, home, school, and general self-esteem, respectively (Shoemaker, 1980).

Chapter 10: Participation

1. The report, *One in Four,* by Douglas E. Hall, was released by the [State] Center for Public Policy Studies, in June 2002.

Chapter 11: Ability Grouping

1. Lemann also refers to a 1948 article in *Scientific Monthly*, "[The authors, Davis and Havighurst] argued that intelligence tests were a fraud, a way of wrapping the fortunate children of the middle class and upper middle class in a mantle of scientifically demonstrated superiority. The tests, they said, measured only 'a very narrow range of mental activities' and carried a strong cultural handicap for pupils of the lower socioeconomic groups" (p. 66).

2. *The Concise Oxford Dictionary*, ninth edition (1995), describes a yurt as, "a circular tent on a collapsible framework."

References

Addison, Richard B. "Grounded interpretive research: An investigation of physician socialization." In M. J. Packer and R. B. Addison (Eds.) *Entering the Circle: Hermeneutic Investigation in Psychology*. Albany: State University of New York Press, 1989.

Allyn, Cathy. "Bused kids exhausted, excluded." Part 2 of a 3-part series, "Problems of regional schools." [Local newspaper] January 26, 2000.

Andrews, Charles. *History of the New York African Free School*, 1830 (Cited in Carl Kaestle, 1983).

Asher, Steven and V. A. Wheeler. "Children's loneliness: A comparison of rejected and neglected peer status." *Journal of Consulting and Clinical Psychology* 53 (1985): 500–505.

Ashton-Warner, Sylvia. *Teacher.* New York: Touchstone Books, Simon and Schuster, 1986 [originally published in 1963].

Bandura, Albert. "The stormy decade: Fact or fiction?" In *Issues in Adolescent Psychology*, edited by D. Rogers, Second edition. New York: Appleton-Century-Crofts, 1972.

Bandura, Albert. "Self-efficacy: Toward a unifying theory of behavioral change." *Psychological Review* 84 (1977): 191–215.

Becker, Howard S. "Social class variation in teacher-pupil relationship." *Journal of Educational Sociology* 25 (1952): 451–465.

Blyth, Dale A., Roberta G. Simmons, and Diane M. Bush. "The transition into early adolescence: A longitudinal comparison of youth in two educational contexts." *Sociology of Education* 51 (1978): 149–162.

Blyth, Dale A., Roberta G. Simmons, and Steven Carlton-Ford. "The adjustment of early adolescents to school transitions." *Journal of Early Adolescence* 3, no. 1–2, (1983): 105–120.

Bolman, Lee G. and Terrance E. Deal. *Reframing Organizations: Artistry, Choice, and Leadership*. San Francisco: Jossey Bass Publishers, 1991.

299

Bourdieu, Pierre and Jean Claude Passeron. *Reproduction in Education, Society, and Culture*. Beverly Hills, CA: Sage, 1977.

Bowers, Q. David. *The History of [Lakeview] 1170–1994: A Chronological History of the Town and its People*. Vol. 1. [Lakeview] Historical Society, 1996.

Bowers, Q. David. *The History of [Lakeview] 1170–1994: Places and People*. Vol. 2. [Lakeview] Historical Society, 1996.

Bowlby, John. *Attachment and Loss*. (Vol. 1: *Attachment*) New York: Basic Books, 1982 [originally published in 1969].

Bowles, Samuel and Herbert Gintis. *Schooling in Capitalist America: Educational Reform and the Contradictions of Economic Life*. New York: Basic Books, 1976.

Bronfenbrenner, Urie. *The Ecology of Human Development*. Cambridge, MA: Harvard University Press, 1979.

Brophy, Jere E and Carolyn M. Evertson. *Learning From Teaching: A Developmental Perspective*. Boston: Allyn and Bacon, 1976.

Brown, Lyn Mikel and Carol Gilligan. *Meeting at the Crossroads: Women's Psychology and Girls Development*. Cambridge, MA: Harvard University Press, 1992.

Carnegie Council on Adolescent Development. *Turning Points: Preparing American Youth for the 21st Century*. Task Force on the Education of Young Adolescents. Washington, DC, 1989.

Cartwright, Dorwin (Ed.) *Field Theory in Social Science: Selected Theoretical Papers by Kurt Lewin (1890–1947)*. Westport, CT: Greenwood Press, 1951.

Chiu, Ming Ming. "Effects of status on solutions, leadership, and evaluations during group problem solving." *Sociology of Education* 73 (July, 2000): 175–195.

Coie, John D. and Kenneth A. Dodge. "Continuities and changes in children's social status: A five-year longitudinal study." *Merrill-Palmer Quarterly* 29 (1983): 261–282.

Coladarci, Theodore and Casey Cobb. "Extracurricular participation, school size, and achievement and self-esteem among high school students: A national look." *Journal of Research in Rural Education* 12, no. 2 (1996): 92–103.

Coleman, James. *Equality of Educational Opportunity*. Washington, DC: Government Publications Office, 1966.

Coleman, John. *The Nature of Adolescence*. New York: Methuen, 1980.

Cook, Edward M. *[Hillside] 1785–1985: A History*. Portsmouth, NH: Peter E. Randall Publisher.

Coopersmith, Stanley. *The Antecedents of Self-Esteem*. San Francisco: W. H. Freeman, 1967.

Corwin, Miles. *And Still We Rise: The Trials and Triumphs of Twelve Gifted Inner City Students.* New York: Harper Perennial, 2001.

de los Reyes, Eileen and Patricia Gozemba. *Pockets of Hope: How Students and Teachers Change the World.* Westport, CT: Bergin and Garvey, 2001.

Delpit, Lisa. *Other People's Children: Cultural Conflict in the Classroom.* New York: Free Press, 1995.

Dennison, George. *The Lives of Children: A Story of the First Street School.* New York: Random House, 1969.

DeYoung, Alan J. *The Life and Death of a Rural American High School: Farewell Little Kanawha.* New York: Garland Publishers, 1995.

DeYoung, Alan J., Craig Howley, and Paul Theobald. "The cultural contradictions of middle schooling for rural community survival." *Journal of Research in Rural Education* 11, no. 1 (1995): 24–35.

Dreeben, Robert. *On What is Learned in School.* Reading, MA: Addison-Wesley Publishing Company, 1968.

Dryfoos, Joy G. *Adolescents at Risk: Prevalence and Prevention.* London: Oxford University Press, 1990.

Duncan, Cynthia M. *Worlds Apart: Why Poverty Persists in Rural America.* New Haven, CT: Yale University Press, 1999.

Eccles, Jacquelynne S., Terry F. Adler, Robert Futterman, Susan B. Goff, Caroline M. Kaczala, Judith L. Meese, and Carol Midgley. "Expectancies, values, and academic behaviors." In *The Development of Achievement Motivation,* edited by J. T. Spence, 75–146. San Francisco: W. H. Freeman, 1983.

Eccles, Jacquelynne S., Carol Midgley, and Terry F. Adler. "Grade related changes in the school environment: Effects on achievement motivation." In *Advances in Motivation and Achievement,* edited by J. G. Nicholls, 283–331. Greenwich, CT: JAI Press, 1984.

Eccles, Jacquelynne S. and Carol Midgley. "Stage/environment fit: Developmentally appropriate classrooms for early adolescents." In *Research on Motivation in Education,* edited by R. E. Ames and C. Ames, 139–186. San Diego, CA: Academic Press, 1989.

Eccles, Jacquelynne S., Carol Midgely, Allan Wigfield, Christy M. Buchanan, David Reuman, Constance Flanagan, and Douglas Mac Iver. "Development during adolescence: The impact of stage environment fit on young adolescents experiences in schools and in families." *American Psychologist* 48, no. 2 (1993a): 90–101.

Eccles, Jacquelynne S., Allan Wigfield, Carol Midgely, David Reuman, Douglas Mac Iver, and Harriet Feldlaufer. "Negative effects of transitional middle schools on students' motivation." *Elementary School Journal* 93, no. 5 (1993b): 553–574.

Eccles, Jacquelynne S., Allan Wigfield, David Reuman, and Douglas Mac Iver. "Changes in students' beliefs about four activity domains: The influence of the transition to junior high school." Paper presented at the annual meeting of the American Educational Research Association. Washington, DC, April 1987.

Elias, Maurice J., Michael Ubriaco, Ann M. Reese, Michael A. Gara, Peggy A. Rothbaum, and Martha Haviland. "A measure of adaptation to problematic academic and interpersonal tasks of middle school." *Journal of School Psychology* 30 (1992): 41–57.

Elkind, David. "Egocentrism in adolescence." *Child Development* 38 (1967): 1025–1034.

Entwisle, Doris R. and Nan Marie Astone. "Some practical guidelines for measuring youth's race/ethnicity and socioeconomic status." *Child Development* 65 (1994): 1521–1540.

Erikson, Erik H. *Childhood and Society.* New York: Norton, 1950.

Erikson, Erik H. *Identity, Youth, and Crisis.* New York: W. W. Norton, 1968.

Fenzel, L. Micky. "Role strains and the transition to middle school: Longitudinal trends and sex differences." *Journal of Early Adolescence* 9 (1989): 211–226.

Finn, Jeremy D. "Withdrawing from school." *Review of Educational Research* 59, no. 2 (1989): 117–142.

Forte, Imogene and Sandra Schur. *The Definitive Middle School: A Handbook for Success.* Nashville, TN: Incentive Publications, 1993.

Freire, Paulo. *Pedagogy of the Oppressed.* New York: Continuum, 1970.

Freud, Anna. "Adolescence." *Psychoanalytic Study of the Child* 13, 255–278. New York: International Universities Press, Inc., 1958.

Gans, Herbert J. *The Urban Villagers: Group and Class in the Life of Italian-Americans.* New York: The Fee Press of Glencoe, 1962.

Garbarino, James. *Lost Boys: Why Our Sons Turn Violent and How We Can Save Them.* New York: Free Press, 1999.

Garbarino, James and Robert H. Abramowitz. "Sociocultural risk and opportunity." In *Children and Families in the Social Environment,* edited by J. Garbarino, 35–70. New York: Aldine de Gruyter, 1992.

Garbarino, James and Joanne L. Benn. "The ecology of child-bearing and child-rearing." In *Children and Families in the Social Environment,* edited by J. Garbarino, 133–177. New York: Aldine de Gruyter, 1992.

Garbarino, James and Claire Bedard. *Parents Under Siege: Why You Are the Solution, Not the Problem, In Your Child's Life.* New York: The Free Press, 2001.

Garbarino, James and Ellen deLara. *And Words Can Hurt Forever: How to Protect Adolescents From Bullying, Harassment, and Emotional Violence.* New York: The Free Press, 2002.

Gardner, Howard. *Frames of Mind: The Theory of Multiple Intelligences.* New York: Basic Books, Inc., 1983.

Geertz, Clifford. *The Interpretation of Cultures.* New York: Basic Books, A Division of Harper Collins Publishers, 1973.

George, Paul, Terry Jenkins, and Joyce Morgan. "Detracking Troup County: Providing an exemplary curriculum for all students." *Equity and Excellence in Education* 30, no. 2 (1997): 60–67.

Giroux, Henry A. *Theory and Resistance in Education: A Pedagogy for the Opposition.* South Hadley, MA: Bergin and Garvey, 1983.

Giroux, Henry A. "Critical theory and the politics of culture and voice: Rethinking the discourse of educational research." In *Qualitative Research in Education,* edited by R. R. Sherman and R. B. Webb. New York: The Falmer Press, 1988.

Gitlin, Andrew and Robyn Russell. "Alternative methodologies." In *Power and Method: Political Activism and Educational Research,* edited by A. Gitlin. New York: Routledge, 1994.

Glaser, Barney G. and Anselm L. Strauss. *The Discovery of Grounded Theory: Strategies for Qualitative Research.* Chicago: Aldine Publishing Co., 1967.

Goodlad, John. *A Place Called School.* New York: McGraw-Hill, 1984.

Grant, Gerald. *The World We Created at Hamilton High.* Cambridge, MA: Harvard University Press, 1988.

Greene, Anita L. "Self-concept and life transitions in early adolescence." Paper presented at the biennial meeting of the Society for Research in Childhood Development. Toronto, April 1985.

Hare, Bruce R. "Black and white child self-esteem in social science: An overview." *The Journal of Negro Education* 46, no. 2 (1977): 141–156.

Hare, Bruce R. "Self-perception and academic achievement: Variations in a desegregated setting." *American Journal of Psychiatry* 137, no. 6 (June 1980): 683–689.

Hare, Bruce R. "Development and change among segregated adolescents: A longitudinal study of self-perception and achievement." In *Advances in Motivation and Achievement* 1, edited by D. E. Bartz and M. L. Maehr, 173–201. Greenwich, CT: Jai Press, 1984.

Harter, Susan. "A new self-report scale of intrinsic vs. extrinsic orientation in the classroom: Motivational and informational components." *Developmental Psychology* 17 (1981): 300–312.

Harter, Susan. "The Perceived Competence Scale for Children." *Child Development* 53 (1982): 87–97.

Harter, Susan. "Self and identity development." In *At the Threshold: The Developing Adolescent,* edited by S. S. Feldman and G. R. Elliott, 352–387. New York: Harvard University Press, 1990.

Heath, Shirley Brice. *Ways With Words: Language, Life, and Work in Communities and Classrooms.* Cambridge, UK: Cambridge University Press, 1983.

Heidegger, Martin. *Being and Time,* translated by J. Macquarrie and E. Robinson. New York: Harper and Row, 1962.

Hektner, Joel. "When moving up implies moving out: Rural adolescent conflict in the transition to adulthood." *Journal of Research in Rural Education* 11, no. 1 (1995): 3–14.

Hinsdale, Mary Ann, Helen M. Lewis, and S. Maxine Waller. *It Comes from the People: Community Development and Local Theology.* Philadelphia: Temple University Press, 1995.

Hollingshead, August B. *Elmtown's Youth.* New York: John Wiley and Sons, 1949.

Horney, Karen. *Neurosis and Human Growth: The Struggle Toward Self-Realization.* NY: W. W. Norton and Company, 1950.

Howley, Craig B. "An agenda for studying rural school busing." *Journal of Research in Rural Education* 16, no. 1 (2000): 51–58.

Jackson, Philip W. *Life in Classrooms.* New York: Holt, Rinehart, and Winston, 1968.

Jackson, Philip W. *The Practice of Teaching.* New York: Teachers College Press, 1986.

John Harvard's Journal. "Harvard to applicants: Chill!" *Harvard Magazine* (March–April 2001): 68–70.

Johnson, Jerry D., Craig B. Howley, and Aimee A. Howley. "Size, excellence and equality: A report on Arkansas schools and districts." Athens, Ohio: Education Studies Department, College of Education, 2002.

Kaestle, Carl F. *Pillars of the Republic: Common Schools and American Society 1780–1860.* New York: Hill and Wang, 1983.

Kazdin, Alan E. "Adolescent mental health: Prevention and treatment programs." *American Psychologist* 48, no. 2 (February 1993): 127–141.

Killeen, Kieran and John Sipple. "School consolidation and transportation policy: An empirical institutional analysis." *A working paper for the Rural Schools and Communities Trust Policy Program. www.ruralchallenge.org,* 2000.

Kohlberg, Lawrence. "Stage and sequence: The cognitive-developmental approach to moral education." In *Handbook of Socialization Theory and Research*, edited by D. Goslin. Chicago: Rand-McNally, 1969.

Krantz, David O. "Separate is not equal." Reprinted from *Education Week* 12, no. 39 (June 23, 1993). In *Inclusion: Moving Beyond Our Fears*, edited by J. Rogers. Phi Delta Kappa: Hot Topics Series, Center for Evaluation, Development, and Research, 1994.

Larson, J. C. *Middle School Evaluation: Final report, technical appendix.* Rockville, MD: Montgomery County Public Schools, 1983.

Lawrence-Lightfoot, Sara. *Worlds Apart: Relationships Between Families and Schools.* New York: Basic Books, 1978.

Lawrence-Lightfoot, Sara. *The Good High School: Portraits of Character and Culture.* New York: Basic Books, 1983.

Lawrence-Lightfoot, Sara and Jessica H. Davis. *The Art and Science of Portraiture.* San Francisco: Jossey-Bass Publishers, 1997.

Leacock, Eleanor Burke. *The Culture of Poverty: A Critique.* New York: Simon and Schuster, 1971.

Lemann, Nicholas. *The Big Test: The Secret History of the American Meritocracy.* New York: Farrar, Straus, and Giroux, 2000.

Lewin, Kurt. *A Dynamic Theory of Personality.* New York: McGraw-Hill, 1935.

Lewin, Kurt. (1946) "Behavior and development as a function of the total situation." In *Field Theory in Social Science: Selected Theoretical Papers by Kurt Lewin*, edited by D. Cartwright, 238–303. Westport, CT: Greenwood Press Publishers, 1951.

Lightfoot, Cynthia. "The clarity of perspective: Adolescent risk taking, fantasy, and the internalization of cultural identity." In *Sociogenetic Perspectives on Internalization*, edited by B. D. Cox and C. Lightfoot, 135–156. Mahwah, NJ: Lawrence Erlbaum Associates, 1997.

Lincoln, Yvonna and Ebon Guba. *Naturalistic Inquiry.* Beverly Hills, CA: Sage, 1985.

Lipsitz, Joan. "Educating the early adolescent: Why four model schools are effective in reaching a difficult age group." *American Education* 17 (1981): 13–17.

Lynch, Michael and Dante Cicchetti. "Children's relationships with adults and peers: An examination of elementary and junior high school students." *Journal of School Psychology* 35, no. 1 (1997): 81–99.

Maag, John W., Stanley F. Vasa, Robert Reid, and Gregory K. Torrey. "Social and behavioral predictors of popular, rejected, and average children." *Educational and Psychological Measurement* 55, no. 2 (April 1995): 196–205.

Marsh, Herbert W. "Extracurricular activities: Beneficial extension of the traditional curriculum or subversion of academic goals?" *Journal of Educational Psychology* 84 (1992): 553–562.

Marshall, Catherine and Gretchen B. Rossman. *Designing Qualitative Research.* Thousand Oaks, CA: Sage, 1995.

Maxwell, Joseph. *Qualitative Research Design: An Interpretive Approach.* Thousand Oaks, CA: Sage Publications, 1996.

McLaren, Peter. "Multiculturalism and the post-modern critique: Toward a pedagogy of resistance and transformation." In *Between Borders: Pedagogy and the Politics of Cultural Studies*, edited by H. Giroux and P. McLaren, 192–222. New York: Routledge, 1994.

Merton, Robert K. *Social Theory and Social Structure.* New York: The Free Press, 1957.

Metz, Mary Haywood. *Classrooms and Corridors: The Crisis of Authority in Desegregated Secondary Schools.* Berkeley: University of California Press, 1978.

Midgley, Carol and Harriet Feldlaufer. "Students' and teachers' decision-making fit before and after the transition to junior high school." *Journal of Early Adolescence* 7 (1987): 225–241.

Midgley, Carol, Harriet Feldlaufer, and Jacquelynne S. Eccles. "The transition to junior high school: Beliefs of pre- and post-transition teachers." *Journal of Youth and Adolescence* 17 (1988): 543–562.

Midgley, Carol, Harriet Feldlaufer, and Jacquelynne S. Eccles. "Student/teacher relations and attitudes toward mathematics before and after the transition to junior high school." *Child Development* 60 (1989): 375–395.

Miles, Matthew B. and Michael A. Huberman. *Qualitative Data Analysis: An Expanded Sourcebook* (2nd edition). Thousand Oaks, CA: Sage, 1994.

Miller, Bruce. "The role of rural schools in community development: Policy issues and implications." *Journal of Research in Rural Education* 11, no. 3 (1995): 163–172.

Moll, Luis C., Cathy Amanti, Deborah Neff, and Norma Gonzalez. "Funds of knowledge for teaching: Using a qualitative approach to connect homes and classrooms." *Theory Into Practice* 31 (1992): 132–141.

Moos, Rudolf H. *Evaluating Educational Environments.* San Francisco, CA: Jossey-Bass, 1979.

Moses, Robert P. and Charles E. Cobb. *Radical Equations: Math Literacy and Civil Rights.* Boston, MA: Beacon Press, 2001.

Muller, Chandra and Kathryn Schiller. "Leveling the playing field? Student's educational attainment and state's performance testing." *Sociology of Education* 73 (April 2000): 196–218.

Nakkula, Michael J. and Sharon Ravitch. *Matters of Interpretation: Reciprocal Transformation in Therapeutic and Developmental Relationships with Youth.* San Francisco: Jossey-Bass, 1998.

Natriello, Gary, Aaron Pallas, and Karl Alexander. "On the right track? Curriculum and academic achievement." *Sociology of Education* 62 (April 1989): 109–118.

Noam, Gil, Sally Powers, Robert Kilkenny, and Jeffrey Breedy. "The interpersonal self in life-span developmental perspective: Theory, measurement, and longitudinal case analysis." In *Life-Span Development and Behavior,* edited by P. B. Baltes, D. L. Featherman, and R. M. Lerner. New Jersey: Lawrence Erlbaum Associates, 1990.

Nottlemann, Editha D. "Competence and self-esteem during the transition from childhood to adolescence." *Developmental Psychology* 23 (1987): 441–450.

Oakes, Jeannie. *Keeping Track: How Schools Structure Inequality.* New Haven: Yale University Press, 1985.

Oakes, Jeannie. "Can tracking research inform practice? Technical, normative, and political considerations." *Educational Researcher* (May 1992): 12–20.

Oakes, Jeannie, Adam Gamoran, and Reba Page. "Curriculum differentiation." In *Handbook of Research on Curriculum,* edited by P. Jackson. New York: MacMillan, 1992.

Paley, Vivian. *Molly Is Three.* Chicago: University of Chicago Press, 1986.

Parker, Jeffrey G. and Steven R. Asher. "Peer relations and later adjustment: Are low-accepted children 'at-risk'?" *Psychological Bulletin* 102 (1987): 357–389.

Parsons, Talcott. "The school class as a social system: Some of its functions in American society." *Harvard Educational Review* 29 (1959): 297–313.

Patton, Michael Q. *Qualitative Evaluation and Research Methods.* Newbury Park, CA: Sage, 1990.

Pearlin, Leonard I. "Role strains and perceived stress." In *Psychosocial Stress: Trends in Theory and Research,* edited by H. B. Kaplan. New York: Academic Press, 1983.

Petersen, Anne C. and Lisa Crockett. "Pubertal timing and grade effects on adjustment." *Journal of Youth and Adolescence* 14 (1985): 191–206.

Piaget, Jean. *The Moral Judgment of the Child.* Glencoe, IL: Free Press, 1965.

Putnam, Robert D. "The prosperous community: Social capital and public life." *American Prospect* 13 (1993): 35–42.

Ravitch, Diane. *The Great School Wars: A History of Public Schools as Battlefield of Social Change.* NY: Basic Books, Inc., 1974.

Ricoeur, Paul. "The model of the text: Meaningful action considered as a text." In *Interpretive Social Science: A Reader,* edited by P. Rabinow and W. M. Sullivan. Berkeley: University of California Press, 1979.

Rist, Ray C. "Student social class and teacher expectations: The self-fulfilling prophecy in ghetto education." *Harvard Educational Review* 40 (1970): 411–451.

Rogers, Annie. "Voice, play, and a practice of ordinary courage in girls' and women's lives." *Harvard Educational Review* 63, no. 3 (1993): 265–295.

Rosenbaum, James E. *Making Inequality: The Hidden Curriculum of High School Tracking.* New York: Wiley, 1976.

Rosenberg, Morris. *Society and the Adolescent Self-Image.* Princeton, NJ: Princeton University Press, 1965.

Rosenberg, Morris. "Which significant others?" *The American Behavioral Scientist* 16, no. 6 (July–August 1973): 829–860.

Rosenberg, Morris and Leonard I. Pearlin. "Social class and self-esteem among children and adults." *American Journal of Sociology* 84, no. 1 (1978): 53–77.

Rosenthal, Robert and Lenore Jacobsen. *Pygmalion in the Classroom.* New York: Holt, Rinehart, and Winston, 1968.

Rumberger, Russell W. "High school drop-outs: A review of issues and evidence." *Review of Educational Research* 57 (1987): 101–121.

Rutter, Michael. *Changing Youth in a Changing Society: Patterns of Adolescent Development and Disorder.* Cambridge, MA: Harvard University Press, 1980.

Rutter, Michael. "Resilience in the face of adversity: Protective factors and resistance to psychiatric disorder." *British Journal of Psychiatry* 147 (1985): 598–611.

Rutter, Michael. "Protective factors in children's responses to stress and disadvantage." In *Primary Prevention of Psychopathology,* vol. 3: *Social Competence in Children,* edited by M. W. Kent and J. E. Rolf. Hanover, NH: University Press of New England, 1980.

Rutter, Michael, Barbara Maughan, Peter Mortimore, Janet Ouston, with Alan Smith. *Fifteen Thousand Hours: Secondary Schools and Their Effects on Children.* Cambridge, MA: Harvard University Press, 1979.

Schulenberg, John E., C. Elliot Asp, and Anne C. Petersen. "School from the young adolescent's perspective: A descriptive report." *Journal of Early Adolescence* 4 (1984): 107–130.

Schwarzer, R., M. Jerusalem, and B. Lange. "The development of academic self-concept with respect to reference groups in school." Paper presented at the International Society for Behavioral Development meetings. Toronto, Canada, 1981.

Seeley, John R., R. Alexander Sim, and Elizabeth W. Loosely. *Crestwood Heights: A Study of the Culture of Suburban Life.* New York: Basic Books, 1956.

Seidman, Edward, Allen LaRue, J. Lawrence Aber, Christina Mitchell, and Joanna Feinman. "The impact of school transitions in early adolescence on the self-system and perceived social context of poor urban youth." *Child Development* 65 (1994): 507–522.

Selman, Robert L. *The Growth of Interpersonal Understanding.* New York: Academic Press, 1980.

Selman, Robert L and Lynn Hickey Schultz. *Making a Friend in Youth: Developmental Theory and Pair Therapy.* Chicago: University of Chicago Press, 1990.

Sennett, Richard and Jonathan Cobb. *The Hidden Injuries of Class.* New York: Alfred A. Knopf, Inc., 1972.

Sher, Jonathan P. and Rachel B. Tompkins. *Economy, Efficiency, and Equality: The Myths of Rural School and District Consolidation.* Washington, DC: National Institute of Education, U.S. Department of Health, Education, and Welfare, 1976.

Shoemaker, Allen. "Construct validity of area specific self-esteem: The Hare Self-Esteem Scale." *Educational and Psychological Measurement* 40 (1980).

Simmons, Ruth G. "Blacks and high self-esteem: A puzzle." *Social Psychology* 41, no. 1 (1978): 54–57.

Simmons, Ruth G. and Dale A. Blyth. *Moving Into Adolescence: The Impact of Pubertal Change and School Context.* Hawthorne, NY: Aldine de Gruyter, 1987.

Simmons, Ruth G., Morris Rosenberg and Florence Rosenberg. "Disturbance in the self-image at adolescence." *American Sociological Review* 39, no. 5 (1973): 553–568.

Simmons, Ruth G., Leslie Brown, Diane M. Bush, and Dale A. Blyth. "Self-esteem and achievement of black and white early adolescents." *Social Problems* 26, no. 1 (1978): 86–96.

Simmons, Ruth G., Dale A. Blyth, Edward F. Van Cleave, and Diane M. Bush. "Entry into early adolescence: The impact of school structure, puberty, and early dating on self-esteem." *American Sociological Review* 44, no. 6 (1979): 948–967.

Sizer, Theodore. *Horace's Compromise.* Boston, MA: Houghton-Mifflin, 1984.

Slavin, Robert E. "Ability grouping in the middle grades: Achievement effects and alternatives." *Elementary School Journal* 93 (1993): 535–552.

Smith, Beverly J. "Raising a resister." In *Women, Girls, and Psychotherapy: Reframing Resistance,* edited by C. Gilligan, A. Rogers, and D. Tolman. Binghamton, NY: Harrington Park Press, 1991.

Stacey, Judith. "Can there be a feminist ethnography?" In *Women's Words: The Feminist Practice of Oral History,* edited by S. B. Gluck and D Patai, 111–119. New York: Routledge, 1991.

Stern, Joyce D. *The Condition of Education in Rural Schools.* Washington DC: U.S. Department of Education, U.S. Government Printing Office, 1994.

Suskind, Ron. *A Hope in the Unseen: An American Odyssey from the Inner City to the Ivy League.* New York: Broadway Books, 1998.

Tatum, Beverly D. *Why Are All the Black Kids Sitting Together in the Cafeteria?* New York: Basic Books, 1997.

Taylor, Jill M., Carol Gilligan, and Amy Sullivan. *Between Voice and Silence.* Cambridge, MA: Harvard University Press, 1995.

Test of Cognitive Skills Technical Report. Monterey, CA: CTB MacMillan/McGraw Hill, 1973.

Thornburg, Herschel D. and Randy M. Jones. "Social characteristics of early adolescents: Age vs. grade." *Journal of Early Adolescence* 2 (1982): 229–239.

Tyack, David B. and Larry Cuban. *Tinkering Toward Utopia: A Century of Public School Reform.* Cambridge, MA: Harvard University Press, 1995.

Tye, Kenneth. *The Junior High School in Search of a Mission.* Lanham, MD: University Press of America, 1985.

Vygotsky, Lev S. *Thought and Language,* edited and translated by E. Hanfmann and G. Vakar. Cambridge, MA: MIT Press, 1962 [originally published in 1934].

Waller, Willard. *The Sociology of Teaching.* New York: Russell and Russell, 1961 [originally published in 1932].

Warner, W. Lloyd, Robert J. Havighurst, and Martin B. Loeb. *Who Shall Be Educated? The Challenge of Unequal Opportunities.* New York: Harper and Brothers Publishers, 1944.

Wehlage, Gary G. and Robert A. Rutter. "Dropping out: How much do schools contribute to the problem?" *Teachers College Record* 87 (1986): 374–392.

Wells, Cyrene M. *Literacies Lost: When Students Move From a Progressive Middle School to a Traditional High School.* NY: Teacher's College Press, 1996.

Werner, Emmy E. "Protective factors and individual resilience." In *Handbook of Early Childhood Intervention,* edited by S. Meisels and J. Shonkoff. New York: Cambridge University Press, 1990.

White, Karl. "The relation between socioeconomic status and academic achievement." *Psychological Bulletin (of APA)* 91, no. 3 (1982): 461–477.

Wigfield, Allan, Jacquelynne S. Eccles, Douglas Mac Iver, David Reuman, and Carol Midgely. "Transitions at early adolescence: Changes in children's domain specific self-perceptions and general self-esteem across the transition to junior high school." *Developmental Psychology* 27 (1991): 552–565.

Wihry, David F., Theodore Coladarci, and Curtis Meadow. "Grade span and eighth grade academic achievement: Evidence from a predominantly rural state." *Journal of Research in Rural Education* 8, no. 2 (1992): 58–70.

Williamson, Marianne. *Healing the Soul of America: Reclaiming Our Voices As Spiritual Citizens.* New York: Touchstone, 1997.

Willie, Charles V. *Black and White Families: A Study in Complementarity.* Dix Hills, NY: General Hall, Inc., 1985.

Willie, Charles V. "Educators who are not afraid to bring good news." *Equity and Excellence in Education* 27, no. 1 (1994): 9–15.

Willie, Charles V. with Jerome Beker. *Race Mixing in the Public Schools.* New York: Praeger Publishers, 1973.

Willis, Paul E. *Learning to Labor: How Working Class Kids Get Working Class Jobs.* New York: Columbia University Press, 1981.

Youngman, Michael B. "Six reactions to school transfer." *British Journal of Educational Psychology* 48 (1978): 280–289.

Index

Abandonment, 181

Achievement: academic, 2, 15; effect of low-income student population on, 7; influences on, 15; school size and, 7

Adaptation. *See also* Transition to middle school: adolescence and, 100–102

Addison, Richard, 19

Administrator(s), 116

Adolescence: adaptation to new environment and, 100–102; capacity for higher level cognitive work in, 106; changes in, 104; depression in, 15, 264; developmental needs during, 96, 97, 106; expansion of life-space in, 101; expectations for autonomy in, 104; identity development in, 100; as inopportune time to leave familiarity of prior school, 109; intellectual challenge during, 133; interest in autonomy, 133; multiple changes during, 100; need for success at primary tasks of, 123; operation within institutional bounds in, 102; parental experiences during, 101; as problematic stage of development, 100; self-awareness in, 101; self-esteem in, 15, 101; shift from primary to secondary contexts, 105; social development in, 15; stresses of puberty in, 100

Affluence, 3, 77; perceived/observed, 28–30

Alexeia (student), 172, 189, 208, 216–220

Algebra Project, 233

Alienation, 166, 205; socioeconomic status and, 205–206

Allen (student), 189

Allyn, Cathy, 206

Altruism, 1, 171–172, 197; opportunities for, 173

Amber (student), 208, 209

Analysa (student), 208

Anxiety, 15, 264

Appearance: attempts to create unique, 160, 161; deemphasis on, 197; gender and, 255; Gothic, 181; importance to girls, 184, 185; vulnerability over, 163

Arianna (student), 31, 156, 189, 216–220

Ashton-Warner, Sylvia, 96

Autonomy: adolescent interest in, 133; desire for, 106, 107, 173; expectations of, 104; student need for, 118

Awareness: diversity, 173; social, 173, 258

Bandura, Albert, 15, 102, 123

Becka (student), 208

Becker, Howard, 11

Behavior: in context, 245–247; gender and, 185; influence of environ-

DATE DUE